ELIE WIESEL'S
SECRETIVE TEXTS

———

ELIE WIESEL'S SECRETIVE TEXTS

———

Colin Davis

University Press of Florida

Gainesville • Tallahassee • Tampa • Boca Raton

Pensacola • Orlando • Miami • Jacksonville

99 98 97 96 95 94   6 5 4 3 2 1

Library of Congress Cataloging-in-Publication Data

Davis, Colin.
    Elie Wiesel's secretive texts / Colin Davis.
        p.   cm.
    Includes bibliographical references and index.
    ISBN 0-8130-1303-8
    1. Wiesel, Elie, 1928–   —Criticism and interpretation.
    I. Title.
    PQ2683.I32Z655   1994   94-8400
    813'.54—dc20

The University Press of Florida is the scholarly publishing agency for the State University
System of Florida, comprised of Florida A & M University, Florida Atlantic University,
Florida International University, Florida State University, University of Central Florida,
University of Florida, University of North Florida, University of South Florida, and
University of West Florida.

University Press of Florida
15 Northwest 15th Street
Gainesville, FL 32611

FOR SARAH

———

We are most unwilling to accept mystery, what cannot be reduced to other
and more intelligible forms. Yet that is what we find here: something
irreducible, therefore perpetually to be interpreted; not secrets to be found
out one by one, but Secrecy.
Perhaps that secrecy is nothing more than our own bewilderment
projected into the text.
Frank Kermode, *The Genesis of Secrecy*, 143

———————

The better the story is, the more it appears clothed. The secret must remain
in a pure state.
Wiesel, *Entre deux soleils*, 248

———————

Usually, Rabbi Bounam would explain his parables, whilst indicating that
their true and deep meaning eluded explanation. The secret of the secret
cannot be divulged, he would say.
Wiesel, *Célébration hassidique*, 228

———————

CONTENTS

Acknowledgments   xi

Abbreviations   xiii

Introduction   1

ONE   After the Event   7

TWO   Storytelling   31

THREE   The Conversion to Ambiguity (Early Works)   52

FOUR   Crises of Narration (Later Fiction)   86

FIVE   Victims and Executioners   113

SIX   Impaired Meaning   141

Conclusion: Secrecy   175

Notes   185

Bibliography   193

Index   199

ACKNOWLEDGMENTS

Some of the material in chapter 3 appeared previously in "Understanding the Concentration Camps: Elie Wiesel's *La Nuit* and Jorge Semprun's *Quel Beau Dimanche!*" in *Australian Journal of French Studies* 28, no. 3 (1991): 291–303; my thanks to the editor for permission to reprint the material.

I also thank all those who have helped, advised, or encouraged me during the preparation of this book, particularly Sarah Kay, Simon Gaunt, Leslie Hill, Mark Treharne, Christina Howells, Bill Calin, Raymond Gay-Crosier, and Ellen Fine.

ABBREVIATIONS

Full references to works cited are given in the bibliography. Translations from the French are my own. I have attempted as far as possible to reproduce the format of Wiesel's texts; however, I have not retained original italics in passages. In quotations from Wiesel's works, ellipses enclosed in brackets denote omitted text; unbracketed ellipses are in the original.

Works frequently cited have been identified by the following abbreviations:

A	*L'Aube*
AS	*Against Silence*
CB	*Célébration biblique*
CH	*Célébration hassidique*
Chant	*Le Chant des morts*
Crépuscule	*Le Crépuscule, au loin*
CT	*Célébration talmudique*
Discours	*Discours d'Oslo*
EDS	*Entre deux soleils*
Fils	*Le Cinquième Fils*
J	*Le Jour*
Job	*Job ou Dieu dans la tempête*
JS	*Les Juifs du silence*
ME	*Le Mal et l'exil*
Mélancolie	*Contre la mélancolie*
Mendiant	*Le Mendiant de Jérusalem*
N	*La Nuit*
O	*L'Oublié*
Paroles	*Paroles d'étranger*
Portes	*Les Portes de la forêt*
Qui êtes-vous?	*Elie Wiesel: Qui êtes-vous?*
Serment	*Le Serment de Kolvillàg*
Signes	*Signes d'exode*
Silences	*Silences et mémoire d'hommes*
Testament	*Le Testament d'un poète juif assassiné*
Un Juif	*Un Juif, aujourd'hui*
Ville	*La Ville de la chance*
Zalmen	*Zalmen ou la folie de Dieu*

INTRODUCTION

ELIE WIESEL was born on 30 September 1928 in Sighet, Romania. The teeming Hassidic community in which he was reared and where he began his lifelong study of the sacred Jewish texts was destroyed during World War II. Transylvania, in which Sighet is located, was annexed by Hungary in 1940; it was occupied by the German army in 1944, and eventually Wiesel and his family were deported to Auschwitz. He would never see his mother or younger sister again. He managed to remain with his father; but as the Russians approached Auschwitz, the camp was evacuated and the prisoners taken eventually to Buchenwald. There, Wiesel's father died between 28 and 29 January 1945. In April the camp was liberated and Wiesel released. Because of British policy on immigration, he was not allowed to go to Palestine; instead he was sent to France but not given French citizenship. He learned French, studied at the Sorbonne, and earned a meager living from teaching and journalism. After a dramatic encounter with the novelist François Mauriac in 1954 (recounted in *Un Juif, aujourd'hui*), he was persuaded to write about his experiences in the concentration camps. His account, originally written in Yiddish, was published in Buenos Aires in 1956 under the title *Un di Velt Hot Geshvign* (And the World Remained Silent). *La Nuit*, a much shorter version written in French, initially failed to find a publisher but appeared in 1958 with the support of Mauriac. This heralded the beginning of Wiesel's career as a writer.

L'Aube (1960), his second book, marked an important development in that the text is a fictional work. Set in Palestine during the struggle for the foundation of Israel, it uses fiction as a way of dealing with issues beyond Wiesel's own experience. Nevertheless, the Holocaust constitutes the essential background to Wiesel's novels. Elisha, the protagonist of *L'Aube*, is a Holocaust survivor like Wiesel, studied in Paris as Wiesel had, and has a name with strong connections to Wiesel's first name. The Holocaust is never absent from Wiesel's work, even if it is rarely directly described; and he has referred to his writing as "a *Matzeva*, an invisible tombstone set up in memory of those who died without burial" (*Chant*, 15).

Although Wiesel has been an American citizen since 1963, he has continued to write mainly in French. His work as a novelist has been accompanied by an increasing involvement in human rights campaigns. His essays on the situation of the Jews in the Soviet Union, collected in *Les Juifs du silence* (1966), have been followed by numerous articles, speeches, and interventions on Jewish and non-Jewish issues. In 1979 he was appointed chairman of the U.S. President's Commission on the Holocaust by Jimmy Carter; and in 1984 he was made Commandeur de la Légion d'honneur by François Mitterand. His fictional works have won numerous prizes: the Prix de l'Université de la Langue Française (Prix Rivarol) and the National Jewish Book Council Award for *La Ville de la chance* (1963), the Prix Médicis for *Le Mendiant de Jérusalem* (1968), the Prix du Livre Inter and the Prix des Bibliothéquaires for *Le Testament d'un poète juif assassiné* (1980), the Grand Prix du Roman de la Ville de Paris for *Le Cinquième Fils* (1983). In 1986 his uncompromising commitment to human rights was recognized by the award of the Nobel Peace Prize. Wiesel has been described by Irving Abrahamson as "by far the most significant writer to have made the Holocaust the major theme of his work"; and Michael Berenbaum has written that he may be "the single most important Jew in America."[1]

A fairly substantial body of secondary material has been devoted to his writing. The theological context of Wiesel's work has been admirably and thoroughly analyzed in Michael Berenbaum's *The Vision of the Void: Theological Reflections on the Works of Elie Wiesel*. Robert McAfee Brown's *Elie Wiesel: Messenger to All Humanity* concentrates on the moral power of Wiesel's writing for Jews and Christians. The relationship between Wiesel's fiction and other Holocaust literature has been extensively discussed in intelligent and useful studies such as Alan Berger's *Crisis and Covenant: The Holocaust in American Jewish Fiction* and Sidra Dekoven Ezrahi's brilliant *By Words Alone: The Holocaust in Literature*. Some writers have used Wiesel to help define their own theological positions; fairly typical in this respect are Maurice Friedman's *Abraham Joshua Heschel and Elie Wiesel: You Are My Witnesses* and Graham B. Walker's *Elie Wiesel: A Challenge to Theology*.

Although such authors do discuss Wiesel's literary texts, they show little interest in the methodological and theoretical questions that have dominated debate in literary studies in recent years. Indeed, Wiesel's fiction often appears as little more than an adjunct to the campaigning for human rights for which he won the Nobel Peace Prize. Ellen Fine's excellent *Legacy of Night: The Literary Universe of Elie Wiesel* is a notable exception; and important themes have been analyzed extensively, such as laughter in Joë Friedemann's *Le Rire dans l'univers tragique d'Elie Wiesel* and madness in Vincent Engel's *Fou de Dieu ou Dieu des fous: L'Oeuvre tragique d'Elie Wiesel*.

On the whole, however, Wiesel's fiction remains curiously unexplored despite an apparent consensus in France and the United States that Wiesel is one of the most important novelists of the post-Holocaust period. I suggest two reasons for this critical silence: an understandable fear of trivializing the Holocaust by subjecting it to literary-critical enquiry, and the ambiguity and difficulty of Wiesel's fiction itself. In this book I suggest that Wiesel's novels are too complex and problematic to be assimilated readily to the more straightforward (even if also consciously paradoxical) positions adopted in his essays and articles.

Given the vast amount of written material that Wiesel has produced, there will inevitably be omissions in my account; most notably, perhaps, I say relatively little about the massive importance of the Jewish tradition for everything that Wiesel thinks, does, and writes. There are several reasons for this omission: partly because such issues have already been discussed at length; partly because my aim in this study is to show the substantial interest of Wiesel's fiction when examined according to protocols of reading that are not those of the author himself; and partly because I am not able to undertake such a task, despite its undoubted importance.

This book is primarily concerned with problems of intelligibility and interpretation raised by Wiesel's fictional texts, as well as with the causes and consequences of those problems. The critic who has most influenced my view of interpretation has been Frank Kermode, particularly through his book *The Genesis of Secrecy*, to which the title of this study alludes. Because the notion of secrecy plays an important role in my reading of Wiesel's fiction, I briefly outline the account that Kermode gives of it. Kermode derives what he calls "two kindred but different secrecy theories" from his discussion of parables in the Gospels of Mark and Matthew: "One says that stories are obscure on purpose to damn the outsiders; the other, even if we state it in the toughest form the language will support, says that they are not necessarily impenetrable, but that the outsiders, being what they are, will misunderstand them anyway."[2]

In both secrecy theories the story is assumed to have a hidden meaning of crucial importance; yet inevitably (according to Mark) or probably, almost to the point of certainty, (according to Matthew) the outsiders will fail to grasp the secret meaning. Interpretation is an activity for outsiders aspiring to become, or masquerading as, insiders; its practitioners hope to acquire knowledge that, if they had it, would terminate the need to interpret. Kermode argues that " 'narrativity' always entails a measure of opacity." All narratives exhibit a degree of secrecy, although they may attempt to conceal it and interpreters may contrive to overlook it. The narrative may be too short, in which case it will not explain itself fully and thereby encourage readers to fill in the gaps for themselves; or it may be too long, with the consequence that it will contain apparent redundancies that call out for explanation. The inherent, though perhaps unwelcome, secrecy of narratives is precisely what solicits interpretation; at the same time, because secrecy is a property of narrative and not governed by the signifying intention of an author, it does not permit full and final elucidation. Secrecy remains, in Kermode's words, "the source of the interpreter's pleasures, but also of his necessary disappointment."[3]

Kermode is, I think, the most urbane and insidiously persuasive representative of a skeptical hermeneutics that portrays interpretation in terms of inevitable failure: inevitable, because we cannot help but interpret; a failure, because we will never achieve the total reduction of mystery and arrive at the full understanding that is the goal of interpretation. I am aware—acutely—that Kermode's account of secrecy can in no way provide an adequate framework for a full understanding of Wiesel's fiction. Reflections on the secrecy of narrative in the work of other thinkers (such as Blanchot or Derrida) would, I believe, be no less ineffectual in unlocking texts that are at once radiantly clear (pain appears on every page) and disturbingly enigmatic.[4] Instead of seeking full comprehension, I have chosen to focus more narrowly on what impedes such comprehension: not in the hope that this will replace all other readings, but in the belief that it may displace the premature security—hermeneutic and ethical—that I have found (however paradoxical it may seem) in some writing on Holocaust fiction.

The first chapter of this book takes one of Wiesel's short stories ("Une vieille connaissance") and two of his essays ("Notre commune culpabilité ..." and "Plaidoyer pour les morts") in order to illustrate the disjunction between the uncertainties of his fiction and the polemical confidence of some of his nonliterary writing. The difficulties of the fiction are then discussed in the context of intellectual and artistic problems caused by the Holocaust, which Wiesel conceives as a radical disruption of the meaning and coherence of history. Subsequent chapters continue the discussion of how this disruption affects Wiesel's literary practice. Chapter 2 deals with the central theme of storytelling, and with the associated problems of belief, interpretation, and effectiveness, as illustrated by three stories recounted in Wiesel's texts: Moché's account of Nazi atrocities in *La Nuit*, Katriel's parable from *Le Mendiant de Jérusalem*, and a Hassidic story concerning the power of storytelling itself.

Chapters 3 and 4 deal respectively with Wiesel's early texts and some of his later fiction. In the first I trace the beginnings of what I call a "conversion to ambiguity" in *La Nuit*, *L'Aube*, *Le Jour*, and *La Ville de la chance*; in the next chapter I consider some of the consequences of this for Wiesel's later aesthetics, with particular reference to *Les Portes de la forêt*, *Le Serment de Kolvillàg*, *Le Mendiant de Jérusalem*, and *Le Crépuscule, au loin*. Chapters 5 and 6 are more general. Chapter 5 returns to the relationship between Wiesel's fiction and his nonfictional texts, discussing his commitment to human rights and comparing views of violence in his essays with attitudes suggested in *L'Aube* and *L'Oublié*. Chapter 6 takes an important theme of Wiesel's writing, the death of the father figure, and shows how it is related to the loss of meaning and the telling of stories; the second section of the chapter continues the discussion in a framework provided by Wiesel's interest in biblical commentary. The final chapter draws some tentative conclusions about secrecy and interpretation through a brief consideration of Wiesel's most recent novel, *L'Oublié*.

Inevitably, some risks are involved with the kind of reading I am proposing in this book. David Hirsch has remarked that "writing about the Holocaust has become an insuperable problem for deconstructionists because their belief that 'human dignity' is nothing but a 'humanist' fiction deprives them of a viable point of view."[5] Despite this rather crude simplification of deconstruction, Hirsch's assertion pinpoints a crucial difficulty. The antihumanism of much recent thought may be considered (wrongly, I believe) to entail a rejection of the values on which we implicitly rely when we express our horror at the Holocaust. Worse still, some critical stances, with their denial that there is anything "outside the text," may appear uncomfortably close to sanctioning the position of those revisionists who have denied the reality of the Holocaust. Even if these dangers are avoided, to concentrate on formal and narrational aspects of Holocaust fiction, or on local and general problems of interpretation, may seem to miss the point entirely. Some readers may think (indeed, at least one reader of this book in manuscript has thought) that I have trivialized my subject by discussing issues such as the formal organization of *La Nuit* rather than emphasizing the chilling experiences recorded in that text.

The dangers are well expressed by James Young in his pioneering work *Writing and Rewriting the Holocaust: Narrative and the Consequences of Interpretation.* Young observes "an unmistakable resistance to overly theoretical readings of [Holocaust] literature":

> Much of this opposition is well founded and stems from the fear that too much attention to critical method or to the literary construction of texts threatens to supplant not only the literature but the horrible events at the heart of our inquiry. . . . To concentrate on the poetics of a witness's testimony, for example, over the substance of the testimony seems to risk displacing the events under discussion altogether. . . . Other potential and equally unacceptable consequences of an unlimited deconstruction of the Holocaust include the hypothetical possibility that events and texts never existed outside each other and that all meanings of events created in different representations are only relative. . . . Applied carelessly, however, contemporary theory and its often all-consuming vocabulary can obscure as much as it seeks to illuminate in this literature.[6]

This book has been written in full awareness of the pitfalls outlined by Young, although this does not of course guarantee that I have been able to avoid them. It nevertheless seemed to me important to take the risks involved. Studies of Holocaust literature have often responded to their subject with moral passion but without theoretical sophistication; on the other hand, theoretically informed criticism has often been intellectually exhilarating but ethically inconsequential. By concentrating on hesitations and indeterminacies in Wiesel's writing, I do not for a moment intend to deny the awful reality of the Holocaust, nor to detract from Wiesel's remarkable work as a human rights activist. But it seems to me just as wrong to overlook the most enigmatic aspects of Wiesel's writing as it would be to let them dominate everything else. I have attempted to contribute to the understanding of Wiesel's work by demonstrating that the disturbances it records are textual and semantic as well as thematic, that fictional form plays a crucial role in the catastrophe that Wiesel's writing commemorates. It is of course for the reader to decide whether the results are worthwhile or merely trivial.

ONE

After the Event

Elie Wiesel's fiction has been described as a form of teaching through storytelling. Ted Estess writes that "Wiesel intends with his storytelling to teach, to speak wisdom and voice insight." Robert McAfee Brown concurs: "If we are to learn from Elie Wiesel, we must listen to stories." Most of the published material on Wiesel's writing, particularly that published in the United States, emphasizes its theological and moral aspects; and Wiesel himself seems to accept, and sometimes even to encourage, the extraordinary moral authority accorded him by his commentators and admirers.[1] However, essential to my argument in this book is the idea that Wiesel's fiction does not serve as the vehicle for his teaching. On the contrary, it questions its own ability to affirm simple or complex truths; in the process it forces a revision of the foundations of the authority that Wiesel, in his work as a human rights campaigner, seems to exploit. My focus here is hermeneutic rather than theological; and the silences that interest me in Wiesel's texts are not the mystical silences that point to a truth beyond language, but the gaps that indicate the absence of fully retrievable meaning.[2] I argue that Wiesel, particularly in his later fiction, adopts an aesthetics of secrecy rather than of revelation.

Before discussing the role of the Holocaust in this aesthetics of secrecy, I give a first illustration of the disruption of ethical authority in Wiesel's fiction through an account of the story "Une vieille connaissance," printed in *Le Chant des morts*. In this story the narrator (whether we should take this narrator as Wiesel is not clear) is traveling on a bus caught in a traffic jam in Tel Aviv. To pass the time he tries to imagine what might be the life of one of the other passengers. After a while he recognizes the man he has been considering. Despite the man's desire to be left alone, the narrator confronts him and begins to evoke their past in Monowitz-Buna. The man had been a sadistic and violent block leader, a prisoner given power and authority over other prisoners. The two men eventually get out of the bus, and the narrator tries to decide what to do: to let the man go or hand him over to the police. Finally, the man begins to shout at him and threaten him in German, as he did when they were in the concentration camp. The narrator turns and walks, and then runs, away.

"Une vieille connaissance" has evident moral resonance. Published only a few years after the Eichmann trial (Eichmann was sentenced in 1961 and executed in 1962), it alludes to the continued well-being of war criminals in the postwar period, in this case even in Israel. The story then develops into a reflection on how best to confront such criminals: should they be hounded and persecuted, or should the search for vengeance be halted? The threats of violence made by the former block leader at the story's end might suggest that the criminals remain unchanged and unrepentant; the narrator's failure to summon the police could be read as indicating the futility or sterility of the desire for revenge. But such a reading makes sense of the story too easily. It extracts a moral message at the expense of psychological complexity. In fact, the narrator makes no conscious decision regarding the arrest of the man; he allows and seems to want the man to make his decisions for him. It is not the narrator who releases the man, but the other way around:

> I tell myself suddenly that this must end, but how? [. . .] What should he say to make me let him go? I've no idea. It's up to him to know [. . .] He let me go. He granted me my freedom. (*Chant*, 70–71)

The story loses in moral clarity as it gains in psychological subtlety: the narrator, still haunted by the past, is paralyzed when confronted with the prospect of making choices. In this light, rather than proposing a clear moral standpoint, the story expresses a desire to be exonerated from the responsibility of decision making.

This is already disruptive for a moral reading of the story. But even this psychological account remains unsatisfactory, because the story also indicates the instability of autonomous psychological identities, and hence the inadequacy of a psychological "key" to the text. This can be seen in the theme of doubling in the story. The first instance occurs before the narrator recognizes the man. To ward off boredom he indulges in what he calls his "favorite game" (*Chant*, 56). He attempts to imagine himself in the identity of the inconspicuous man sitting opposite:

> I end up by substituting myself for him: I think and I dream in his place. It is I whom his wife will greet with love or rancor, it is I who will drown my sorrow in sleep or in solitary drunkenness; it is I who am betrayed by my workmates and detested by my subordinates; it is I who have ruined my life and now it is too late to start again. (*Chant*, 56)

This identification precedes the crucial act of recognition, and may even provoke it: "Caught in the game [*Pris au jeu*], the traveler suddenly seems familiar to me" (*Chant*, 56). The narrator enters into an identification that will exceed his control; and the phrase *pris au jeu* is echoed later in the story by references to the trap, suggesting the phrase *pris au piège* [caught in the trap], into which both characters have fallen:

> The trap closes on him [*Le piège se referme sur lui*] [. . .] That's the trap [*Voilà le piège*]: at the point I am at now, it is impossible to step back. (*Chant*, 61, 64)

Doubling, introduced apparently innocuously into the text, dominates the rest of the story and establishes a dangerous interchangeability between the roles and identities of the two characters. The former block leader attempts to make himself inconspicuous; the narrator recognizes this strategy:

> This traveler, I can place him, I know him; this defense, *in the past I used it myself*. The best way to avoid catching the attention of the torturer [*bourreau*] was not to see him [. . .] He's acting dumb, blind, dead. *As I did in the past* [. . .] The point: hide your pain, for it excites the torturer [*bourreau*] more than it appeases him. With me that will not be of any help to him: *I know the tricks of the trade*. (*Chant*, 57–58; my emphasis)

The narrator recognizes strategies he himself has employed. Moreover, a reversal of roles has occurred: the former torturer has now taken the place of the victim; and the victim, here the narrator, has adopted the stance of the torturer, as his repeated use of the word *bourreau* suggests. Like the narrator at the end of the story, the man is now incapable of decision, expecting all initiative to come from the other: "He prefers to let me act, to let me decide for him" (*Chant*, 62).

This role reversal is possible because of the structural interdependence of identities: both characters are defined by relation to the changing position they occupy in the victim/torturer dichotomy. Each requires the other; and the two may in a sense be doubles because they have more in common than is at first apparent. The narrator acknowledges that in the camp he was both the "slave" and the "accomplice" of the block leader (*Chant*, 66), that he was "happy at his intervention" (*Chant*, 66) when obliged by him to eat his own father's food; and the man even suggests, when referring to the narrator, that he might himself become block leader: "one day perhaps he will succeed me" (*Chant*, 67). The identities of victim and victimizer are, then, dangerously close, interdependent, even interchangeable. The moral problems that this reversibility of roles involves are explored further in Wiesel's longer fiction: in *L'Aube* a Holocaust survivor kills a British officer; in *Le Cinquième Fils* two survivors help in the attempted murder of a former Nazi; in *L'Oublié* Jews become partisans and take revenge on the Germans.

In its anxious exploration of ethical dilemmas Wiesel's story reflects one of the central preoccupations of twentieth-century French literature; in texts such as Gide's *L'Immoraliste*, Camus's *Les Justes* or "L'Hôte" (published in *L'Exil et le royaume*), the plays of Sartre, or the novels of Malraux, the themes of moral responsibility and the legitimacy of violence have been foregrounded in ways that expose the insecurity—even the risk—involved in any moral judgment. Wiesel's fiction often seems no more assured of its moral authority than these texts. In "Une vieille connaissance" the potential proximity of victim and torturer serves to undermine the grounding upon which the narrator might pass any unequivocal judgment on the other man. This disruption of the security or even possibility of judgment is intensified by another passage that appears to be a digression and distraction from the action of the narrative, but that is in fact central to its development. The narrator considers the possibility of handing the man over to the authorities; he comments that he has been to several trials of former war criminals and imagines an exchange between prosecutor and defense lawyer. The narrator can see both sides of the argument at once:

> The prosecutor was telling the truth, so was the defense lawyer; the witnesses were all right, whether they were appearing for the prosecution or the defense. The verdict sounded just and yet a flagrant injustice emerged from these confused and difficult trials, one had the impression that no one had told the truth, because the truth was to be found

elsewhere, with the dead, and who knows if the truth didn't die with them? (*Chant,* 64)

The narrator has now put himself in a position where he must judge the former block leader, even though he knows no foundation on which to base his judgment, and even though his ability to judge is corroded by his sense of complicity and guilt, and by the impression that both defense and prosecution are equally correct or equally incorrect. The destabilization of identity ("I will assume all the roles, that of the witnesses first, then those of the prosecutor and the defense lawyer," *Chant,* 65) is accompanied by a disruption of moral authority and paralysis when faced with the need to act or judge. And this in turn is related to an absence of truth ("and who knows if the truth didn't die with them?") originating, as Wiesel's texts consistently suggest, in the Holocaust.

This passage governs the subsequent development of the story, as the narrator attempts to conduct an imaginary trial while undergoing a crisis of faith in his ability to pass judgment. This explains his dilemma at the end of the story: he *must* make a decision, but his ability to do so has been eroded. The final role reversal, when the block leader reassumes his former violent persona and takes command of the situation, is the best solution for the narrator because it relieves him of the need to make his own decisions. "Une vieille connaissance," then, dramatizes an anxiety of identity and judgment through the unstable play of complicity, identification, and role reversal. This obstructs the capacity of the text to adopt any assured moral standpoint; and the story revolves around a secret—the intelligible key to its action—that is ultimately withheld. When the block leader prepares to speak, the narrator expects revelation:

Sharply, he stiffens. I know that his eyes regained their coldness, their hardness. He is going to speak. At last. By defending himself, he is going to shed full light on that mystery [*jeter toute la lumière sur ce mystère*] to which we shall remain chained for ever. I know that he will speak without moving the thin line of his lips. At last, he is speaking. No: he is shouting. No: he is yelling. Without preparation, without warning. He insults me, he abuses me. (*Chant,* 70)

The narrator gets insults rather than explanations; and this precipitates his ultimate failure to find an intelligible principle underlying what has happened and even to understand his own actions:

> It's something else, it's worse: suddenly I am aware of my power-
> lessness, of my defeat. I know that I will leave him in freedom, but I
> will never know whether it's because of courage or cowardice. I will
> never know whether, confronted with the torturer, I acted as judge or
> victim. (*Chant,* 71)

Secrecy, here, is not just, as for Kermode, an inevitable by-product of the
narrative act. In all Wiesel's fiction the difficulties of interpretation posed
by the text are related specifically to a crisis of intelligibility envisaged as
originating in the Holocaust. In the rest of this chapter I discuss the
importance of the Holocaust as the background to Wiesel's fiction. First,
however, I comment on the disjunction between Wiesel's fictional and
nonfictional writing. Although in the latter he does admit to doubts and
uncertainties, these serve in the main to underline his honesty and hence
to strengthen his authority. The corrosion of ethical certainty in Wiesel's
fiction contrasts sharply with the moral assurance often to be found in his
nonliterary writings. This is illustrated briefly in two essays, "Notre
commune culpabilité . . ." and "Plaidoyer pour les morts," which
conclude *Le Chant des morts,* the collection of short texts in which "Une
vieille connaissance" also appears.

These two essays are rather different from other texts in the *Le Chant
des morts* in that they adopt an openly argumentative stance. "Notre
commune culpabilité . . ." opens with a series of reflections on the
Eichmann trial, which also formed an important part of the background
to "Une vieille connaissance." The question of guilt, which the short
fiction explores, is examined more discursively in "Notre commune
culpabilité . . . ," and the title of the essay already anticipates Wiesel's
answer to the fundamental question he poses: to whom should guilt for
the Holocaust be ascribed?

Some had criticized the Eichmann trial for being too restricted in its
scope, for concentrating on the guilt of one man rather than on the more
general historical, philosophical, and theological questions of responsibility that are also inevitably involved. Wiesel asserts that everyone is to
some extent guilty for what happened: "we maintain that, to different
degrees, we all bear a part of the responsibility for what happened in
Europe" (*Chant,* 177). As with the word *notre* (our) in the title of the
essay, the use of *we* here would seem to implicate the author of the essay
in the universal guilt he is describing, although the qualifying phrase "to
different degrees [*à des degrés divers*]" makes it clear that responsibility
is not equally shared. Wiesel goes on to demonstrate how everyone bears

a measure of responsibility: some countries occupied by the Germans actively collaborated in the extermination of the Jews; the Allies failed to take effective measures to impede the progress of the Holocaust; the Palestinian Jews were too absorbed by their own local concerns to become involved in events in Europe. Moreover, most cruelly, even the survivors of the Holocaust cannot rid themselves of a sense of guilt, knowing as they do that their own survival necessarily meant that others died in their place.

In "Notre commune culpabilité . . ." and "Plaidoyer pour les morts" Wiesel describes how the judges and the judged, the accused and the witnesses, all share some measure of responsibility for the Holocaust. This poses a problem about who has the right to judge when all are guilty. So far, then, the essays describe the same corrosion of secure judgmental positions as is depicted in narrative form in "Une vieille connaissance." The essays nevertheless differ from the story in that the implication of the speaking voice in the guilt being described (*"Notre* commune culpabilité . . ."*) does not seem to inhibit the authority with which Wiesel continues to pronounce judgment and deliver instructions to the reader. On the one hand the speaker accepts his absence of competence to judge, he concedes—indeed insists upon—the inability of the intellect to comprehend the Holocaust (thereby combatting what he sees as hasty, fashionable explanations); on the other hand, his rhetoric exhibits both verbal and moral self-confidence, as if his position were not damaged by the generalized absence of authority that his essays describe. He delivers essential truths about the nature of the Holocaust ("Events at that time did not obey any law and no law can be derived from them," *Chant,* 200), informs us of our duty ("To turn aside from these questions is to fail in our duty, it is to lose our only chance of being able, one day, to lead an authentic life," *Chant,* 200), issues prohibitions ("I forbid you to ask him the question," *Chant,* 203) and instructions ("So, learn to be silent," *Chant,* 220).

The apparently confident rhetoric of authority adopted here is in tension with the potential subversion of such confidence glimpsed in the speaker's acknowledgment that his own position is itself compromised. At one moment Wiesel approaches a justification of his procedure when he imagines what those concerned with the Eichmann trial should say in order to acquire the right to judge and attain the "valid moral level—that of absolute truth": "Before judging others we must first recognize our own errors, our own weaknesses" (*Chant,* 183). Only by his own acknowledgment of guilt, then, is the speaker empowered to assert and judge the guilt of others. The legal implications of the title "Plaidoyer pour les morts" suggest an analogy between the speaker and a lawyer with a case to argue; this contrasts with the narrator of "Une vieille connaissance" who found himself persuaded by both defense and prosecution lawyers, unable to judge one case against the other, and ultimately made powerless by the resultant indecision (see *Chant*, 63–64).

Wiesel's suggestion that acknowledging one's own errors makes it possible to judge others might strike a disturbing chord in readers familiar with French literature; for this is precisely the strategy adopted by Jean-Baptiste Clamence, the narrator of Camus's novel *La Chute*. Clamence, who presents himself as having been formerly a successful Parisian lawyer, now practices the paradoxical profession of the judge-penitent. He confesses his own shortcomings in order the better to judge those around him; his self-condemnation is used to authorize his condemnation of others: "Since one could not condemn others without immediately judging oneself, it was necessary to burden oneself with guilt in order to have the right to judge others [. . .] The more I accuse myself, the more I have the right to judge you."[3] *La Chute*, which displays a disorientating fascination with the logic and rhetoric of Clamence's monologue, can be read as an attack on Camus's existentialist critics; it is also a ruthless deconstruction of the authority of judgment and the power of discourse.

As such, it consistently exposes the tension between the assertion and denial of authority that remains partly occluded in Wiesel's essays. And this is one of the fundamental differences between his essays and his fiction. Whereas "Une vieille connaissance," like Camus's *La Chute*, foregrounds the collapse of assured ethical positions, essays such as "Notre commune culpabilité . . ." and "Plaidoyer pour les morts" require and attempt to reestablish some secure judgmental position, which Wiesel refers to as "absolute truth" (*Chant*, 183). The self-problematization (the implication that all positions, judgments, or interpretations are compromised) is still present in the essays, but it is not allowed to endanger the rhetorical power and moral impact of the text. In other words, the essays contain the material that *could* be used to deconstruct the rhetoric of the text, whereas "Une vieille connaissance" *foregrounds* its own deconstruction.

I prefer the problems of understanding raised in Wiesel's fiction to the assertive clarity of the essayist. There are of course good reasons for the persuasive strategies he adopts in his essays. The rhetoric of authority, whatever its simplifications, may be the price Wiesel has to pay in order to participate in the formation of opinion through his essays and to exercise an influence in his human rights campaigning. To put it in other terms: the confrontation with ambiguity may be ultimately more honest than a display of certainty, but it might also endanger the practical effectiveness of Wiesel's activism.

The comparison between "Une vieille connaissance" and Wiesel's essays illustrates a tension between his fictional practice and the ethical stance for which he has received most attention. I return to this tension in chapter 5; but in this study I concentrate mainly on Wiesel's fiction, in the conviction that the hermeneutic problems that it raises have significance beyond academic disputes over points of detailed interpretation. That significance is largely due to the importance of the Holocaust for Wiesel's writing.

THE HOLOCAUST AND THE CRISIS OF HUMANISM

If history were just One Damned Thing After Another, the Holocaust would be one event in a random and meaningless sequence. However, the Holocaust was too vast in scale and terrible in nature to be dismissed as an event without significance. It demands explanation precisely because the conceptual paradigms by which we normally understand experience do not apply to it; even the pogroms that periodically decimated the European Jews seem trifling in comparison.[4] The Holocaust provokes an urgent need for explanation. This section considers aspects of the significance attached to it, and shows how some of Wiesel's critics have dealt with the problems it poses for the establishment of positive values.

For some religious Jews the Holocaust represents a challenge to their traditional faith that history was governed by a superintending God who had entered into a binding covenant with them on Mount Sinai. It was difficult to understand how God could allow the Holocaust to happen; and so part of its significance derives from the theological challenge it poses to Jewish, and to a lesser extent Christian, thinkers. For such thinkers it would be wrong to explain what happened simply by cultural or sociological factors, because it was also metaphysical and ontological in character. Steven Katz outlines nine responses: (1) the Holocaust is not unique, it is like all other tragedies; (2) it is a punishment for sin; (3) it represents a vicarious atonement for the sins of others; some die so that others may be cleansed; (4) it is a test of faith; (5) it demonstrates the eclipse of God, or (6) shows that God is dead; (7) God is not implicated because human evil is the price that must be paid for human freedom; (8) it is a revelation to the Jews of their duty to survive; (9) it is an inscrutable mystery that demands faith and silence rather than explanation.[5]

The Holocaust has been described as the third element in a "three caesura paradigm" of Jewish history, after the destruction of the Temple and the expulsion from Spain; these three events brought shifts in Jewish thought, which, in Arthur Cohen's account, progressed from guilt, to hope, to meaninglessness.[6] Even Wiesel, who according to Alan Berger remains within the covenantal framework of traditional Jewish faith, has claimed that God broke his covenant with the Jews during the Holocaust.[7] The most extreme position in this theological debate is represented by Richard Rubenstein. He has argued that the Holocaust marks the demise not only of the covenant, but also of God himself; after the Holocaust we live in the time of the death of God.[8]

The Holocaust has also been discussed in the context of secular values. According to Sidra Dekoven Ezrahi, "No symbolic universe grounded in humanistic beliefs could confront the Holocaust without being shaken to its foundations." All humanistic belief systems are undermined. Berger has described the Holocaust as "the death of reason and the defeat of man."[9] Science is compromised by the fact that it was used to perfect the techniques of killing; technology, rather than advancing the establishment of a society based on humane and rational principles, was harnessed in the construction and operation of the death camps. Belief in individual conscience also carries little weight in the light of the indifference or collusion of those who knew about the murders. If, after the Holocaust, it was hard to believe in God, it was hard also to believe in Man; as Wiesel has written, "At Auschwitz not only man died, but also the idea of man" (*Chant*, 210).

Western culture seems hollow if it creates the ground on which the Final Solution may be implemented. This raises particular problems for the writer who uses literature to express the failure of culture; Ezrahi writes that the "writer who touches such events with his inheritance of words appears to be reaffirming if not the sanities then the forms of civilised existence." To communicate with the reader, the Holocaust writer must at least in part follow linguistic and literary conventions; but to follow such conventions is also to distort the truth of what is being communicated. Holocaust literature, then, runs the risk of diminishing the horror of its subject by succumbing to what Ezrahi calls "the dissonance between aesthetic and formalistic conventions of order and beauty and the chaos and ugliness which were the essence of Auschwitz."[10]

The Holocaust has given rise to a wide range of literary responses. The chapters of Ezrahi's *By Words Alone* are devoted to seven broad categories: documentary literature, which sticks as close as possible to factual detail; concentrationary realism, which deals with experiences in the death camps; literature of survival, which describes the lives of survivors of the death camps; texts within the tradition of Jewish lamentation literature; Jewish texts concerned with the covenantal implications of the Holocaust; texts that mythologize the Holocaust; and works written by authors who were not themselves in the death camps. Different categorizations or further refinements are possible: in *Crisis and Covenant*, for example, Berger subdivides Ezrahi's fifth category by distinguishing between those Jewish writers who maintain, modify, or break with the traditional covenant. Some writers (for example, Blanchot, Jabès, Duras, Perec), undoubtedly affected by the Holocaust, have chosen to refer to it only rarely or obliquely; indeed, the impossibility of writing directly and truthfully about the Holocaust has become a commonplace among writers of the modern period.

Critics are equally prone to feelings of anxiety and inadequacy as they approach the subject. At the beginning of his book *The Holocaust and the Literary Imagination* Lawrence Langer expresses an unease that can be taken as characteristic of Holocaust literature and its criticism: "There is something disagreeable, almost dishonourable, in the conversion of the suffering of the victims into works of art which are then, to use Adorno's pungent metaphor, thrown as fodder to the world ('der Welt zum Fraß vorgeworfen') that murdered them."[11] The danger of art is that it may give order, coherence, and meaning, and thereby uphold, by its very status as art, the culture that seemed endangered; so Holocaust literature may implicitly assert the continuation of the humanistic belief systems that thematically it undermines. By its very existence it may reaffirm the survival of values that have been shown to be without purchase on the real. Not surprisingly, this paradox has provoked radical responses. The best known is Adorno's proscription of poetry after Auschwitz. Other writers and thinkers have echoed this view, insisting that the Holocaust either cannot or should not be represented in literature: "In the presence of certain realities art is trivial or impertinent. . . . The world of

Auschwitz lies outside speech as it lies outside reason." "It is forbidden to make art out of Auschwitz because art takes the sting out of suffering." "The task is to save [the Holocaust] from becoming literature."[12]

The inadequacies of humanist values would be of limited and strictly historical interest if we had something with which to replace them. However, humanism is notoriously difficult either to pin down or to reject; and the critique of humanism reproduces and relies on humanist attitudes. Derrida, for example, in an essay on Heidegger, acknowledges that humanism is not easily escaped despite its contradictions: "Is it possible to escape from it? No sign permits us to think we can. . . . Is it possible to transform the programme? I do not know."[13] Derrida even concedes that humanism may have played a crucial role in the establishment of antiracist values that make possible the denunciation of Nazism.[14]

Adorno shows the same ambivalence in his discussions of art in the post-Holocaust era. On the one hand he defends his view that it is barbaric to write poetry after Auschwitz: culture has been revealed to be trash, art may have lost its right to exist; it has the potential for producing pleasure from even the most horrific material; it may make an unintelligible destiny ("das unausdenkliche Schicksal") appear meaningful, thereby diminishing its horror; even morally committed literature is in collusion with the culture that gave birth to murder: it affirms human values ("das Menschliche") when no such affirmation can be justified.[15] On the other hand Adorno insists that the suffering of the victims must not be forgotten, and that survivors have the right to (try to) express their suffering through art: "But that suffering . . . demands the continuation of the art which it forbids; hardly anywhere else does suffering still find its own voice, the comfort which does not immediately betray it." In *Negative Dialectics* Adorno continues this line of thought: "Perennial suffering has as much right to expression as a tortured man has to scream; hence it may have been wrong to say that after Auschwitz you could no longer write poems." Adorno insists that culture has been revealed as "radically culpable and shabby," but it may be dangerously barbaric (as well as impossible) simply to abandon our cultural baggage; we are left with a choice of barbarisms: "All post-Auschwitz culture, including its urgent critique, is garbage."[16]

In his discussion of art and culture after the Holocaust Adorno adopts a paradoxical stance that is, I think, characteristic of the best and most honest thinking on the subject. (We see in the next section that Wiesel also considers paradox to be the inevitable condition of humanity after Auschwitz.) Writing on the Holocaust is, I suggest, motivated by a double necessity: to confront the irrecuperability of what happened to traditional cultural and religious values, and at the same time to maintain those values against the odds (because we might be even worse off without them). The reemergence of humanist and religious positions that seemed to have been made untenable can be seen with particular clarity at the end of the general introduction to a reader of Holocaust literature, edited by Albert Friedlander:

> We cannot sustain the old belief in man, nor the old belief in God and His moral ordering of the world, but we can search for new beliefs. And once we have wept for man, we can also glory in the indomitable spirit of man which yet endures. As we turn to this dark period, we recognize that in confronting the worst, man has produced the best within himself. We look at the Age of Evil and we come to celebrate the vision of man's goodness, the songs of the night that join together with the morning stars and sing of the crowning glory of God's creation— the human soul.[17]

The "but" in the first sentence signals an imminent reversal of perspectives. Crisis leads to reconstruction, and the confrontation with Evil culminates in the rediscovery of Good. Whatever the intentions of the author, the process of writing about the Holocaust seems to involve a renewed affirmation of the values that seemed most endangered (faith in man and God, the redemptive power of art), and to avoid this may require a boldness and rigor that are impossible to sustain. And readers share the writers' ambivalence toward post-Holocaust art and culture, as Sidra Dekoven Ezrahi suggests at the end of her book *By Words Alone:* "Are we still searching for redemption in literature? Or do we rather condemn the writer who finds it in the darkest regions?"[18]

I now discuss how the reaffirmation of endangered values can be seen in critical accounts of Wiesel's writing. The problem for the humanist critic is Wiesel's first book, *La Nuit*. This autobiographical *témoignage* (testimony) gives a bleak, uncompromising depiction of life and death in Auschwitz and Buchenwald. There is broad consensus among Wiesel's critics that all his subsequent works can be read as a gloss, or Midrash, on this initial text and the experiences to which it refers.[19] It can also be argued, I think, that Wiesel himself has been trying, in his later fictional works, to distance himself from the trauma of *La Nuit*. (I discuss some aspects of this in relation to the death of the narrator's father in chapter 6). In order to affirm their own humanist stance, Wiesel's critics need to be able to read *La Nuit* through the perspective of his later revisionary texts. The meaning of the first work is not permitted to lie within the work itself; it must be found through its relation to later, less bleak texts. This requirement, then, commits the critics to a view of Wiesel's writing as a unified corpus in process of organic development. Alan Berger, for example, refers to *La Nuit* as Wiesel's "Rubenstein phase," alluding to Richard Rubenstein's "death of God" theology; but the designation of the text as a "phase" already implies that other phases will follow, that the less negative phases will mitigate the initial rejection of God. And indeed, Berger goes on to describe *Le Jour* as "the first attempt to enter a new phase which permits the reconstruction of a covenant tradition."[20] Wiesel subsequently espouses messianism and becomes "a covenant revisionist," revising but reaffirming God's covenant with the Jews.[21]

Berger's use of the word "phase" is not a neutral choice; on the contrary, it actually preinscribes the conclusion that restores Wiesel to the tradition from which he had seemed to deviate in *La Nuit*. This is most commonly achieved by Wiesel's critics through the metaphor of a journey. The dominant reading of Wiesel's fiction uncovers a progression from trial to wisdom, darkness to light, despair to hope. The chapter headings from Ted Estess's short book indicate this progression: "The Journey into Night" (chapter 2), "A New Beginning" (chapter 4), "Choosing Life" (chapter 5). Ellen Fine, in what is the best single study of Wiesel's fiction, isolates "a progression in the author's own thinking from the individual to others, from isolation to communication, from resignation to regeneration." Edward Grossman describes Wiesel's work as "a forced march from despair to affirmation."[22] Robert McAfee Brown describes how, in Wiesel's writing, "Darkness that Eclipses Light" (chapter 2) is relieved by "Light that Penetrates Darkness" (chapter 3); and he describes a "moral journey—not only an affirmation of humanity, won back by Michael [in *La Ville de la chance*] at so great a cost; not only an affirmation of God, won back by Grégor [in *Les Portes de la forêt*] at so great a cost; but an affirmation of humanity and God together, won back by Elie Wiesel at so great a cost." John K. Roth refers to Wiesel's "journey . . . from the despair of [*La Nuit*], where God dies at Auschwitz to the theodicy of [*Célébration biblique*]." And Irving Halperin locates in Wiesel's writing a movement "from Buchenwald to the synagogue, from the image of the corpse-like face in a mirror [at the end of *La Nuit*] to the grandiloquent and serene words of the Kaddish [at the end of *Les Portes de la forêt*]."[23]

I have mentioned here only a handful of Wiesel's critics, but the journey-metaphor occurs with sufficient frequency for it to be more than coincidental; and I am tempted to argue that it actually structures and predetermines readings of his fiction. It corresponds to the deep need that motivates writing on the Holocaust to demonstrate that things are not as bad as they may seem. In contrast to Wiesel's uncompromising maxim quoted above ("At Auschwitz not only man died, but also the idea of man," *Chant*, 210), here, if men died in Auschwitz, then the values of Man seem to have survived relatively unscathed. The journey-metaphor makes of *La Nuit* a starting point; and what is important of course is not the starting point but the destination. The metaphor predestines (and perhaps dooms) Wiesel to arrive, ultimately, in the homeland of covenantal Judaism and liberal humanism.

In this book I argue that, even if Wiesel himself might accept (even encourage) such a reading of his work, it is not necessarily borne out by the texts themselves. I suggest that a great deal of the enthusiasm generated by Wiesel's writing derives from its susceptibility to humanist or theological recuperation. The critics appear almost embarrassingly grateful that Wiesel has returned to the fold:

> Elie Wiesel is not an ordinary writer. We cannot read him without the desire to change, to lead better lives. His books are of the kind that save souls.[24]

> I believe that my meeting with [Elie Wiesel] has been, for me, on the level of destiny. . . . For me, Elie Wiesel has made the great act of faith of his century.[25]

> His courage forces us to reexamine who we may claim to be at any given moment, and such self-evaluation may one day save us from a nuclear holocaust.[26]

> After reading Elie Wiesel my faith may be less sure of itself, because no one can read his books without being shaken. On the other hand, I think my faith is also more passionate than before. I am grateful to him for moving me, for setting my soul on fire.[27]

It is strange that Wiesel's literary journey has turned out to be so predictable, and so easily reconciled with the values it seemed to endanger. The story told by Wiesel's critics is a coherent, morally uplifting tale imbued with significance, made intelligible by the community of values in which reader and author participate. Wiesel's fiction appears as a limpid mirror reflecting the author's gradual conversion to hope, communicated and understood without loss or distortion of meaning. However, Wiesel's texts are often neither as clear, nor as uplifting, nor as intelligible, as the dominant reading of his fiction would suggest. His stories often entail confusion, disbelief, and misunderstanding, rather than the linear progression from despair to hope attributed by the critics to Wiesel himself. And those critics contrive to mitigate the most challenging aspects of Wiesel's conception of the Holocaust as a radical hiatus.

WIESEL AND THE HOLOCAUST

In his study of Holocaust theology Dan Cohn-Sherbok criticizes Wiesel's treatment of the Holocaust on the grounds that "he seems to adopt contradictory positions." Cohn-Sherbok identifies three main contradictions. (1) Wiesel portrays God as unconcerned with human history, yet also castigates him for not intervening to prevent Nazi atrocities. Such criticism presupposes an interventionist God, which Wiesel's texts deny. (2) In some texts Wiesel presents God as being on the side of violence and destruction, yet in the cantata *Ani Maamin* he appears as a compassionate comforter: "God is either a remorseless tyrant or a merciful father. He cannot be both." (3) Wiesel believes that modern man lives in a religious void, yet he remains committed to the Jewish way of life; this is inconsistent since Judaism is sustained by, and untenable without, belief in a God who cares for his people. Wiesel refuses traditional faith, deism (belief in God as Prime Mover who does not intervene in human affairs), and atheism. He thus leaves himself with no coherent theological position. Cohn-Sherbok criticizes Wiesel for being "unable to accept the consequences of his own views," and for proposing a theology of protest that is "not only inconsistent, but also devoid of any clear basis for a dedication to the Jewish heritage and Jewish existence."[28]

There may be some justification for Cohn-Sherbok's criticisms, but his understanding of Wiesel is severely vitiated by his naive approach to fiction. He unquestioningly assumes that the views expressed by Wiesel's characters are also unproblematically attributable to Wiesel himself. The narrator of *Le Jour* may depict God as cruel, but such a depiction does not automatically commit Wiesel to the same view. At the same time, the impossibility of abstracting a coherent theological stance from Wiesel's work is hardly a failing, at least in Wiesel's terms, because he argues that the impossibility of theoretical coherence is itself one of the consequences of the Holocaust. Not only does Wiesel not have a consistent theory of the Holocaust (though he does make comments that might be incorporated into such a theory), but, as he has frequently insisted, the Holocaust demarcates the limits and failure of all theory: "Answers, I say that there is none. Each of these theses contains perhaps an element of truth, but their sum remains beneath and outside what was, at the time of night, the truth" (*Chant*, 200); "its mystery is condemned to remain entire, inviolable" (*Un Juif*, 191). The Holocaust is an essential mystery, an enigma that cannot be explained, the stumbling block of all philosophical, theological, sociological, historical, or ethical reflection. Wiesel, then, is less concerned with explanations than with the question of how, and whether, it is possible or permissible to talk about something that defies both language and thought.

Wiesel's writing is characterized by what Ellen Fine calls "an underlying tension between the compulsion to tell the tale and the fear of betraying the sanctity of the subject."[29] The Holocaust demands both silence and language, awe and outrage. Wiesel feels that survivors such as himself have a moral obligation to tell of their experiences; yet he also argues that they will inevitably fail in that obligation. Wiesel invokes a number of reasons for their failure, which can be found, with different degrees of emphasis, in the essays "Plaidoyer pour les morts" (in *Le Chant des morts*), "Une génération après" (in *Entre deux soleils*), and "Plaidoyer pour les survivants" (in *Un Juif, aujourd'hui*), as well as in his numerous interviews. Taken together they constitute what he calls "the drama of the messenger incapable of delivering his message" (*EDS*, 249):

1. The Holocaust lies beyond language. Wiesel has repeatedly insisted that the Holocaust is radically alien to language, and even that it marks a decisive point of separation between words and meaning. Any attempt to describe it also deforms it (see *EDS*, 246; *Un Juif*, 191).
2. The survivor risks madness by talking about his or her experiences (see *Un Juif*, 193).
3. Since the Holocaust is a sacred mystery, to talk about it is sacrilege (see *EDS*, 248).
4. Talking about it may trivialize it and thereby blunt its importance and impact (see *Chant*, 195–96).
5. Even if survivors did talk about their experiences, people would not believe them (see *EDS*, 246).
6. People could not understand what the survivors were saying; their experiences are beyond our grasp, and their use of language is

unintelligible to us: "The survivor expresses himself in a foreign tongue. The code that he uses, you will never break it" (*Un Juif*, 191).

Wiesel, then, preempts any discussion by indicting the coherence of the message, the adequacy of the medium, and the competence of both speaker and listener. The argument in favor of silence is disconcertingly reminiscent of what is known in French as *le raisonnement du chaudron*, which derives from Freud's *Interpretation of Dreams*. Freud recounts a dream that seems to relieve him of responsibility for the persistence of suffering in one of his patients; yet the dream offers inconsistent and even mutually exclusive explanations for the patient's pain. This reminds Freud of the defense given by a man accused by a neighbor of giving back a borrowed kettle in a damaged condition: "The defendant asserted first, that he had given it back undamaged; secondly, that the kettle had a hole in it when he borrowed it; and thirdly, that he had never borrowed a kettle from his neighbour at all."[30] Individually, any of these arguments might be accepted; taken together they indicate how the powerful desire for exculpation overrides strict logic. Wiesel, adopting what might be called *le raisonnement du silence*, calls upon a series of at least partially incompatible arguments: the Holocaust cannot be described; the Holocaust should not be described; if it were described we would not believe or understand; to describe it risks trivializing it. What emerges is a *desire for unrepresentability*, which would relieve the survivor of responsibility and justify a silence that he believes to be culpable.[31] This does not diminish the survivor's duty to bear witness, though it condemns it to paradox and failure; and it suggests that the need to tell and the obligation to tell will remain in constant tension with the impossibility of telling and the desire to forget.

Fiction plays a particularly important role in this simultaneous need to speak and desire to remain silent. On the surface the reservations about literature expressed by Wiesel would seem to make it a totally inappropriate medium for him to adopt. He accepts and even radicalizes Adorno's strictures on poetry and culture after Auschwitz: "Adorno was perhaps right. After Auschwitz poetry is no longer possible. Nor literature. Nor friendship. Nor hope. Nor anything" (*Un Juif*, 202). Secular literature rarely appears in a positive light in Wiesel's writing. To the pious Jewish child it seemed trivial; to the adult Holocaust survivor it seems a dangerous distraction or distortion. Wiesel's literary project involves, paradoxically, the refusal of literature: "No literature, above all not to make literature [*ne pas faire de la littérature*]" (*Silences*, 18). He insists that "any testimony [. . .] is worth more than any novel" (*Qui êtes-vous?* 70); and Holocaust literature is a nonsensical notion because the Holocaust is not susceptible to literary representation: "Unique experience, the Holocaust defies literature" (*EDS*, 248–49).

> At the risk of shocking you, I will tell you that so-called Holocaust literature does not exist, cannot exist.
> With a generation's distance, one can still say it, one can already affirm it: Auschwitz negates all literature as it negates all systems, all doctrines; to imprison it in a philosophy is to restrict it; to replace it by words, no matter which words, is to denature it. So-called Holocaust literature? The very term is a nonsense. (*Un Juif*, 190)

> A novel about Auschwitz is not a novel, or else it is not about Auschwitz. The two do not go together. (*Qui êtes-vous?* 49)

A passage at the beginning of *Entre deux soleils* illustrates Wiesel's unease about fiction and his career as writer, particularly in the context of the Jewish tradition to which he still claims adherence. The narrator has gone to see his grandfather's rabbi who questions him about his life; the rabbi is taken aback to hear that the narrator is a writer. He asks what sort of stories the narrator writes and receives the reply: "- No idea, Rabbi" (*EDS*, 10). He asks whether the stories are true or not: "- Yes . . . and no, I stammered with difficulty. I do not know . . ." (*EDS*, 10); he asks whether or not the narrator knew the characters involved: "- Yes . . . and no. I would have liked to have known them" (*EDS*, 10); and he asks whether or not the events described really took place: "- Yes . . . and no. They could have taken place" (*EDS*, 10). The rabbi is not impressed by the narrator's responses:

> His eyes darkened:
> - I see . . . You invent characters and stories . . . You spend your time hiding reality, divine or human reality, with words created for other ends. In other words: you write lies.
> Under the shock, I waited for a long moment without saying a word. The child in me, caught red-handed, had nothing to say in his defence. But the adult had to justify himself:
> - All that, Rabbi, is not as simple as you seem to think. You see, certain events have taken place but are not true; others, on the contrary, are true but have not taken place. (*EDS*, 10–11)

"Poor Rebbe. He missed the whole point," observes Robert McAfee Brown.[32] However, the narrator's unease here, coupled with Wiesel's need to recount the story, indicates that the rabbi may after all have a point. The narrator's evasions and contradictions ("Yes . . . and no") expose the ambiguity of his relationship to writing; and the rabbi's "you write lies" suggests the same equation of literature with falsehood (or at best unnecessary ornament) as Wiesel's own "above all not to make literature" (*Silences*, 18).

This unease concerning the value and status of literature raises the question of why Wiesel has chosen to write fiction rather than, for example, engaging in historical research or making documentaries. Wiesel has suggested that ambiguity lies at the root of his fiction: "In effect, this will to say and this impossibility of saying are at the origin of all my novels. I am like Kafka's messenger who does not manage to deliver his message" (*Qui êtes-vous?* 70). Literature, then, is characterized by its exclusion from truth; rather than proclaiming a message, it foregrounds its inability to communicate: "I know that words do not have the power to transmit the message that I carry within me, nor even a fragment of the message. I try in vain to say the unsayable in order to express my inability to say" (*Qui êtes-vous?* 69). On his own account, then, Wiesel's fiction is the product of a tension between the will to say (*la volonté de dire*) and the impossibility of saying (*l'impossibilité à dire*); however, in the light of what I called above *le raisonnement du silence*, I would add a third factor: the desire *not* to speak, the desire to keep silent. Despite the condemnation of literature in Wiesel's writing, fiction appears as the only possible compromise between the need to speak and the desire not to speak; it allows Wiesel to bear witness to imaginary lives, to fulfil his obligation to preserve the memories of the dead while maintaining the sanctity of his own experiences and remaining reticent about his own grief. In this light, the rabbi's "you write lies" acquires its full force: the mendacious quality of fiction, or at least its inassimilability to a simple truth/ falsehood paradigm, makes it possible for Wiesel to fulfil his self-imposed double bind to speak and to remain silent. The secrecy of literature is as crucial for Wiesel as its ability to deal with urgent historical, theological, and ethical questions.

On occasions, Wiesel has himself acknowledged that the function of literature, and even the source of its value, lies in its ability to conceal as well as to reveal. He states this as a general principle:

To take on the project of recreating the unbelievable reality of one sole person, you or someone else in one sole camp, that borders on sacrilege. The better the story is, the more it seems clothed. The secret must remain in a pure state [*Plus le récit est bon, plus il paraît habillé. Le secret doit demeurer à l'état pur*]. Once revealed, it becomes myth and can only become tarnished, diminished. (*EDS*, 248)

And in *Paroles d'étranger* he admits that this desire for secrecy may motivate his own writing: "Sometimes it seems to me that I speak of other things in the sole aim of keeping silent about the essential: lived experience" (*Paroles*, 12).

In order to protect the silent universe which is mine, I recount that of others. In order not to speak of that which hurts me, I explore other subjects: biblical, talmudic, Hassidic or contemporary. I evoke Abraham and Isaac in order not to reveal the mysteries of my relationship with my father. I recount the adventure of the Besht [the founder of Hassidism] in order not to have to insist on how his descendants ended. In other words, literature has become for me a way of making you look aside. The stories I reproduce are never those that I would like, that I ought, to tell. (*Paroles*, 187–88)

Wiesel's use of language is itself implicated in the dual imperative of revelation and concealment. Wiesel is one of a number of writers with direct experience of the Holocaust, including Anna Langfus, Piotr Rawicz, and Jorge Semprun, who have chosen to write in French although they were not native speakers of the language. Wiesel lived for only a relatively short period in France, but French was the first language he learned after the Holocaust; it seems to offer a medium not directly associated with or compromised by previous experiences. Even so, his sometimes tortuous French style seems to bear traces of the trauma of the Holocaust.[33] His use of language often seems contrived and awkward, deprived of fluency and harmony; his texts stutter rather than flow. Paradox is preferred to simple affirmation; and Wiesel's texts are full of portentous-sounding phrases that may mean nothing. Three elements of style in particular contribute to the stuttering rhythms of Wiesel's prose: repetition, the use of periods to isolate individual phrases, and apparent self-contradiction. Wiesel frequently uses repetition for rhetorical emphasis; but it also marks an absence of progression or development in an argument that continually revolves around the same compulsive thoughts:

> Yet it can happen that the survivor feels remorse. He has tried to bear witness; it was for nothing. He has said what he knew; it was for nothing [. . .] [The witnesses] have spoken. And it was for nothing. (*Paroles*, 13)

Wiesel uses periods to interrupt the flow of the sentence and throw into relief individual words and phrases, connected to but disjoined from what precedes:

> And yes, like him, sometimes I use words. Against my will. Words separate me from myself. They signify absence. And lack. (*Paroles*, 7)

> And the survivors, powerless and overwhelmed, have only to be submissive. And accept. And say thank you. (*Un Juif*, 176)

Moreover, the isolated phrase may introduce a reversal or contradiction of the perspective adopted up until that point. This is particularly apparent in Wiesel's use of the word *pourtant* ("yet, nevertheless") and the phrase *Et pourtant* ("And yet"). Vincent Engel has drawn attention to Wiesel's almost compulsive use of *Et pourtant* in his writing since the publication of *Le Serment de Kolvillàg*; and Robert McAfee Brown has also commented on the importance of the phrase: "They may be Wiesel's most important words. For they signal that conclusions do not have to follow from premises, that directions can be reversed, that there are new possibilities beyond what we anticipated, that we are not locked into ineluctable patterns."[34]

Brown emphasizes the positive aspect of this reversal of perspectives; he concedes that "Et pourtant" sometimes signals a change to a negative view, but he argues that its most common use is to mark the survival of positive values: everything is bleak, *and yet* there is still reason to hope.[35] Brown's view is, I think, too schematic, and it concords with his determination to find hopeful messages in Wiesel's writing. It is a simplification to suggest that the positive dominates the negative, just as it is equally simplistic to maintain the opposite. "Pourtant" and "Et pourtant" signal an instability of meaning, the reversibility of perspectives and the near inevitability of paradox; and it is striking how many of the examples revolve around the need to speak about something that negates language:

> I only know that Treblinka and Auschwitz cannot be recounted. Yet I've tried, God knows that I've tried. (*Paroles*, 11)

The true witness can only be dumb.

And yet. Right at the beginning, on a continent still in ruins, he did violence to himself and told his story, or at least raised the veil. (*Un Juif*, 192)

A treacherous situation: impossible to be indifferent to it and impossible to envisage it without being indifferent to it. To refer to it raises as many problems as turning aside from it.

Yet, yet. It would be necessary to speak to you. (*Serment*, 55)

And at its most enigmatic, the device may be used to reverse an affirmation that itself was already mysterious:

Every story has an end as every end has a story. Yet, yet . . . (*Serment*, 254)

These elements of Wiesel's style also govern longer sequences of his writing. Phrases, ideas, characters, and episodes recur in similar or identical forms in different texts. The repetitiveness, the staccato rhythms, and the fragmented composition of his texts have been criticized.[36] To some, Wiesel appears to have nothing new to say, to be repeating public pronouncements he first made thirty years ago and using the same material over and over again in his fiction. Whether such criticisms are justified, repetition, paradox, and fragmentation are essential to his writing and are signs of an unease about signification and communication that his texts evince on the levels of theme and style. This is particularly evident when Wiesel discusses the Holocaust. His essays constantly shift perspective. He mimics the French academic mode of argumentation, which progresses from thesis to antithesis to synthesis, but with a crucially missing final element; at one moment he argues for silence, at the next for the necessity of speech, but there is no resolution of contradictory views. This instability within the very structure of his arguments conflicts with the polemical tone of his essays; his desire to argue clear positions and impose the "correct" attitudes is threatened by the unease that pervades everything he writes. A passage from *Signes d'exode* illustrates the semantic insecurity that is provoked by the attempt to write and think about the Holocaust:

What for Orwell was a matter of fantasy or foreboding, is the lived experience of the Auschwitz survivor. Orwell, that was before; for us it is after. And before. In other words: for us time seems to have stopped between Auschwitz and Hiroshima.

> Be careful [*Attention*], we mustn't compare them. Where the con-
> centration camps are concerned, every analogy can only be false. And
> blasphemous. Despite—or because of [*En dépit—ou en raison*]—its
> universal implications and applications, the Holocaust remains unique:
> it is in its singularity that its universality is to be found. And yet [*Et
> pourtant*]. Negating History, Auschwitz represents a sort of aberration
> and culminating point to History. (*Signes*, 221)

The text cannot settle down into a set of stable, unproblematized proposi-
tions. It seems to suggest, but then to withdraw from, a comparison
between Auschwitz and Hiroshima. Twice, it interrupts its own flow and
shifts perspective ("Attention," "Et pourtant"). Opposites seem on the
verge of collapsing into one another: the distinction between *before* and
after is denied; *despite* and *because* ("En dépit—ou en raison") cannot be
told apart; and the Holocaust appears as both singular and universal,
universal because singular, outside history but also part of it, its end and
its culminating point.

Wiesel insists on the impossibility of talking truthfully about the
Holocaust; and consistent with his reservations about Holocaust literature, he treats the subject obliquely and with reticence. Even so, it affects
everything he writes; what cannot be said will continue to haunt what is
said through the shadow of a meaning that cannot quite be grasped.
Exegetes of the Hebrew Bible distinguish between four stages in the
process of understanding; the fourth of these is concerned with the
hidden meaning of the text.[37] The Holocaust, for Wiesel, makes such
hidden meanings unattainable: "Still today, my reason fails; it is unable
to grasp the hidden meaning [*le sens caché*], the brutal truth of what I
have seen" (*Signes*, 241). It is in the elusiveness of hidden meanings and
the consequential frustration of the intellect, rather than in its importance as a theme, that the Holocaust makes its most important impact on
Wiesel's writing.

Auschwitz, according to Wiesel, signifies "the defeat of the intellect
that wants to find a Meaning—with a capital—to history" (*Chant*, 202).
The evacuation of meaning from history leads ultimately to Wiesel's
aesthetics of secrecy; his texts constantly return to the exclusion of both
author and reader from a lost domain of intelligible secrets: "No, I do not
understand. And if I write it is to warn the reader that he will never
understand either" (*Paroles*, 11). This book addresses some of the ways
in which Wiesel's texts confront the reader with the limits of understanding.

TWO

Storytelling

TESTIMONY

The Holocaust raises the question of the adequacy of narrative in its most acute form, and I return to this question on numerous occasions. All writers (indeed all speakers) touched by the Holocaust directly or indirectly have had to confront this dilemma; the impossibility of narrating was already taken for granted in the earliest accounts of experiences in the concentration camps, such as David Rousset's *L'Univers concentrationnaire* or Robert Antelme's *L'Espèce humaine*.[1] Wiesel himself is intensely aware of the tension between the need to narrate and the impossibility of narrating, and his writing can be seen as a sustained reflection on this tension. In this chapter I discuss three stories recounted in Wiesel's texts and the different perspectives that they give on the problem of storytelling and the respective perplexities of narrators and listeners.

The first story is from *La Nuit*, and it is introduced by the first occurrence of the keyword *raconter* (to recount) in Wiesel's writing. The story of Moché the Beadle, who returns "miraculously" after his deportation, overshadows all Wiesel's subsequent texts:

> He recounted his story [*Il raconta son histoire*] and that of his companions. The train carrying the deportees had crossed the Hungarian frontier and, once in Polish territory, had been put in the charge of the Gestapo. There, it had stopped. The Jews were ordered to get out and climb into lorries. The lorries drove off toward a forest. They were told to get out. They were told to dig huge ditches. When they had finished their work, the men of the Gestapo began theirs. Without passion, without haste, they slaughtered their prisoners. Each had to

approach the ditch and bare the back of his neck. Babies were thrown in the air and the machine gunners used them as targets. It was in the forest of Galicia, near Kolomaye. How had he, Moché the Beadle, succeeded in escaping? By miracle. Wounded in the leg, he was thought to be dead. (*N*, 16)

Moché's narrative, coming at the beginning of *La Nuit*, serves as a reflection of Eliezer's situation as narrator, and even of the storytelling impulse that underlies Wiesel's writing in general. Saved from death by chance, or "by miracle [*par miracle*]" as we are twice told (see *N*, 16 and 17; chapter 3 this book), the narrator feels impelled to recount the outrages he has witnessed. Storytelling is portrayed as truthful witnessing, practiced by a narrator more dead than alive, but charged with an urgent ethical mission ("I wanted to return to Sighet to recount my death to you," *N*, 17; see also the end of *La Nuit*, when Eliezer looks in a mirror and sees "a corpse," *N*, 121).

We are invited to read *La Nuit* as a témoignage (testimony), not a novel; for its impact, the text requires our belief in the literal truth of the facts that are described. In consequence, we should identify the Eliezer who narrates *La Nuit* with the Elie given on the title page as the author of the text. The events described in *La Nuit* are authenticated by the experience of the narrator, who claims to be describing what he has seen with his own eyes. This is first indicated in Moché's tale: "He no longer spoke of God or the Kabbalah, *but only of what he had seen [mais seulement de ce qu'il avait vu]*" (*N*, 16; my emphasis); and the same claim underlies and justifies the truth of the whole text, as Eliezer/Elie recalls the horror of Birkenau: "A lorry approached the hole and tipped its load into it: it was children. Babies. Yes, I had seen it, seen it with my own eyes . . . [*je l'avais vu, de mes yeux vu*]" (*N*, 42). If we do not accept the identification of Eliezer with Elie, then the direct link between the text and historical reality will be broken. Moreover, the moral urgency of the text depends upon our acceptance of it as truthful; without that claim to truthfulness the ethical underpinning of the témoignage would be lost; it would become fiction, a novel rather than a historical document. And Wiesel certainly wants to avoid this reading of *La Nuit* as fiction (though the difference between Eliezer and Elie is striking because it *encourages* such a reading, and perhaps indicates after all the desire for the text to be read as fiction; this issue is addressed in chapter 3).

The model of the survivor-witness who tells of disastrous occurrences is provided by the biblical Book of Job, which is in fact one of the most important points of reference for Wiesel's writing in general. Wiesel has discussed the story of Job at length, both in his *Célébration biblique* and with Josy Eisenberg in *Job ou Dieu dans la tempête*. Near the beginning of the Book of Job no fewer than four messengers appear in rapid succession to tell of the disasters that have befallen Job's property and family; and each declares "I alone have escaped to tell you" (Job 1. 13–21). In discussion of this passage Wiesel draws attention to Job's readiness to believe the stories he is told, which means, for Wiesel, that he cannot be a Jew:

> There is the witness, his way of bearing witness, but there is also the attitude of him who receives the account. And here, you see, Job amazes me: he believes everything he is told. For me, that proves that he is not a Jew. A Jew would have exclaimed: "It's impossible, it's unimaginable, why me? What? The same scenario, the same message. It's impossible!" (*Job*, 59)

The tragedy of the witness is to be disbelieved; and what Wiesel describes as the typical reaction of the Jew to the narrative of disaster recalls the reaction of the Jews of Sighet to Moché's story in *La Nuit*. Through Moché, Wiesel introduces into his writing the motif (and also the anxiety) of the disbelieved witness, thereby anticipating, and perhaps also disarming, skeptical receptions of his own témoignage:

> People refused not only to believe his stories but even to listen to them.
> - He's trying to make us feel sorry for him. What an imagination . . .
> Or else:
> - The poor man, he has gone mad. (*N*, 16–17)

Here, the listeners pose the fundamental question that Wiesel's later narrators, in disbelief of their own experience, will ask themselves: did it really happen? In this instance the Jews of Sighet are simply and tragically wrong to ascribe Moché's story to the madness or overactive imagination of its narrator. But they do have a point: the events described by Moché are unintelligible in a world believed to be governed by reason or divine ordinance. By contrast, Job appears anomalous in his immediate acceptance of the truth of what he is told. The atrocities described by Moché may be true, but they are inconceivable, unimaginable, and unbelievable. To accept Moché's story requires a revision of the reader-listener's conception of the world, which the Jews of Sighet are unwilling to undertake. Rather than believing the story, they attempt to understand the storyteller and thereby to undermine his credibility. Understanding, however, is precisely what Moché's story defies and precludes:

> I didn't believe him either. I would often sit down with him, in the evening after the service, and listen to his stories, trying to understand his sadness. I just felt sorry for him.
> - People think I'm mad, he would murmur, and tears, like drops of wax, would flow from his eyes.
> Once I asked him:
> - Why are you so keen that people should believe what you say. If I were you, I wouldn't care whether people believed me or not . . .
> He closed his eyes, as if to escape time:
> - You don't understand, he said in despair. You can't understand.
> (N, 17)

The witness requires belief and defies comprehension. Faced with a skeptical audience that makes understanding a condition of belief, Moché chooses silence: "Even Moché the Beadle had gone silent. He was tired of speaking" (N, 18).

Moché's listeners, including Eliezer, adopt strategies of misreading that make them blind to the dangers that his story reveals: "What an imagination [. . .] he has gone mad [. . .] I just felt sorry for him" (N, 16–17). Wiesel's struggle is to avoid the fate of Moché, to continue storytelling beyond and despite the critical trial of doubt and self-doubt. Nevertheless, it is inevitable that Wiesel's stories will be misunderstood because readers will continue to rely upon a presumption of intelligibility (i.e., interpretability within a preestablished code) that the material itself tends to disqualify. Moché does not require his story to be interpreted; on the contrary, he insists that it is beyond understanding ("You can't understand," N, 17). His story parallels that of Eliezer; and *La Nuit* resists accommodation by secure systems of belief and interpretation. Nevertheless, accommodation seems bound to occur, even if it is doomed to repeat the errors of the Jews of Sighet. One such repetition can be seen in Ellen Fine's account of *La Nuit* as an expression of the redemptive value of culture: "[The survivor] has been able to relate and to order the events so as to transmit a coherent literary work. Language and memory are mobilized as instruments of healing, and telling the story becomes an act of restitution, as well as a protest against forgetfulness. By bearing witness the author transforms his voice into a life-giving force, so that he may infuse his dead father, the hanging child, the other victims of the Holocaust with breath."[2]

The strategies of misreading adopted by Wiesel's academic critics are perhaps more sophisticated and better informed, but not fundamentally more enlightened, than the tragic incredulity encountered by Moché. The journey-metaphor (discussed in chapter 1) that makes it possible to read *La Nuit* as not only "the zero point of existence," but also "the point of departure for [Wiesel's] future works," offers a particularly astute means of overlooking the radical challenge to humanist values that the book represents.[3] The journey-metaphor implicitly makes claims about the coherence, direction, and meaning of the author's development. However, reading the despair of *La Nuit* through the perspective of the more ambiguous later texts is one way of *not* reading Wiesel's first book. Moché's story, like *La Nuit*, does not communicate a message that is intelligible to its skeptical listeners; rather it exposes an inadequacy within understanding, its potentially fatal failure to comprehend inassimilable data, and it reveals the incapacity of the storyteller to deliver readily accessible truths. This can also be seen in the more sophisticated stories; contrary to Moché's narrative they do invite and require completion through interpretation, though they prove ultimately to be no more intelligible.

PARABLE

The second story I consider is the parable narrated by Katriel in *Le Mendiant de Jérusalem*. Ten years separate *La Nuit* and *Le Mendiant de Jérusalem*, and in that time Wiesel's view of storytelling has been modified by his reflections on Hassidism, particularly on Hassidic stories, as well as on biblical stories and the tales of the Midrash. Four years after the publication of *Le Mendiant de Jérusalem* Wiesel collected together some of the fruits of his reflection in his *Célébration hassidique* (1972), to be followed by *Célébration biblique* (1975) and *Contre la mélancolie* (1982). I will discuss the significance of this meditation in a moment. First, here is Katriel's parable in full:

> One day, a man leaves his home, the village where he was born, where time does not exist, and goes off in search of a rainbow, of an adventure. He heads in the direction of the great city, distant and unknown. By evening he is in the middle of the forest. He chooses a

dense fir tree to sleep under, safe from the wind and from thieves. Before falling asleep, he takes off his shoes and puts them nearby, pointing in the direction to take in the morning. Could he predict that, around midnight, in order to confuse, to punish or to save him, a joker would turn his shoes around so that they pointed to the village? At dawn, suspecting nothing, he rises, thanks God for giving him back life and soul, and with a light foot he continues his journey. After a certain time, from the top of a hill, he finally sees the mysterious, promised city. He says to himself that he had imagined it to be larger, different. Seen from a closer perspective, from inside the city, it seems strangely familiar to him: the rivers, the gardens, the crossroads. The same as in his own village. Moreover, he has the impression of recognizing every building and being able to guess what is inside it. To the right: the inn and its drunkards, who are filthy not because they like it but because they have no confidence in water. Further on, the town hall with its faded tricolor flag that hangs on its flagpole like the head of a horse sagging with exhaustion. To the left: the police station, where the brave occupants are at daggers drawn by tradition rather than by necessity. At the market, behind the village hall, the visitor knows in advance what every housewife will buy, at what price, from which farmer. Surprised rather than disappointed, he thinks: oh well, I've been told lies; the great city has got nothing to boast about, there is no great secret; perhaps it doesn't even exist; only my village exists, its image is reflected back to me by the rest of the world. From then on, he is no longer surprised by anything. He knows that, as he turns the next corner, after the cobbler's abode, he will find himself in front of a house similar to his own. The door is slightly ajar: the lock needs fixing; just like at my house. From the inside, a voice invites him to enter: you must be hungry, come and eat. It was like the nasal, authoritative voice of his wife. It's enough to drive you mad, but since his stomach is empty, he may as well obey, not make a fuss. Besides, he has always obeyed his wife. So he crosses the kitchen, enters the living room, where the windows look out onto the tree-lined courtyard. He sits at table. Children smile at him, and that fills him with sadness. The smallest climbs onto his knees, plays with his beard and whispers into his ear: won't you stay with us? You're going to stay with us, aren't you? In order not to hurt his feelings, and also because he feels trapped, and because he says to himself "what's the use?", the stranger caresses the child's golden hair and finally promises him everything. (*Mendiant*, 112–14)

Katriel's story is described at the beginning and the end as a parable:

He recounted to me a parable that made me uneasy [. . .] Something
in his parable troubled me [. . .] Was it his fault if his parable had set off
an alarm bell in me? (*Mendiant*, 112, 114, 115)

This in itself aligns the story to a tradition of biblical narrative. It also
marks an important difference from Moché's story and the principles of
storytelling as exemplified in *La Nuit* as a whole. The truth of the
témoignage lies in its reference, and our belief in its reference, to events
actually witnessed. Katriel's parable, on the other hand, makes no such
appeal to the experience of narrator. The Greek *parabole* means a placing
of one thing by another, and it could be translated as "comparison,"
"illustration," or "analogy"; in the Greek Bible it is the equivalent of the
Hebrew *mashal*, which means "riddle," "dark saying," or even "exem-
plary tale."[4] Whereas Moché's "true" story required belief, not commentary or understanding, the parable elicits interpretation; as Frank
Kermode writes, "the parable-event isn't over until a satisfactory answer
or explanation is given; the interpretation completes it." The parable
offers neither self-evident truth nor witnessed experience; it is justified
by the interpretative response that it provokes. It presents an enigma that
demands elucidation; and it raises the crucial hermeneutic question of
whether the enigmatic narrative can ever be fully or adequately explained
by the commentary that it elicits. Kermode maintains, in relation to
Kafka and the Gospel of Saint Mark, that the parable retains an uninter-
pretable residue and withholds its full meaning: "This interpretation
maintains that interpretation, though a proper and interesting activity, is
bound to fail; it is an intrusion always, and always unsuccessful. . . . The
opinion of Mark is quite similar: he says that parables are about every-
body's incapacity to penetrate their sense."[5]

Katriel's parable, as I have quoted it, may seem like a faintly humorous story about a naive man's error; but Katriel adds a final observation
that overturns the apparent logic of the story and draws attention to a
different level of meaning. The man has promised the child that he will
stay, and Katriel concludes his parable:

- Yes, he kept his promise, Katriel continued. He did not return to
his own village. Death went to fetch him from his house but did not
find him. (*Mendiant*, 114)

Surely death *would* have found the man in his house, because, by mistake
and naively, he has returned to his own village? Katriel's conclusion

defeats the primary logic of the story and indicates the necessity of other approaches. At the same time, he is merely underlining an enigmatic element that permeates the whole story. The description of the man's village as a place "where time does not exist" (*Mendiant,* 112), or of the town to which he is traveling as "the mysterious, promised city" (*Mendiant,* 113), or the reference to the man at the end of the story as "the stranger [*l'étranger*]" (*Mendiant,* 114) may alert the reader to different levels of meaning or possibilities of interpretation. Such details seem to require explanation. Rather than openly *given,* the truth of the parable is to be *found* through interpretation. The parable is completed by the interpretation; and Wiesel's text goes on to dramatize the struggle over meaning occasioned by the enigmatic tale:

> - All that doesn't make sense, someone objected. When he arrives at his "new" home, your traveler should logically have run into his double.
> - You don't understand anything, Gdalia sniggered. The double had also gone looking for adventure . . .
> - . . . Looking for a stranger, perhaps?
> - Or for death?
> - You're getting on all our nerves, said Gdalia, the self-appointed protector of Katriel [. . .]
> Ignoring his interruption, I continued:
> - Your story draws a veil over the real wife, the real children who, abandoned in their obscure village, wait in vain for the traveler to return. Their fate is as important to me as his; their distress is worth as much as his quest. (*Mendiant,* 114–15)

Each of the interpreters quoted above assumes there are two identical villages, and this is justified by Katriel's comment that the man "did not return to his own village" (*Mendiant,* 114). None of the listeners seems to recall that the man's shoes, which were pointing in the direction he should have followed the next morning, had been turned around by a "joker" during the night. The central contradiction of the parable is that it justifies a realistic reading, in which there is only one village, and, simultaneously, a second reading in which there may be two identical villages. In consequence the parable solicits interpretation but also maintains the primacy of story over commentary in as far as it obstructs any attempt to achieve unifying interpretation. (The sleight of hand practiced by my own reading lies, of course, in the implicit privileging of the interpretation that foregrounds ambiguity.)

An important literary forerunner of Katriel's tale is the "Vor dem Gesetz" episode in chapter 9 of Kafka's *Der Prozße*. The priest recounts the brief story of a man waiting to enter a court of law and then, in a manner that resembles rabbinical debates over Holy Scripture, disputes with Josef K. about its possible meanings. In the course of the discussion the priest warns Josef K. that he should distinguish carefully between the story and the opinions that surround it: " 'Don't misunderstand me,' said the Priest, 'I'm only indicating the opinions that exist. You mustn't pay too much attention to opinions. The text is unchanging, and opinions are often only an expression of despair about it.' "[6] The text is given and unalterable, but it may give rise to contradictory responses. Wiesel has drawn attention to the variety of interpretations that Kafka's fiction permits:

> In truth there are thousands of readings of Kafka. Kafka is a seminal author. It is natural that each reader, each interpreter finds in Kafka what he wants. [. . .] All interpretations are possible, all are valid, even those that seem aberrant. (*ME*, 139)

Wiesel's practice of storytelling is also influenced by the Hassidic tales with which he first became acquainted as a child in Sighet. One of the Hassidic masters in particular, Rabbi Nachman of Bratslav, throws important light on Wiesel's use of the parable. In his admiration for Rabbi Nachman, Wiesel belongs to an imposing lineage. Martin Buber adapted his stories into German, and it has often been suggested that Kafka was influenced by them, probably through knowledge of Buber's versions.[7] Rabbi Nachman is a constant point of reference in Wiesel's novels, and he is named on several occasions in *Le Mendiant de Jérusalem* (see *Mendiant*, 19, 34, 37, 38). Wiesel particularly likes Nachman's description of a laughing man:

> In one of his stories, we read this tale: once upon a time there was a country that contained all the countries of the world; and in this country there was a town that incorporated all the towns of the country; and in this town there was a street that combined all the streets of the town; and in this street there was a house that brought together all the houses in the street; and in this house there was a room, and in this room there was a man, and this man personified all men in all countries, and this man was laughing, laughing, and no one has ever laughed like him. (*CH*, 204; see also *Mendiant*, 34)[8]

Rabbi Nachman's story is quoted as an epigraph to Le Testament d'un poète juif assassiné (Testament, 9); and that novel could be seen as a retelling of the story on a larger scale. Paltiel's life traverses the crucial moments of twentieth-century history in Nazi Germany, Palestine, Spain during the Civil War, and the Stalinist Soviet Union. The individual destiny acquires general significance, and the novel, like Nachman's story, ends with laughter:

> I have a bizarre feeling; my heart is broken, but I feel that I am going to laugh, and there it is, I am laughing, I am laughing at last [. . .] It's stupid, it's even unjust, but it's the dead, the dead poets who will force men like me, and all the others, to laugh. (Testament, 290)

The novel ends with laughter, but laughter, like silence, is deeply ambiguous in Wiesel's writing, with a series of modulations ranging over violence, despair, and hope.[9] Laughter is problematic rather than unequivocally joyful; rather than giving answers, it raises questions and demands interpretation. Ending on laughter, then, is a way of not concluding the story, an admission that the final explanations have not been given; the story is still awaiting its meaning.

Wiesel's account of his response to Rabbi Nachman's stories gives a personal illustration of this sense of frustrated intelligibility. Wiesel argues that Nachman's stories are a way of propagating his teaching (see CH, 180), but he admits that he can no longer understand their meaning:

> I remember: as a child, I read these stories and, captivated, I thought I understood them. Now I reread them and, still captivated, I no longer understand them. Some seem too simple, others too complex, and sometimes it's the same ones. Sometimes it's appearances which deceive; sometimes it's the invisible framework. The more I read, the more I have the impression of remaining on the near side, of not being able to get all the way to the end. There will always be a mute zone, a dark zone to which I will not gain access. (CH, 186)

The parable, then, is an ambiguous text, rich in meaning, but never permitting final revelation. Like its biblical forerunners, which Wiesel continues to study, it encourages an open series of readings; and this is not the result of authorial inadvertence—an unwilled ambiguity introduced by error—as is explained by an elegant story recounted by Wiesel in Célébration biblique in relation to the Torah:

A legend: When Moses rose to heaven to receive the Law, he found God busy adding various symbols and ornaments. Aware of his role as spokesman, he asked timidly:

- Why not give the Torah as it is. Isn't it rich enough with meanings, sufficiently obscure, why add more complications?

- I must, replied God. After numerous generations there will be a man called Akiba, son of Joseph, who will seek and find all sorts of interpretations in each word, in each syllable, in each letter of the Torah. So that he can find them, I have to put them there. (*CB*, 151)

When Wiesel recounts this same legend again in *Célébration talmudique*, he draws a comparison between Moses and himself, putting his own interpreter in the flattering position of Akiba who finds meanings in the text that are incomprehensible even to its author:

I love this legend. It is the author in me who loves it. I am not Moses, no one is, but sometimes I read commentaries on what I try to write, and I do not understand a word. . . . (*CT*, 143)

To some extent Wiesel is evidently speaking ironically of his own commentators. But he is also making a serious point. In the Jewish exegetical tradition the meaning of the source text is not conceived as something that can be fully revealed through any individual act of interpretation, even one that might gain the support of the author of that text, be he Moses or Wiesel himself. The value of commentary is measured by its provisional success, its action in and on the world, rather than its ultimate and inevitable failure to reveal a single, unambiguous meaning.[10] The role of the text is to solicit new interpretations for new situations. In this perspective, the meaning of the story is not entirely given in the text; it is also produced by the interpreter's recognition that the story speaks to him or her personally. The individual listener or reader is always the privileged hermeneut, the sole competent *destinataire* of the narrative, however inadequate his or her interpretations may be for the use of others. The narrator of *Le Mendiant de Jérusalem* is made uneasy precisely because he perceives the relevance of the story to himself:

- I don't like your story, I said to him to provoke him.
- Because you recognize yourself in it? said Gdalia, raising himself up on his bed. (*Mendiant*, 114–15)

The anxiety that occupies David in the following pages is the distress of the interpreter solicited by the text but not yet able to understand its significance for his own life:

> Then I felt my anguish swell up and fill my chest. Within myself, I guessed that it wasn't to do with particular facts, but with the story that I had just heard. It seemed to me to have a distant origin, linked to other landscapes, other encounters. How could I make sense of it? (*Mendiant*, 118)

Later, David believes he has discovered the meaning of the parable:

> Then, in a flash, I saw the solution to the enigma [. . .] Sharply, I understood that the traveler was perhaps me. I had perhaps lived disguised as a stranger, alongside women who took me for someone else. My real self had remained back there, in the kingdom of night, the prisoner of the dead. The living person I was, that I thought I was, had lived a lie; I was no more than an echo of the voices long extinguished. (*Mendiant*, 121)

In a striking image of the appropriation inherent in every act of interpretation, David understands the parable by making himself its hero; perhaps it is the interpreters' characteristic delusion to see themselves as uniquely enabled to understand the text. David's reading in fact involves a sophisticated resolution of the central enigma of the parable: the question of whether the traveler returns to his own village or discovers a second, identical village in which he takes the place of his double. David's life is dominated by two towns: the "little town lost somewhere in Transylvania" (*Mendiant*, 19) where he was brought up (Sighet is inevitably suggested), and Jerusalem. The towns are different, but also united. This is suggested in the first reference to Rabbi Nachman in the novel:

> Rabbi Nachman of Bratslav, the visionary storyteller of Ukrainian Hassidism, liked to say that it was enough for him to walk in any direction in order to be heading for Jerusalem. As for me, it was in the holy word that I discovered Jerusalem. Without moving. (*Mendiant*, 19)[11]

As a child, David discovers Jerusalem without leaving his hometown, and as an adult he rediscovers his past while living in Jerusalem. The journey is a return, although the points of departure and arrival are geographically separate. After the recapture of the Old City, David insists that everything is different and nothing has changed: "The decor is immutable" (*Mendiant*, 178). David's identity partakes of the same paradox. Like all Wiesel's protagonists, he is both himself and other than himself, living and dead. Part of him has died with those he has left behind, and at the same time he carries the dead within him. Doubled with Katriel, part of him disappears with Katriel, while at the end of the novel the surviving self prepares, perhaps, to replace his double as the partner of Malka. Like the traveler of the parable, David is *l'étranger*, a man whose existence is proven by his ability to doubt his own reality: "The victor in me seemed to me to be alien [*étranger*] as well as unreal" (*Mendiant*, 174).

In this presentation Katriel's parable appears as a *mise en abyme* of *Le Mendiant de Jérusalem* as a whole. The enigmatic details can be resolved by the paradoxes of time, travel, and identity that underlie the novel. The reference to the village "where time does not exist" (*Mendiant*, 112) reflects a view of history as stasis within crisis: "It is always the same people, its journey is always the same" (*Mendiant*, 178); the "mysterious, promised city" (*Mendiant*, 113) is Jerusalem, which contains and was contained in the narrator's hometown and which is the point of departure and arrival of every journey; and the reference to the traveler as "the stranger [*l'étranger*]" (*Mendiant*, 114) reflects David's estrangement from himself. The "solution to the enigma" (*Mendiant*, 121) discovered by David involves the recognition that Katriel's parable tells fundamentally the same story as *Le Mendiant de Jérusalem*. The novel is a commentary on the parable, just as the parable distills key elements from the novel. However, the novel *displaces* rather than *resolves* the enigma of the parable. The contradictions of the latter are explained by the paradoxes of the former, which in turn require further explanation: "someone has died within me, I still don't know who it is" (*Mendiant*, 187). The explanation of the parable is given through a new narrative, commentary turns out to be another form of storytelling; and this is also reflected in the relationship between Wiesel's writing and its commentators. The meaning of the story turns out to be another story: the journey from despair to hope, or (the story recounted in the next chapter) the conversion to ambiguity.

Wiesel's stories, like biblical parables and the tales of Rabbi Nachman, invite completion through commentary by their abundance of interpretable details or by their silences; but they also question the principle of underlying coherence—that is, the faith that all acceptable interpretations are ultimately anticipated and sanctioned by the text—which is fundamental to rabbinical biblical commentary (I discuss this more fully in chapter 6). In other words, Wiesel's stories solicit interpretation but also tend to subvert the possibility of assured understanding. This can be shown by the elements in Katriel's parable that directly address the problem of interpretation. The traveler's shoes, which are pointing in the direction he should follow in the morning, are turned around during the night; three possible reasons are given for this: "in order to confuse, to punish or to save him [*pour l'embrouiller, le punir, ou le sauver*]" (*Mendiant*, 113). Punishment and salvation, despite the differences between them, suggest the existence of a coherent moral order of reward and retribution; confusion, however, suggests ill will or simple arbitrariness. The implied finality of the act, carried out *in order to* achieve a specific result ("*pour* l'embrouiller") is belied by the absence of insight into what the desired result might have been. The act may have been purposeful, but its purpose is not revealed. Later, the traveler becomes the interpreter of his own experience as he looks at what he believes to be the goal of his journey: "oh well, I've been told lies; the great city has nothing to boast about, there is no great secret; perhaps it doesn't even exist; only my village exists" (*Mendiant*, 113). The journey leads the traveler to doubt the reality of his destination; the secret of the city is that it has no secret; and interpretation has led to the point where it denies the very existence of the object it was aiming to understand. Perhaps this is the true secret of the story: the disclosure that it has nothing to disclose. The end of the journey is no advance on the beginning; we have learned nothing, and the traveler's parable results in the interpreter's disorientation.

THE STORY

The third story is one of the best known Hassidic tales, which Wiesel recounts as an epigraph to *Les Portes de la forêt* and again in *Célébration hassidique*. Below is the version from *Célébration hassidique*:

> When the great Rabbi Israël Baal Shem Tov saw that some misfortune was about to befall the Jewish people, he used to go and reflect at a certain place in the forest; there, he would light a fire, recite a certain prayer, and the miracle would be accomplished, revoking the misfortune.

Later, when his disciple, the famous Maggid of Meseritz, had to call on heaven for the same reasons, he would go to the same place in the forest and say: "Master of the universe, listen to me. I do not know how to light the fire, but I am still capable of reciting the prayer." And the miracle would be accomplished.

Later, Rabbi Moshe-Leib of Sassov, to save his people, would also go into the forest and say: "I do not know how to light the fire, but I can find the place and that should be enough." And it was enough: there again the miracle would be accomplished.

Then it was the turn of Rabbi Israël of Rishin to avert the danger. Seated in his armchair he would take his head in his hands and speak to God: "I am incapable of lighting the fire, I do not know the prayer, I cannot even find the place in the forest. All that I can do is tell this story. That should be enough." And it was enough. (*CH*, 173; also, with minor differences, in *Portes*, 7)

In *Major Trends in Jewish Mysticism*, Gershom Scholem quotes this story and gives the following gloss: "You can say if you will that this profound little anecdote symbolizes the decay of a great movement. You can also say that it reflects the transformation of all its values, a transformation so profound that in the end all that remained of the mystery was the tale." Hassidism, in Scholem's view, represents the decline of Jewish mysticism, and this is reflected in the story told here: the powers of the Baal Shem Tov are gradually lost until Rabbi Israël of Rishin recalls only the story of his predecessor's actions; as Scholem puts it, "nothing at all has remained theory, everything has become a story."[12]

Scholem's preference for theory over story is one of the main causes of the disagreement between himself and Martin Buber in their debate about Hassidism. Buber insists on the primacy of the tale over other forms of speculation or discourse; Scholem counters that Hassidic theoretical writings predate and are more voluminous than the stories. Scholem is presumably correct; however, Buber's belief in the primacy of the story in Hassidism is not necessarily undermined by the historico-empirical factors invoked by Scholem. Buber argues that "the legend is no chronicle, but it is truer than the chronicle for those who know how to read it."[13] According to Buber, then, the best way of understanding Hassidism is through its legends rather than, as Scholem argues, through its theoretical writings or historical determinants.

When Wiesel examines the sources of Hassidism he seems more on Buber's side, as he openly acknowledges his indifference to the question of historical truth. Having recounted a story about the Baal Shem Tov, the founder of Hassidism, Wiesel admits that he neither knows nor cares whether the story is true or false:

> And then, I must say it, this fable is typical in that none can guarantee its truthfulness. No, I do not know whether or not it is true, whether or not it really took place in this way; and it isn't very important to me to find out. I would say the same of most of the stories concerning the Baal Shem—or, for short: the Besht—and his successors: unfathomable from the outside, their authenticity can be measured only from the inside. (*CH*, 19)

The story neither allows nor requires verification by reference to external criteria. In Wiesel's version of the origins of Hassidism, "the theories could wait" (*CH*, 45); the story has greater urgency and influence because it appeals to lived experience and human imagination rather than to historical truth or abstract theory.

Scholem's view of Hassidism influences his comments on Rabbi Israël's story; most significantly, he fails to take account of the fact that the *story* has the same effect as the Baal Shem Tov's *actions* ("And it was enough"), even if that effect is not explicitly qualified as a miracle (the phrase "the miracle was accomplished" is not repeated in the final episode). The comment with which Wiesel concludes his version of the story reverses Scholem's interpretation of "the decay of a great movement": "God created man because he likes stories" (*Portes*, 7). In the reading that this suggests, the story realizes God's aim—mankind's discovery of its role as storyteller—rather than betokening a process of decline and loss. Rabbi Israël does not share the Baal Shem Tov's mystical knowledge, but he has not entirely lost the powers of the founder of Hassidism.

Wiesel transforms the story into a metafictional statement about the value of storytelling. The enigmatic aspects of the tale do not impair its power; this is suggested in a passage of *Les Portes de la forêt* that, particularly in its final words, echoes the story of Rabbi Israël recounted as an epigraph to the novel:

> The Rabbi speaks quickly, using an obscure, distant language; he quotes the Midrash and the Zohar, tells stories that are disturbing and wonderful in their apparent simplicity, not bothering to provide the key to understanding them. Fascinated, people listen feverishly, with passion, little caring if they understand, if they can pursue the Master's

thoughts to its ultimate point: they are purified in his voice, in his secret. That must be enough, so it is enough. (*Portes*, 213)

The role of storytelling seems independent of the intelligibility of the story. The value of the story is not in its message or teaching, but in the continuity of tradition and the bond of community between storyteller and listener.

The comment at the beginning of *Les Portes de la forêt* that "God created man because he likes stories" (*Portes*, 7) represents, then, the positive pole of Wiesel's interpretation of storytelling. Inevitably, there is also a negative pole. When he repeats the story of Rabbi Israël in *Célébration hassidique*, he gives a less optimistic gloss. Picking up the final "And that was enough," he adds in parentheses:

That is no longer enough. The proof: the threat has not been averted. Perhaps we no longer know how to tell the story? Could we all be guilty? Even the survivors? Especially the survivors? (*CH*, 173)

Here, Wiesel seems closer to a reading of the story in terms of decline; moreover, by extending the story into the present he shows that the decline has continued, with the result that narrating the story is no longer sufficient. The two comments on this same anecdote indicate an uncertainty within Wiesel's attitude toward storytelling. The storyteller is alternatively fulfilling a divine plan and combatting forgetfulness, or engaging in a marginal, ineffectual activity.

The tension within Wiesel's attitude toward storytelling is the motive force behind his novel *Le Serment de Kolvillàg*, published in 1973, the year after *Célébration hassidique*. In *Le Serment* Wiesel puts the storyteller, Azriel, in a situation where he must choose between conflicting responsibilities: by telling the story of Kolvillàg he may save a life, but he will damn himself for breaking his oath of silence. Azriel's hesitations reflect a general unease within Wiesel's fiction concerning the validity of storytelling:

The story that I have to tell you, I was forbidden to tell it. Tell me what I am supposed to do. I would like to be able to speak without going back on my oath, without lying. I would like to be able to live without reproaching myself for it. I would like to be able to be silent without making even of silence a lie or a betrayal. (*Serment*, 42)

The importance of témoignage in Wiesel's aesthetics has often been taken for granted. Wiesel frequently draws attention to its central importance, and Ellen Fine takes the motif of the witness as the organizing principle for her study of his fiction.[14] Témoignage gives Wiesel's texts their moral and referential authority: this happened, I know that this happened because I was there. However, the critique of témoignage undertaken by Moshe indicates that the imperative of bearing witness is countered by a desire to remain silent (see *Serment*, 216–18; it is ironic that his name recalls that of Moché the Beadle, the first witness to appear in Wiesel's writing). This can be seen in a variety of ways. One is through the desire to forget, when témoignage depends upon memory: "Consciously I have done everything in order not to forget; unconsciously I have done no less in order to forget" (*Fils*, 228–29). Another is in the temptation of madness or silence that pervades Wiesel's writing, when both madness and silence represent the refusal or inability to narrate experience in an intelligible form. And most significantly in the present context, another way of not bearing witness is through telling stories. Forbidden to describe the destruction of the Jewish community of Kolvillàg, Azriel makes up stories that resemble the tales of the Hassidic masters; he does this *in order not to tell* of what he has seen: "I told all sorts of stories except my own: by inventing them I gave free rein to my imagination" (*Serment*, 51).

The witness sees, survives, and tells of what he has seen; the storyteller makes no such claims to firsthand experience, or even to the literal truth of the stories he recounts. Katriel's parable made no claim to be an account of experience; and the story told by Rabbi Israël of Rishin, and subsequently of course by Wiesel, was something they had heard or read rather than something they had seen. The discrepancy between the witness and the storyteller is suggested on the one hand by Eliezer's "I had seen it, seen it with my own eyes . . ." (*N*, 42) and on the other by Zalmen's words at the end of Wiesel's play *Zalmen ou la folie de Dieu*: "The story that I have just told you, it did not really happen!" (*Zalmen*, 174). The witness asks for belief, even if understanding is impossible; the storyteller encourages interpretation. In his fiction Wiesel establishes himself principally as storyteller rather than witness. Only in *La Nuit* does he talk at any length about his experiences in the concentration camps, and *La Nuit* is not, or at least is not presented as, a novel. Fiction offers Wiesel a medium through which he can *avoid* talking about his own experiences. In fact, the choice of literature as a means of expression is directly related to the *refusal* to describe Auschwitz, since—Wiesel himself argues—Auschwitz can have no place in literature (see chapter 1).

Like Azriel in *Le Serment de Kolvillàg,* Wiesel invents stories in order not to tell his own. At the same time, storytelling gives rise to moral anxiety. This can be seen in echoes of the assertion "God created man because he likes stories" (*Portes,* 7) in Wiesel's fictional texts: the phrase "I like stories [*J'aime les histoires*]" is used in *Le Crépuscule, au loin* by the madman who believes he is God (*Crépuscule,* 275); it is repeated in *L'Aube* when John Dawson is killed (*A,* 140); and in *Le Cinquième Fils* it is uttered by a former sadistic Nazi (*Fils,* 218). That the love of stories may be a characteristic of God or of a Nazi does not in itself constitute a moral position. This is perhaps why, in his second gloss on the story of Rabbi Israël, Wiesel associates storytelling with guilt; the story may be just a story, an abdication of the duty to bear witness to history: "Could we all be guilty? Even the survivors? Especially the survivors?" (*CH,* 173).

In his book *Heidegger et "les juifs,"* Jean-François Lyotard proposes an addition to the story of Rabbi Israël as it is recounted by Wiesel in order to make it relevant to the problem of art after the Holocaust:

> What art can do is to make itself witness not to the sublime but to this aporia of art and to its pain. It does not say the unsayable, it says that it cannot say it. "After Auschwitz," we must, with Elie Wiesel in mind, add another verse to the story of the forgetting of the meditation by the fire in the forest (*Célébration* [*hassidique*], 173). I cannot light the fire, I do not know the prayer, I can no longer find the place, I cannot even recount the story. All I can do is recount that I can no longer recount this story. And that should be enough. It will have to be enough.[15]

Lyotard turns the story into an account of the situation of the modern artist, who is not capable of témoignage, the recounting of experience, but only "the negative testimony that the 'prayer' is impossible and so is the story of the prayer"; all that remains possible is "the testimony of that impossibility." And so Lyotard confines Wiesel within the postmodern aporia: "Here, as in Wiesel, the only story that is left to tell is the story of the impossibility of the story."[16]

Lyotard's comments reflect a crucial problem in Wiesel's aesthetics. The urgent moral imperative of témoignage is shadowed by a lucid awareness of its impossibility (and in some respects also its undesirability). In *Un Juif, aujourd'hui,* for example, Wiesel describes the dilemma of those who survived the Holocaust in terms that echo Lyotard's analysis: "Rather than communicating the experience of the Holocaust, they transmitted their sense of the impossibility of communicating it" (*Un Juif*, 194). Lyotard shares Wiesel's conviction that the Holocaust cannot, can never, be fully explained.[17] And this is associated for both authors with a radical acknowledgment of the inadequacy that inhabits the aesthetics of representation, made most urgent by the problem of describing the Holocaust: "to say 'that's how it was' is impossible, without referentialist credulity bordering on stupidity."[18] "I only know that Treblinka and Auschwitz cannot be recounted" (*Paroles*, 11). However, knowing that Treblinka and Auschwitz cannot be narrated, Wiesel does not abandon the attempt: "Yet I've tried, God knows that I've tried" (*Paroles*, 11). Lyotard seems uneasy with Wiesel's *La Nuit* precisely because it does attempt to represent the experience of the Holocaust.[19]

This marks an important difference between Lyotard and Wiesel. Lyotard concedes, somewhat grudgingly, that the survivor can and must attempt to save his or her experience from oblivion: "It is necessary, certainly, it is necessary to inscribe, in words, in images. No question of escaping the necessity of representing";[20] but the danger of this, in Lyotard's view, is that it risks making the Holocaust an "ordinary," recountable event. Lyotard's addition to the Rabbi Israël anecdote asserts the unrecountability, the intractability to narrative, of the Holocaust; the narrator does not recount the story of the forgotten prayer, but recounts that he can no longer recount it. For Lyotard, then, the story tells of the failure of stories and of storytelling; and the continuation of storytelling involves the repetition of that failure (perhaps because the repetition of failure is the only alternative to silence). However, telling the story of the forgetting of the story involves, *in some sense*, telling the story itself, as indeed Lyotard does tell the story of Rabbi Israël, if only allusively and depending (rather unreasonably) on his reader's familiarity with Wiesel's text. The narrative act does and must take place, even if it describes its own failure; and the narrative is still to some degree representational, even if representation depends upon a "referentialist credulity bordering on stupidity."

Lyotard's discussion leads to a hesitant acceptance of the artist's failure to recount the story: "And that should be enough. It will have to be enough."[21] However, I believe he is wrong to associate Wiesel with this position. Lyotard makes no mention of Wiesel's comments on the anecdote in *Célébration hassidique* where Wiesel locates the artist's failure in a different domain from that described by Lyotard. For Wiesel, the story can be told, and he does tell it (as does—elliptically— Lyotard);

but Wiesel is categorical about the inadequacy of storytelling: "That is no longer enough. The proof: the threat has not been averted" (*CH*, 173). Wiesel's flat denial of the sufficiency and self-sufficiency of storytelling contradicts Lyotard's hesitant acceptance. Brilliantly and disconcertingly, Lyotard leads his reader into aporia: representation is both inevitable and impossible. Wiesel breaks through aporia with his curt "That is no longer enough." The ambiguity inherent in writing and thought—their shared failure to occupy the open space of truth—is a point of departure, not a dead end. Storytelling, for Wiesel, takes place in the wake of a crisis of meaning and belief, but it is not paralysed by that crisis. It must still act, affect, and alter. Storytelling may not deliver unambiguous messages, but it must still be a form of action in and on the world. The story does not communicate clear meanings; instead it confronts the reader with opacity and enigma, the ambiguity of experience and of the narrative of experience. And thereby a link is formed with the reader and with the world; not a referential link, perhaps, or at least not a reliably referential link, but a bond of shared ignorance based on the inevitable and impossible illusion of representation. Wiesel bypasses Lyotard's aporia by turning failure back upon the reader, by making the ambiguity of the story its principal message, by transmitting unintelligibility to a readership unlikely to be willing to receive it, and by communicating an anxiety of living through the textual intermediary of an anxiety of meaning.

THREE

The Conversion to Ambiguity (Early Works)

Chapter 2 illustrated a change in Wiesel's practice as a storyteller from the autobiographical témoignage to the parabolic narrative of *Le Mendiant de Jérusalem*. By examining Wiesel's early texts, specifically *La Nuit* (1958), *L'Aube* (1960), *Le Jour* (1961), and *La Ville de la chance* (1962), this chapter shows how the origins of the ambiguity of his later fiction can be seen in tensions that appear in the early texts.

LA NUIT

More than thirty years after its first publication, *La Nuit* is still a shocking and remarkable book. It also occupies a unique and ambiguous position in the corpus of Wiesel's work. It is the only text in which Wiesel talks at length about his experiences in the concentration camps. At the same time it can be read as integral to Wiesel's fictional corpus. It constitutes the nonfictional basis of Wiesel's subsequent fiction, it is the center around which his later works revolve and to which they always implicitly refer.

Critics have implied that *La Nuit* should be *read*, but not *interpreted*. Robert McAfee Brown and Ted Estess, for example, both preface their commentaries on *La Nuit* with disarming remarks on the inappropriateness of critical analysis: "Of all Wiesel's works, [*La Nuit*] is the one that most cries out not to be touched, interpreted, synthesized. It must be encountered at first hand." "One is reluctant to apply the usual conventions of literary analysis to the book, for by doing so one runs the risk of blunting the impact of its testimony by too quickly speaking of secondary matters. Against the horror of the story, literary considerations seem somehow beside the point."[1]

Some readers have nevertheless insisted that *La Nuit* should be read as a literary text. Denis Boak describes it as "a highly conscious literary artifact," and Zsuzsanna Ozsvath and Martha Satz argue that "the power of [*La Nuit*] as a document of the Holocaust owes much of its intensity to its literary quality."[2] Moreover, despite the scruples of Wiesel's readers, interpretation does inevitably take place, and the text has been interpreted in a variety of ways. Particularly fruitful readings have been generated by the expedient of comparing the text with biblical stories. *La Nuit* has been read as an inversion of the story of the Exodus and as a version of the story of Abraham and Isaac, the sacrificial drama of father and son played out against the silence of God. And one critic, adapting a phrase from Martin Buber and justified by a reference in *La Nuit* itself (see *N*, 54), describes Wiesel as the "Job of Auschwitz."[3]

La Nuit can be read both as a historical document and a reenactment of biblical stories "by the opaque light of the Night of Auschwitz." There is no contradiction here. Wiesel's account of the Holocaust gives signs of adherence to the belief—essential to the Jewish tradition—that history is not just a random sequence of events; as Paul Johnson puts it, "no people has ever insisted more firmly than the Jews that history has a purpose and humanity a destiny."[4] In the Jewish tradition past and present are linked by the continuing spiritual drama that is enacted through history, and also by a dialectic through which individual experience and biblical story reciprocally illuminate one another. Wiesel expresses this view in his *Célébration biblique*, a work in which he constantly uses episodes from the Bible as a means of reflecting on recent history:

> In Jewish history all events are linked. It is only today, after the whirlwind of fire and blood of the Holocaust, that we can read of the murder of a man by his brother, the questions of a father and his disturbing silences. It is by recounting them now, in the light of certain experiences of life and death, that we can understand them. (*CB*, 11)

The interlinking of historical and spiritual dramas is reflected in the second and third paragraphs of *La Nuit*:

> Physically, [Moché the Beadle] was clumsy like a clown. He raised smiles, with his orphan's shyness. I loved his large dreamy eyes, lost in

the distance. He spoke little. He sang; or rather he murmured tunes to himself. The snatches that one could hear spoke of the suffering of God, of the Exile of Providence that, according to the Kabbalah, would await its redemption in that of man.

I got to know him toward the end of 1941. I was twelve. I was deeply religious. By day I studied the Talmud, and, at night, I ran to the synagogue to cry over the destruction of the temple. (*N*, 13–14)

Both of these paragraphs show the same development from factual description to spiritual meaning. Moché's songs introduce the themes of exile, providence, and deliverance; Eliezer's piety forges a link between the Europe of 1941 and Jerusalem at the time of the destruction of the Temple. Moché sings of exile; Eliezer longs for return.

There is no place for arbitrariness in this world. When Moché comes back to Sighet to describe Nazi atrocities against the Jews, we are told twice that he has escaped "by miracle" (*N*, 16, 17). The choice of the word *miracle* reflects the belief according to which individual actions or events are providential manifestations of a higher order of meaning. Moché's survival, in as far as it is miraculous, confirms the continuing intervention of God in human affairs. However, while adopting verbal and narrative forms that suggest the union of historical event and spiritual meaning, Wiesel's text describes their effective separation. Moché escapes "by miracle," but what he experiences is brute historical reality. The divine order implied by the word *miracle* does not operate when it is most needed—God does not intervene to prevent the massacre of the Jews. The initial fusion of literal and spiritual realities has now been shattered. What Moché sees has no link with the sacred drama: "He no longer spoke to me of God or the Kabbalah, but only of what he had seen" (*N*, 16). Complementary aspects of the same truth have been torn apart, and the rest of the narrative sets out—and fails—to heal this rift.

La Nuit can be read as an attempt to achieve existential self-recognition, as the narrator attempts to understand himself and his place in history. This is emblematized—and its failure underscored—in the final lines of the text when he looks in a mirror and sees a corpse looking back at him. *La Nuit* does not offer unmediated, uninterpreted realities. Events are filtered through the eyes of a narrator, Eliezer, whose primary function is to seize their meaning as he organizes them into a coherent narrative. He exhibits considerable control in his organization of material. The nine short chapters divide the text into manageable units that can be summarized as follows:

Chapter 1. In Sighet. Buildup to deportation.
Chapter 2. In train. Arrival in Birkenau.
Chapter 3. First experiences of Auschwitz. Transfer to Buna.
Chapter 4. Life in Buna. Hangings.
Chapter 5. Selections. Evacuation of camp.
Chapter 6. Evacuation through snow. Arrival in Gleiwitz.
Chapter 7. In train to Buchenwald.
Chapter 8. Death of father.
Chapter 9. Liberation of Buchenwald.

Throughout *La Nuit* Wiesel uses the past historic tense as part of a retrospective narrative. He is "telling a story" in a way that becomes more problematic in his later, more formally sophisticated fiction, with its changing narrative voices, shifting time scales, and unstable tense systems. In *La Nuit* the past historic gives the narrator retrospective command over his material. This allows him to organize and underline its significance, as well as to calculate and control its effect on the reader. Since this narrative mastery is important to the central tension of *La Nuit*, it is worth briefly describing some of the means by which it is achieved.

Direct comment. The narrator interrupts his description of events and comments directly; for example, while life for the Jews in the ghetto is still relatively tolerable, the narrator shows the wisdom of hindsight:

It was neither the German nor the Jew who reigned over the ghetto: it was illusion. (*N*, 21)

Reader's knowledge of history. Much of *La Nuit* is written in a terse, telegraphic style. Eliezer avoids commentary or explanation when the reader's knowledge of history can be expected to fill in gaps. The use of place names provides a clear example:

But we arrived at a station. Those who were near the windows told us the name of the station:
- Auschwitz.
No one had ever heard that name. (*N*, 36)

In front of us, those flames. In the air, that smell of burnt flesh. It must have been midnight. We had arrived. At Birkenau. (*N*, 38)

Warning and premonition. The Jews of Sighet are constantly being warned of what will happen to them. Moché recounts the atrocities of the Nazis, but is not believed. In the train to Auschwitz Mme Schächter has

a premonitory vision ("- A fire! I can see a fire! I can see a fire!" [N, 34]),
but she is bound, gagged, and beaten up by the other Jews. Later, the Jews
are told what will happen to them:

> Sons of dogs, do you understand nothing then? You're going to be
> burned! Burned to a cinder! Turned to ashes! (N, 40)

Eliezer's direct comments also have a premonitory function:

> From that moment everything happened with great speed. The chase
> toward death had begun. (N, 20)

Retrospective viewpoint. Related to the latter point is the way in
which the narrator can explain what he did not know at the time of the
events being described due to knowledge acquired in the period between
experiencing and describing. He uses phrases like "Later we were to
learn" (N, 44), "I learned later" (N, 58), "I learned after the war" (N, 90),
"Many years later" (N, 63).

Repetition of themes. One of the central concerns of *La Nuit* is
Eliezer's relationship with his father and his ambiguous sense of guilt
and liberation when his father dies. Eliezer's feeling that he has betrayed
his father is reflected in other father-son relationships that he compulsively describes. Bela Katz, seconded to the *Sonder-Kommando*, places
his own father's body into the furnace at Birkenau (N, 44); the narrator
refers to a child who beats his father (N, 72); during the long march from
Buna to Gleiwitz, Rabi Eliahou is left behind by his son, who has run on
ahead, Eliezer believes, "in order to free himself from a burden that could
reduce his own chances of survival" (N, 99); and on the train to Buchenwald, a man murders his own father for the sake of a piece of bread (N,
108).

Preparation of effects. Eliezer introduces striking or unexpected details that seem out of place at first, but that reinforce the impact of what
comes later. After the first execution that he witnesses, Eliezer seems
unmoved: "I remember that that evening I found the soup excellent . . ."
(N, 72); later, the cruel execution of a young boy is interpreted as
reflecting the death of God, and Eliezer picks up his words from the
previous page: "That evening, the soup had the taste of corpse" (N, 73).
In Buna the treatment of the children seems to indicate a more humane
attitude than we had been led to expect:

Our convoy contained several children of ten, twelve years of age. The
officer took an interest in them and ordered that some food be brought
for them. (*N*, 57)

A page later, a more sinister explanation for the officer's interest is
suggested as a new character is introduced:

Our block leader was a German [. . .] Like the head of the camp, he liked
children. Immediately after our arrival he had had some bread, soup
and margarine brought for them (in reality, this affection was not
disinterested: children here were the object, amongst homosexuals, of a
real trade, as I was to learn later). (*N*, 58)

Through these devices, the narrator filters, interprets, and assimilates
the experience of the Holocaust. Wiesel adopts a form and techniques
that seem to confirm the Jewish expectation of the meaning of history
and the interpretability of experience. The essential problem of *La Nuit*
derives from the tension between the formal coherence and retrospective
authority of the narrative, and the subject-matter of the work. Wiesel has
always emphasized that the Holocaust can be neither understood nor
described; it is a unique event without precedent, parallel, analogy, or
meaning. This results in a problem of communication, and the survivors'
predicament is particularly acute. They must, and cannot, recount the
experience of the death camps: "Impossible to speak of it, impossible not
to speak of it" (*Un Juif*, 193). *La Nuit*, then, is written in the knowledge
of its own inevitable failure: the survivor must tell his story, but will
never communicate the truth of his experience; what is kept silent is
more true than what is said, words distort and betray, the Holocaust
cannot be understood or described, the constraints of *vraisemblance*
ensure that the story will always fall short of *vérité*. As Wiesel writes in
Un Juif, aujourd'hui, "In order to be realistic [*vraisemblables*], the
stories recounted less than the truth" (*Un Juif*, 192).

The failure of narration to command belief is reflected at the very
beginning of *La Nuit* in the incredulous reaction encountered by Moché
the Beadle (see *N*, 16–17). Moché is disbelieved, his story dismissed as
imagination or madness, utterly contrary to *vraisemblance*. Finally, he
chooses silence rather than futile narrative (see *N*, 18). Later, Eliezer
meets with a similar reaction when he goes to warn a friend of his father's
about the liquidation of the ghetto: "- What are you talking about [*Que
racontes-tu*]? [. . .] Have you gone mad?" (*N*, 24). Eliezer is reduced to

silence: "My throat was dry and the words were choked there, paralysing my lips. I couldn't say another word to him" (*N*, 24); and paradoxically it is this silence that convinces the father's friend: "Then he understood" (*N*, 24). In its opening pages the text describes an anxiety about its own status and its communicative capabilities. The messenger is unwelcome and his story disbelieved or dismissed. The narrative process itself is interrupted. Eliezer's father is recounting a story when he is called away to be told of the deportation of the Jews: "The good story that he was telling us would remain unfinished" (*N*, 22). The father's "good story" is unfinished and supplanted by the less pleasant story that the son will now recount.

The failure of narrative represented at the beginning of *La Nuit* by these incidents is reflected in the writing of the text as a whole. The retrospective stance of the narrator and the control he exhibits over the presentation of his material put him in a privileged position of authority and understanding; at the same time, what he describes is the destruction of all points of certainty, resulting in the collapse of the interpretative authority that his stance as narrator seems to arrogate. *La Nuit* is above all a narrative of loss; in the course of the text, family, community, religious certainty, paternal authority, and the narrator's identity are corroded or destroyed. The theme of loss also has consequences for the validity of the narrative. The narrator constantly expresses the desperate hope that what he is witnessing is not real; thereby he draws attention to the desire to deny the truth of his own experience, to subvert the credibility of his own narrative:

> Wasn't all that a nightmare? An unimaginable nightmare? [. . .] No, all that could not be true. A nightmare [. . .] It was surely a dream. (*N*, 41, 42, 46)

This does not mean that narrated events did not take place; but it does disclose a reluctance within the *témoignage* itself to accept the validity of experience. While *La Nuit* never discredits the authority of its narrator, significant aspects of the text seem to resist acknowledging what Eliezer nevertheless knows to be true. Like the man in *Le Mendiant de Jérusalem* who believes himself mad rather than accepting that what he has seen— the consequences of the Holocaust—can be true (see *Mendiant*, 29–31), the narrator of *La Nuit* seeks to deny the evidence of his senses. The witness simultaneously suggests "this is true" and "this cannot be true."

This tension is compounded by a mistrust of language, which, Wiesel has suggested, was corrupted by the Holocaust: "The absolute perversion of language dates from that period" (*Signes*, 18).

> If our language is corrupted it is because, at that time, language itself was denatured. Innocent and beautiful words designated the most abject crimes [. . .] The first crime committed by the Nazis was against language. (*Signes*, 221)

This corruption of language is reflected in the course of *La Nuit*. The book begins in a world of confident speech: Moché the Beadle teaches Eliezer the mysteries of the Kabbalah; the father gives paternal advice; Eliezer narrates his childhood. However, the precariousness of this confidence in language is signaled by Moché's story of Nazi atrocities, which is true but discredited and disbelieved, and the father's never-finished anecdote. The rest of the text, and indeed all Wiesel's texts, fall under the shadow of these failed narratives. In Auschwitz language itself is devalued and stripped of its conventional meanings. Only one word retains its significance:

> The word "chimney" was not a word empty of sense here: it floated in the air, mixed with the smoke. It was perhaps the only word here that had a real meaning. (*N*, 48)

The degradation of language is shown most clearly in the use of direct speech in the course of *La Nuit*. The advice and teaching of Eliezer's father and Moché are supplanted by the curt imperatives of the concentration camp guards: "Everyone get out! Leave everything in the wagon! Quickly!" (*N*, 38); "- Men to the left! Women to the right!" (*N*, 39). The dialogue between Eliezer and his father acquires a surreal, futile quality as the son repeats the father's imperatives—now devoid of all imperative force—and begins to usurp his father's authority:

> - Don't let yourself be carried off by sleep, Eliezer. It is dangerous to fall asleep in the snow. You can fall asleep for good. Come, my little one, come. Get up.
> Get up? How could I? How could I get out from this good covering? I heard the words of my father, but their meaning seemed empty to me, as if he had asked me to carry the whole hangar in my arms . . .
> - Come, my son, come [. . .]
> - Come, father, let us get back to the hangar . . .
> He did not reply. He was not looking at the dead.

> - Come, father. It's better over there [. . .]
> - There's nothing to fear, my little one. Sleep, you can sleep. I will
> stay awake.
> - First you, father. Sleep.
> He refused. (*N*, 96–97)

As *La Nuit* unfolds the father's speech indicates most dramatically the
decay of linguistic authority and the sources of traditional authority in
general. Initially, the father is presented as a well-respected figure: "The
Jewish community of Sighet held him in the highest consideration; he
was often consulted on public affairs and even on private matters" (*N*,
14). In particular, his authority is reflected in his command of language:

> My father told anecdotes to them and explained his opinion on the
> situation. He was a good storyteller [*un bon conteur*]. (*N*, 22)

Eliezer first disregards his father's authority (he begins to study the
Kabbalah despite his father's warnings), and then in his narrative undermines the validity of his father's views. This is done gently in the early
stages of the text; Eliezer's father sees little to worry about in the decree
ordering Jews to wear the yellow star:

> - The yellow star? So what? You don't die of that . . .
> (Poor father! What did you die of, then?) (*N*, 20)

Subsequently, *La Nuit* narrates the degradation and humiliation of
the father, who becomes an increasingly unwelcome burden on his son.
The growing desire for freedom from his father goes together with
Eliezer's increasing sense of guilt (see *N*, 64, 65, 113, 114, 117). Finally,
Eliezer experiences the death of his father as a terrible liberation, bringing freedom from an unwanted burden but also the loss of his self-respect
and of his closest link with the values of the past:

> I didn't cry, and it pained me not to cry. But I had no tears left. And,
> within myself, if I had searched the depths of my enfeebled mind, I
> would perhaps have found something like: free at last! . . . (*N*, 118)

As this loss of authority is taking place, the father's speech undergoes a
decline from command to incoherence. His first speech in the book
underlines his assurance and confidence with language:

- You are too young for that. It's only when you are thirty, according to Maimonides, that you have the right to explore the perilous world of mysticism. First you must study the basic texts that you are capable of understanding. (*N*, 14)

This contrasts starkly with the unfinished sentences of his final speeches:

- Eliezer . . . I must tell you where to find the gold and silver that I buried . . . In the cellar . . . You know . . . [. . .] I'm wasting away . . . Why do you behave so badly toward me, my son . . . Water . . . [. . .] My son, water . . . I'm wasting away . . . My guts . . . (*N*, 115–18)

The fundamental double bind at the core of Wiesel's writing lies in the fact that he must and cannot write about the Holocaust. His experiences during the war are at the source of his urge to narrate and to bear witness; at the same time, those experiences corrode the foundations of his narrative art as they undermine faith in mankind, God, self, and language. *La Nuit* is a work sustained by its own impossibility: the need to tell the truth about something that entails a crisis of belief in truth. The tension of *La Nuit* lies in its simultaneous assertion that what it narrates is true and that it cannot be true; such events cannot be perpetrated or seen or described. The narrator wants to believe he is mistaken at the very moment when he claims to be most brutally honest. So *La Nuit*, despite its apparent simplicity, is a deeply paradoxical work: a first-person narrative that recounts the destruction of identity, a *témoignage* in which the narrator wants most urgently to undermine his own credibility, a coherent account of the collapse of coherence, an attempt to describe what the author of the text insists cannot be described.

In the opening pages of *La Nuit* Eliezer's narrative suggests the unity of historical event and spiritual meaning; his stance as narrator shows retrospective command and interpretative authority over his material. In this respect, then, *La Nuit* has—paradoxically—a *reassuring* aspect in as far as it preserves the norms of narrative coherence and authorial presence. But the narrative order is shadowed by a counternarrative that denies the foundation of order. The text draws attention to its own impossibility as the narrator describes his own death; when Moché returns to Sighet it is, he says, "to recount my death to you" (*N*, 17), and when at the end of the text Eliezer looks in a mirror he sees a corpse: "From within the mirror a corpse was looking at me" (*N*, 121). Most crucially, and despite the narrator's strategies for conferring order on his

experiences, *La Nuit* describes the origins of disjunction between historical and spiritual dramas, between history and its significance. The story
of Auschwitz can no longer be assimilated to the story of exile and
providence introduced in the second paragraph of the book. The narrative
attempts to establish a command over meaning that the counternarrative
negates; Eliezer tries to understand, but his story does not make sense.

At the beginning of *La Nuit* Moché is saved from death "by miracle"
(*N*, 16, 17). The miracle suggests a divine intervention that the circumstances of the event belie. *La Nuit* is written in this same tension between
the establishment of order in the narrative and the description of order in
process of collapse. The miracle does not take place, though the narrative
forms and strategies that Wiesel adopts in his first work indicate the
continuing desire for the miracle, for the restitution of the union of event
and meaning. Perhaps it would be impossible for him to write without the
presumption of order, so that in writing he is bound to affirm values that
his texts nevertheless show to be without foundation. In his later fiction
Wiesel experiments with ambiguous, fragmented narrative forms more
appropriate to the collapse of meanings that is at the source of his writing.
This entails a growing lucidity on Wiesel's part to the broader implications of narrative technique and an explicit rejection of the attempt to
inscribe historical events within a scheme of miraculous intervention and
divine providence:

> But there was a miracle. Sorry, I withdraw that term: the war broke
> out and, if it saved me from prison, it cost twenty million men, women
> and children their lives and, we now know, it allowed the annihilation
> of six million of my people . . . No, it wasn't a miracle. (*Testament*,
> 218)[5]

L'AUBE AND LE JOUR

La Nuit describes the collapse of coherence from a deceptively stable
standpoint that is itself implicated in and threatened by that collapse. Like
La Nuit, Wiesel's subsequent texts *L'Aube* and *Le Jour* are retrospective
first-person narratives that use the past historic tense. The narrators look
back on their lives and are able to give their experience a degree of order.
Despite the wandering memory of its narrator, *L'Aube* even preserves
the dramatic unities of time, space, and action: the text describes the
events of one night in a house in Palestine. However, the material of
L'Aube and *Le Jour* continues to strain against the semblance of coherence conferred by the retrospective narratives. The progression implied

in the titles of Wiesel's first three works (*La Nuit, L'Aube, Le Jour*) is not borne out by the texts themselves; there is no unambiguous movement from darkness to light, despair to hope. Wiesel's "trilogy" appears to set itself a teleological program with which it fails to comply.

The ambiguity of Wiesel's writing after *La Nuit* is compounded by the fictionalization of the narrative voice. The force of *La Nuit* as a témoignage depends upon the reader's identification of the author Elie with the narrator Eliezer. The claim of the text that "all this really happened," and hence also its moral urgency, flounder if we refuse to invest the narrative voice with the authority of a witness. Interestingly, it is the narrator not the author of *La Nuit* who bears the "proper name" of the historical protagonist, since Elie is a French version of the name given to the child at birth. In a sense then, Wiesel is already playing with his own name by indicating a possible distinction between the victim of the concentration camps (Eliezer) and the author of the text (Elie). Such a distinction does not deny the autobiographical status of the text, though it may indicate the author's desire to dissociate himself from his narrator, while also being identified with him. This process of dissociation continues in *L'Aube* and *Le Jour*, the titles of which suggest a connection with *La Nuit*, with the consequence that Wiesel's first text belongs to a cycle that combines an autobiographical work with two overtly fictional narratives.

The fictional status of *L'Aube* and *Le Jour* is acknowledged on their title pages, which describe the texts respectively as a *récit* and a *roman*. Nevertheless, the divorce between fictional narrator and "real" author remains incomplete; Wiesel names his principal characters Elisha ("I am called Elisha [. . .] Elisha was the disciple of Elijah [*Elie*]," *A*, 21, 118) and Eliezer ("I am called Eliezer, son of Sarah," *J*, 98), and thereby invites some degree of identification between author and narrator (in the same way that Proust does by suggesting that his narrator may be called Marcel), even though the texts in which they appear are presented to the reader as fictional.

The status of the texts is problematic: in as far as they are fiction, we are discouraged from regarding them as historically truthful; in as far as the narrators are, *at least to some degree*, identifiable with the author, we are encouraged not to disregard their value as témoignage (this is reinforced with respect to *Le Jour* by the fact that Wiesel himself was hit by a taxi in 1956). Rather than recording real lives and real selves, Wiesel now begins to explore potential selves that are related to, but not entirely identifiable with, himself. The fictionalization of the narrative voice can be seen as a sort of self-fictionalization. Eliezer becomes Elie, and is refracted, particularly in the recurrence of the constituent /el/ (Hebrew for God), which occurs twice in the name Elie Wiesel, in the names of numerous subsequent fictional characters: Dr. Russel, Avriel, Azriel, Michael, Paltiel, Raphael, Malkiel, Elhanan.

Wiesel's fictional texts constantly reflect upon their own status as fiction. This is already apparent in *L'Aube*. At one point in the *récit* telling stories is described as equivalent to doing nothing at all:

> - What did you do afterward? she asked, suddenly anxious.
> [. . .] - Nothing [*Rien*]. He told me stories. (*A*, 106)

Earlier in *L'Aube*, however, the implication is that storytelling and the process of fictionalization may have a therapeutic aspect. Ilana describes to Elisha a future time when the telling of stories will enable the forgetting, and facilitate the overcoming, of present anxieties:

> You will get married. You will have children. You will tell them stories. You will make them laugh. You will be happy because they will be happy [. . .] And long ago you will have forgotten this night, this room, me and all the rest . . . (*A*, 92)

Storytelling is possible when the present can be forgotten, and it may even contribute to the process of forgetting; it may help to liquidate the memory of a traumatic past. "I am Eliezer, this happened to me," claims the author of the autobiographical *La Nuit*; "I am not Elisha, this never happened," suggests the author of the fictional *L'Aube*.

Disguise, concealment, the swapping of names, and the assumption of false identities are central motifs in Wiesel's writing; the creation of illusions and the telling of lies appear as essential strategies of survival (see in particular *Les Portes de la forêt*). There is a curious discrepancy between Wiesel's public image as a man of impeccable moral integrity (Berenbaum, for example, refers to "Wiesel's compelling honesty as a writer") and the prominent theme of dissimulation in his fiction.[6] Thematically at least, language is not used as a medium of truth, but as a screen to hide what the speaker does not wish to say. The emptiness of language is described on the first page of *Le Jour*:

> I had barely finished my work: a five-hundred-word cable. Five hundred words to say nothing [*pour ne rien dire*]. To mask the void of

the day that had passed [. . .] To say in five hundred words that there was nothing to say [*rien à dire*] was not an easy matter. (*J*, 9–10)

The text itself is at a further remove from the narrator's insistence that he has *rien à dire* (nothing to say). It revolves around an initial text, the journalist's report, which has nothing to say, and it repeats and comments on that absence of message. The use of *rien* (nothing) here recalls the equation of storytelling with doing nothing in *L'Aube* (see above), and is developed in Wiesel's next novel, *La Ville de la chance*. In the course of *Le Jour* the theme of empty language is reinforced by the narrator's decision to tell lies: "I will have to practice lying, I decided" (*J*, 11).

> I will have to learn how to lie, I thought again. Even for the short time I have left. To lie well. Without blushing. (*J*, 12)

The question of lying is related to the status of literature in general, as Wiesel indicates in the anecdote recounted in *Entre deux soleils*, when the rabbi equates fiction with a masking of the truth: "you write lies" (*EDS*, 11). As I suggested in chapter 2, Wiesel's evasive response fails to disarm the rabbi's accusation. Eliezer, the narrator of *Le Jour*, also attempts to make an unconvincing defense of lying:

> I was lying. I was going to have to lie. A lot. She was suffering. It is permissible to lie to those who are ill. (*J*, 122)

In *L'Aube*, as we saw, *raconter des histoires* (to tell stories) is equated with forgetting the past and being happy (see *A*, 92); a similar equation is established on the final page of *Le Jour*, though here *raconter* is replaced by *mentir* (to lie):

> Kathleen will be happy, I decided. I will learn to lie well and she will be happy. It's absurd: lies can give rise to real happiness. Happiness that, as long as it lasts, seems real. The living love lies, like they love to acquire friendship. (*J*, 142)

The change from Eliezer mark one, in *La Nuit*, to Eliezer mark two, in *Le Jour*, signals the transition from autobiography to fiction; and this also marks the shift from a sincere idiom based on individual experience ("Yes, I had seen it, seen it with my own eyes . . ." *N*, 42) to a self-consciously false discourse ("I will learn to lie well," *J*, 142). This entry into fiction develops out of the desire of the narrator of *La Nuit* to discredit and disbelieve the evidence of his senses: "That could not be true" (*N*, 42). Nevertheless, particularly in Wiesel's early fiction, the presumption of intelligibility has not been overcome. This is shown in *L'Aube* and *Le Jour* by the attempts of the respective narrators to assume authority over their narratives. Elisha in *L'Aube* presents himself as someone in search of meaning: "Philosophy attracted me: I wanted to understand the meaning of the events of which I was the victim" (*A*, 23). Elisha lives in anticipation of meaning, and he seems justified in his anticipation when he abandons philosophy in favor of direct intervention in the struggle for the foundation of Israel: "I entered a messianic world [. . .] in which no act was lost, no look was wasted" (*A*, 41). When Elisha kills John Dawson, he hopes to find in his act "a meaning that transcends it" (*A*, 136). Nevertheless, such a meaning is never revealed. John Dawson turns his failure to understand the meaning of his death back onto Elisha: "I don't even know why I am dying [. . .] Do you know why?" (*A*, 139). The question remains unanswered, and thereby the text refuses to confirm the authority over meaning for which the narrator is searching.

An illustration of this potential loss of meaning is also given in *Le Jour* through the contrast between the narrator's two operations, the first of which took place when he was twelve, the second after his accident in New York. At the time of his first operation, while he is under the anaesthetic, he dreams of a meeting with God. He thinks of all the questions he might ask, and God gives him all the answers he wanted: "God had answered all my questions and many others besides" (*J*, 85). When the child awakes, he has forgotten God's response, but his dream nevertheless stands as evidence of hope in the revelation of ultimate meaning. At the time of the second operation, the dream is not repeated:

> And you see, Doctor, this time, stretched out on your operating table, deeply asleep, I did not see God in my dream. He was no longer there. (*J*, 86)

Paul Russel, the surgeon during the second operation, seems to expect "a hidden meaning [*un sens caché*]" in the narrator's story (*J*, 86); but the story concerns the withdrawal or eclipse of transcendent meaning rather than its revelation.

The final page of the novel shows that this loss of intelligibility is at work within the text itself. Gyula has finished his portrait of the narrator, in which the latter sees his grandmother; recognizing the narrator's morbid thoughts, the artist burns his work. This has been read as an important step forward in Wiesel's "choice of life"; but the passage is too enigmatic and ambivalent to fit easily with any such interpretation.[7] The burning of the portrait appears as a second Holocaust in which the grandmother is destroyed once again ("Don't burn Grandmother a second time!" *J*, 142); and as Gyula leaves he does not take the ashes with him ("He had forgotten to take the ashes away," *J*, 142), suggesting perhaps that the traces of the past remain despite the desire to efface them. And the "choice of life" is deeply ambiguous if it involves a destruction that can be compared to the Holocaust. What is certain is that this final page does not offer any unequivocal solutions to unresolvable questions. The retrospective first-person narrator seems to promise a control over meaning that remains elusive. Intimations of significance are not fulfilled; and the reader of Wiesel's fiction is increasingly put in the same position as his narrators: confronted with uninterpreted signs and portents that do not quite make sense.

LA VILLE DE LA CHANCE

The narrators of *La Nuit*, *L'Aube*, and *Le Jour* attempt to maintain an interpretative command over experiences that threaten to undermine the foundations of intelligibility. The tension between coherence and incoherence, narrative authority and narrative subversion comes to a head in Wiesel's next novel, *La Ville de la chance*. I suggest that this novel is a watershed between the tensions of the early texts and the ambiguities of the later fiction.

The central issue of *La Ville de la chance* is the return to origins, and its principal character, Michael, reflects on the motivation and viability of such a return:

> - Since the end of the war, Michael continued, I have done nothing except look for Szerencsevàros. I thought that it was everywhere, except where geography situates it. I told myself that like me it had been deported, transplanted elsewhere, to Germany or to heaven. Now, I would like to go back. To see if it exists, if it has remained similar to itself. (*Ville*, 139)

Michael is convinced of the value of return: "Me, I know, the truth is to be found in Szerencsevàros" (*Ville*, 139). His journey has a purpose, even if he is not fully aware of it himself; Pedro's question "why this desire to go back?" (*Ville*, 49) turns out to have a precise answer, which is revealed toward the end of the novel when Michael begins to realize why he has returned:

> Suddenly, I understood that of all the reasons behind my return, this one was linked to a precise aim, to a specific idea. I was looking for something, but did not know what; someone, but did not know whom. (*Ville*, 168)

When Michael recalls the face of a man who dispassionately observed the deportation of the Jews, the meaning of his return is revealed:

> At last! Everything became clear, laid bare. So this was the reason, the real reason, the one that motivated all the others. So my acts, my desires were obeying a logic that was contained within them. (*Ville*, 171)

Michael's meeting with the man who witnessed the deportation of the Jews in indifference does not end the novel, but it does ensure the coherence and success of Michael's quest. His return now makes sense; and the encounter with the indifferent witness prepares his conversion to a humanist ethic of responsibility. In the final pages of the novel he rejects the temptation of madness and undertakes to restore his cell mate, *le Silencieux* (the Silent One), to the world of human relations. Toward the end of the novel a distinctly moralistic tone is adopted as narration gives way to prescription:

> It is within man that we find both our question and the strength to delimit it or, on the contrary, to make it universal. To take refuge in a sort of Nirvana—whether it be reasoned indifference or pathological apathy—is to oppose man in the most absurd way, the most futile, the most comfortable way. Man is only man amongst other men. It is more difficult to remain a man than to attempt to go beyond oneself [. . .] Don't stay at the window. Leave your nest but don't attempt to reach the heights by distancing yourself from the children who are thirsty and the mothers who don't have a single drop of milk left in their breasts. The true heights are like the true depths: they are to be found at your own level, in the pure and simple dialogue, in a look full of being. (*Ville*, 203)

When the young Michael begins to study Kabbalism, he discovers a world suffused with the meaningful designs of God:

> Suddenly all acts had a meaning, occupied a definite place in that immense mosaic of which even the contours escape our understanding. God was presence. He could be seen in every object, behind every gesture. (*Ville*, 53)

It is this sense of pervasive meaningfulness that *La Ville de la chance* attempts to recover. It is partly provided by the theme of return and Michael's final ethical conversion, which give the novel a degree of coherence; but there is also another aspect to the text that shadows this search for meaning and threatens its success. This is indicated when Michael's father denies the unity of reality sought by the mystics and describes life as "made of laughter, foolishness, daily hopes, childish illusions, adventures without future [*aventures sans lendemain*]!" (*Ville*, 54). The novel contains further examples of the denial or absence of intelligibility, or of incoherent stories and messages that fail to arrive. Pedro waits to hear the end of a story that is in fact already completed (*Ville*, 48); the narrator's father dies murmuring "unintelligible words" (*Ville*, 91); in prison Michael meets *l'Impatient* (the Impatient One) who is awaiting a letter that never arrives. When Michael is reunited with Yankel, a fellow concentration camp survivor, he cannot make sense of his story:

> [Yankel] began to recount to him his life in Paris. Michael, despite his efforts, could not follow the thread of the story [*le fil du récit*]. (*Ville*, 87)

Later Yankel dies without giving the elucidation expected by Michael:

> [Michael] thought: if Yankel could speak now, he would help me unveil mysteries [. . .] But Yankel could not speak. He kept his mouth open, his eyes open: no word, no message came out of them. (*Ville*, 109)

Michael encounters the prototype of the coherent narrative when he listens to an Arab storyteller in Tangiers. The pleasure of the story derives from its familiarity; the audience gets what it knows, expects, and wants: "In the market place, the old storyteller, as he did every evening, was reciting the same story, which caused the same enthusiasm in the listeners as if they were hearing it for the first time" (*Ville*, 123). This pleasure in repetition reaches its climax in the security of a known ending:

> Michael guessed that the story would soon be reaching its end. The happy ending—the merciful intervention of Allah, the miracle—was close. The Arabs were waiting for it avidly, impatiently, to greet it with a deafening roar. All's well that ends well. Up above someone is watching, someone is smiling. (*Ville*, 124)

The coherence of the story depends upon a divine presence, the guarantor that actions are not arbitrary, that a transcendent eye oversees and approves human activity and governs its significance. The story persuades its audience of the connection between the teleology of the narrative, where the ending is crucial to the conferment of meaning, and the teleological order of the universe. The end assures the meaning and meaningfulness of what precedes. The conversion to humanistic responsibility at the end of *La Ville de la chance* reflects the Arab storyteller's aesthetic of "all's well that ends well [*tout est bien, tout finit bien*]." The bond of communication that unites storyteller and audience is assured by the familiarity of the story's conclusion. The Arab delivers what is expected of him and leaves his audience deeply satisfied. In the less coherent world of "adventures without future" (*Ville*, 54), the father dies with only "unintelligible words" on his lips, Yankel dies leaving "no message." Michael, on the other hand, succeeds in delivering his message, as he proclaims the storyteller's version of *veni, vidi, vici*: "I came, I saw, I delivered the message: the cycle is closed. The act accomplished" (*Ville*, 187).

The end of *La Ville de la chance* is not, however, as straightforward as this presentation would suggest. The final page of the novel recounts a legend in which man and God exchange places; taking advantage of his omnipotence, man then refuses to return to his human condition (see *Ville*, 205). This legend and its relation to the main text are enigmatic: does it suggest that man has now acquired the powers of God, hence endorsing Michael's attempt to redeem *le Silencieux*, or does it imply that man's usurpation of God's power is an abuse, an illusion based on a world order that no longer makes sense ("so neither God nor man was any longer what he appeared to be," [*Ville*, 205]) or a betrayal of the initial bargain between man and God? In the latter case the legend might indicate that the redemption of *le Silencieux* is less assured that it seems. Moreover, the conclusion to Michael's story itself raises problems of interpretation that unsettle the coherent reading of the story that I have sketched so far.

The name of the man whom Michael has undertaken to save from silence and solitude turns out to be Eliezer: "The other [*L'autre*] bore the biblical name of Eliezer, which means *God has answered my prayer*" (*Ville*, 204). The name suggests that God has intervened just as Allah's miracle ensured the successful conclusion of the storyteller's tale. However, such an interpretation of this sentence fails to account for some of its most striking and strangest features. Wiesel gives *le Silencieux* his own forename, drawing a connection between the autobiographical Eliezer of *La Nuit* and the fictional Eliezer of *Le Jour*. At the end of *La Ville de la chance*, then, he suggests that the man who does not speak is another fictionalized version of himself. Michael's role, it might seem, is to rescue his own author from silence. And the introduction of the name Eliezer at the end of the novel indicates once again the duality of an identity that is torn between silence (*le Silencieux*) and writing (Wiesel the novelist), and between real and fictional selves. Eliezer is described as "*L'autre*" (the other), reminding us that he is both Wiesel and other than Wiesel. Like *La Nuit*, *La Ville de la chance* ends with the author reflecting on himself; and as in that first text, the mirror reveals the author as other than himself.

The meaning of the name Eliezer is given as "*God has answered my prayer [prière]*," and the use of the word *prière* here contributes to the strangeness of this final sentence. *La Ville de la chance* is divided into four sections, each of which is called a prayer: "Première prière," "Deuxième prière," "Troisième prière," "Dernière prière." And the word *prière* acquires ironic force because it is used to refer to the form of torture adopted by the Hungarian police in their interrogation of Michael:

> So that's the prayer, the famous prayer, thought Michael. Given this name by an erudite torturer, the torture consists in breaking the resistance of the prisoner by obliging him to remain standing until he passes out. It is because Jews stand up when they pray that this torture is now called the prayer. (*Ville*, 16)

The pious assertion "*God has answered my prayer*" has, then, a bitter ring when *prière* refers to a form of torture; and the coherence of the conclusion to the novel, suggested in the reference to a fulfilled prayer, is undercut by the presence of elements with multiple and contradictory resonances: Eliezer (fictional character/real author, silence/writing) and *prière* (pious prayer/cruel torture). In consequence, the sentence itself has an excess of meaning that resists simple explanation and undercuts the reader's anticipated pleasure in the predictable rediscovery that "all's well that ends well" (*Ville*, 124). Michael's ethical conversion does not satisfactorily tie up all the loose ends of the novel; and the intervention of Allah, bringing coherence guaranteed from above, has not un- ambiguously taken place.

What is at issue here is the degree to which *La Ville de la chance* fulfills the anticipation of intelligibility, of which the model is the tale of the Arab storyteller. In this respect there is a revealing difference between *La Ville de la chance* and Wiesel's essay "Le Dernier Retour," in which he describes his first return visit to Sighet in 1964, two years after the publication of *La Ville de la chance*. Wiesel himself makes the connection between the novel and the essay:

> I lived my return a long time previously. I tried to describe it in *La Ville de la chance*. Afterward, reality confirmed the fiction. (*Chant*, 162)

Wiesel, like Michael, anticipates some event or revelation that will justify his return:

> What have I come to do in Sighet, so late at night, so late in life? [. . .] Night is advancing and I am looking for a sign. (*Chant*, 156, 160)

Unlike Michael, however, he finds no hidden purpose that explains his journey: "I came to do something, I still do not know what" (*Chant*, 172–73). This is Wiesel's "dernier retour" (final return)—not because he will never visit Sighet again (he has in fact been back since 1964; see *Qui êtes-vous?* 100–101), but because the return journey confirms the impos- sibility of authentic return. The quest for origins culminates in the knowledge of loss:

> Sighet is no longer Sighet [. . .] I had no home any more [. . .] That town they spoke to me about, it no longer existed [. . .] No possibility of returning again [. . .] For the town that, previously, had been mine, never existed. (*Chant*, 146, 147, 172, 173)

No revelation, other than the revelation of the futility of return, takes place; and Wiesel leaves Sighet after only twenty-four hours. In the novel, Michael seems to be afforded the positive revelation of purpose that is denied to Wiesel: "so that is the reason, the real reason, the one that motivated all the others" (*Ville*, 171). Michael discovers, if not the answers to his questions, at least the faith in the sense of the question and the possibility of an answer: "The depth, the meaning, the salt of man, is to attempt to ask the question in a more and more internal way, to feel in a more and more intimate way the existence of an answer that he does not know" (*Ville*, 202).

This conclusion makes it possible to read *La Ville de la chance* as a larger-scale version of the tale of the Arab storyteller—a coherent story of return and revelation, depending upon the existence of a meaningful universe in which all actions imply one another; the audience belongs to an established community in which each member reacts in the appropriate way at the appropriate moment (see *Ville*, 123). All this depends upon a miracle—"the merciful intervention of Allah, the miracle" (*Ville*, 124). This miracle gives the whole story its meaning; the end explains the beginning, everything coheres thanks to the divine eye that watches over human affairs. But we have seen already, in relation to *La Nuit*, that Wiesel's texts are written in the absence of the redemptive miracle that confers meaning on history and gives wholeness to the story. Michael would like to be a storyteller: "Michael said to himself that if he were to return to earth, he would like to be a teller of legends [*conteur de légendes*]" (*Ville*, 123); but he realizes that his life and story do not conform to the aesthetics of the legend and the assurance of order that it gives to its audience. Michael's insight into this exclusion is shown by his eagerness to avoid witnessing the audience's ecstatic reaction to the divinely inspired dénouement to the story; and as he hurries away from the scene, he also turns his back on the aesthetics of the legend and the unified community of listeners: "Dreading this scene of collective emotion, Michael got up and departed as fast as he could" (*Ville*, 124).

Michael's reaction to the Arab storyteller and his relationship with his audience involves, then, both envy ("he would like to be a teller of legends") and rejection ("Michael got up and departed as fast as he could"). In its formal aspects *La Ville de la chance* reflects this ambivalence toward the aesthetics of the coherent narrative. *La Ville de la chance* contains more formal innovation than Wiesel's earlier books. In *L'Aube* and *Le Jour*, and to a certain extent in *La Ville de la chance*, Wiesel continues to employ narrative forms that give a semblance of coherence to experience. At the same time, *La Ville de la chance* is a more fragmented work. It does not rely exclusively on a first-person retrospective narrative; it oscillates between first- and third-person narrators, between real and imaginary conversations (such as the final conversations with Pedro); and, beginning a practice that Wiesel would adopt more extensively in his later fiction, passages in italics stand apart from and comment on some of the main issues in the principal body of the text. Wiesel's novel begins to adopt formal strategies that disrupt the anticipation of coherence. The first page gives a good illustration of this. It begins by describing the town at dusk:

> Outside dusk has fallen onto the town, like the heavy fist of a malefactor. Rapidly, without warning. Onto the low houses with red and grey roofs, onto the living wall of ants surrounding the cemetery, onto the dogs with anxious looks. No light anywhere. All the windows are dark. The streets: almost deserted. (*Ville,* 11)

The narrator seems in full command of his description. A quasi-divine eye surveys the whole town and describes the darkness everywhere, in every window, without exception. The details given are not arbitrary. The comparison of nightfall to "the heavy fist of a malefactor" prepares us for the most satisfying of literary events: a crime perpetrated under the cover of darkness, a mystery waiting to be explained. The ants encircling the cemetery and the dogs "with anxious looks" reinforce the reader's sense of anticipation: something strange is afoot, something is about to happen. The scene is pregnant with anticipated meanings; we are drawn into the narrative by its promise of an imminent event. In short, we have here a classic beginning to a novel—reminiscent of Roquentin's parody in Sartre's *La Nausée*: " 'It was night, the street was deserted.' The phrase is proffered casually, it seems superfluous; but we aren't deceived and we put it to one side: it's a piece of information of which we will understand the value by what follows. And we have the impression that the hero experienced all the details of that night like forewarnings, like promises, or even that he experienced only those which were promises, deaf and blind to everything that didn't announce the coming adventure."[8]

The opening paragraph of *La Ville de la chance* is rich with such promise. This is no disconnected assortment of facts, but the preparation of an event, the advent of meaning. As "old Martha, the accredited drunkard of the community" begins her drunken dance, the narrative raises its stakes to a universal level of meaning, which unites protagonist and audience in the same joyful anticipation of significance: "Happy, she performs before the universe, as if before an audience, her mirror" (*Ville*, 11).

This opening is followed, however, by what I call a textual stutter, as we realize that the first paragraph was a false start:

> - What did you say?
> Michael opened his eyes. The voice was that of a man who did not live in the town. It brought no memory, no richness.
> - Nothing [*Rien*], he said. I said nothing [*Je n'ai rien dit*].
> He returned to his images. (*Ville*, 11)

The first paragraph turns out to have been only masquerading as narration. The present tense ("All the windows are dark") does not correspond to any observed reality contemporaneous with the time of description. Michael's mind is wandering, and the narrator's command over his material is now revealed as a deception. Michael's "I said nothing" describes what the text itself is doing as it undercuts the validity of its own utterances. What the text has said—its first paragraph—is shown to be *rien* (nothing): the description of something that does not exist.

One of the characteristics of modern self-conscious literature is its tendency to foreground disjunctions between intention, utterance, and world. A clear example of this is given in the final lines of Beckett's *Molloy*, which draw attention to the conscious falsehood of fiction: "Then I returned home and I wrote: It is midnight. The rain is lashing the windows. It was not midnight. It was not raining."[9] The opening paragraphs of *La Ville de la chance* adopt the same self-canceling effect as the passage from Beckett, though it is more elaborately and deceptively prepared. The text speaks, but then declares that it has said nothing to an understandably confused interrogator-reader. The text is an infelicitous speech act aware of its infelicity. As Michael returns to his imagination ("He returned to his images," *Ville*, 11), the description acquires an apocalyptic dimension: "It was as if it were [*On dirait*, literally: One would say] the end of the world" (*Ville*, 12). The condition implied in "On dirait" is fulfilled in the same sentence: as the text suggests that one *might* say "the end of the world," it *does* indeed say it; but this realization of its own prophecy is trivially linguistic rather than properly apocalyptic. And this again provokes the disclosure that the text has nothing to say:

    It was as if it were the end of the world.
    - What did you say?
    - Nothing, replied Michael. I said nothing.
    - I heard you mutter something.
    - I said it was the end of the world. (*Ville*, 12)

Michael's "I said nothing" is reflected in the course of *La Ville de la chance* in a range of similar formulations. For example, when Michael meets his friend Meir:

    - What are you going to tell me now?
    - Nothing, Meir. Nothing. I said nothing. (*Ville*, 78)

Later, when he meets Meir again:

    - How did you get in this state? said Meir. Tell me.
    - There is nothing to tell. (*Ville*, 121)

In a story recounted by Michael about a man hiding Jews from the Germans in the back of a cart:

    "What are you hiding under the hay?"
    "Nothing. Nothing at all. I swear to you. I have nothing to hide."
    (*Ville*, 131)

And in the surprise of an interrogating officer at Michael's refusal to speak when he has nothing to say:

    - The idiot, said the colonel. To keep silent, to play the hero, when
    you have nothing to say, what an imbecile. (*Ville*, 151)

A humorous version of this "nothing to say" occurs in the episode describing Michael's short-lived career as a smuggler. On the outward trip Michael is so terrified by the customs officer's question "Anything [*Rien*] to declare?" (*Ville*, 79) that Meir decides to send him back without contraband. On the return journey Michael discovers the joy of the smuggler who has nothing to declare:

    Michael returned the following day. At the frontier, when the
    customs officer asked him what he had to declare, Michael retorted,
    with a smile, in a proud and loud voice:
    - Nothing, sir. Nothing at all! (*Ville*, 79)

"I said nothing," "nothing to recount," "nothing to hide," "nothing to say," "nothing to declare": the response to the question is "rien," nothing, the absence of substantive reply. This is reminiscent of the journalist's "Five hundred words to say nothing" at the beginning of *Le Jour* (*J*, 9). And on a more somber note, it is also reflected in Michael's reaction to the death of his father:

> - Tell me, Yankel, what was I doing whilst my father was dying?
> - I've just told you. Nothing. You did nothing. You watched. (*Ville*, 91)

This repeated insistence that there is "nothing to say" can be related to the theme of the unanswered question in Wiesel's novel. The importance of the question and the primacy of the question over the answer in Wiesel's writing are well known. At the end of *La Ville de la chance* we are given the clearest expression of Wiesel's thinking on the subject: "The essence of man is to question and the essence of the question is to be without answer" (*Ville*, 202). The ontological openness of the question is crucial to what I would call the "official" Wiesel: it brings with it a moral commitment to enquiry, reflection, and receptivity to others. However, in the main part of *La Ville de la chance* the theme of the unanswered question does not have the moral and intellectual respectability that this account would give it. Indeed, the unanswered question forms a disruptive countertext to the ethical thrust of the novel. It marks the refusal to answer, the interruption, deferment, or avoidance of dialogue. Pedro is able "to elude all questions concerning his identity" (*Ville*, 136), and Michael also "skillfully eluded" questions (*Ville*, 97). Numerous other examples could be quoted from *La Ville de la chance*, illustrating the prohibition on questions: "It is forbidden to ask questions" (*Ville*, 74; see also 27, 32, 61, 95, 115, 159). The most sustained passage that highlights this theme is the nondialogue between Michael and Yankel:

> - You haven't answered me! said Yankel.
> - What did you say?
> - I asked you a question.
> - A question? What was it?
> - You didn't listen to me.
> - Yes, Yankel. I did pay attention. I didn't hear everything, but I did listen to you.
> - Why don't you answer me then? [. . .]

- . . . How can you speak like that? After all that you did for my father? Do you think that I've forgotten?

Yankel left the question unanswered. [. . .]

- Do you remember Karl? said the boy very gently [. . .] It was Michael's turn to leave the question hanging in the air. (*Ville*, 89–91)

The deferred question—suppressed by the questioner or eluded by the addressee—indicates, in opposition to Wiesel's "official" stance, the impulse to hide, to guard one's own secrets, to reject narrative ("- Recount, he said simply. / - No. Not now. Not yet," *Ville*, 134) as Azriel does at the beginning of *Le Serment de Kolvillàg:*

I will not speak, said the old man. What I have to say, I do not want to say it. (*Serment*, 9)

The deferment of unwelcome revelations is a crucial aspect of Wiesel's fiction. His texts withdraw into themselves, using their exclusion from the felicity of successful speech acts to disclose an essential secretiveness within the urge to write. Once again it is worth recalling Wiesel's assertion that "the better the story is, the more it seems clothed. The secret must remain in a pure state" (*EDS*, 248). Wiesel seems actually to value the secretiveness of the text above its potential for revelation; and the emphasis on the withholding of secrets constitutes a disruptive countertext to the ethical conversion recounted in *La Ville de la chance.*

The different versions of Michael's "I said nothing," as well as the unanswered, unasked, forgotten, or eluded questions that fill the text, suggest an evasive aloofness from humanist ethics; and this indifference to the ethical concerns that seem so urgent to Wiesel himself (to judge from his nonliterary texts) is reflected in *La Ville de la chance* by the moral neutrality of the man who witnessed the deportation of the Jews from Szerencsevàros. Not surprisingly *le Témoin* (the Witness) is characterized by his negations and the repeated "rien" (nothing) that recalls Michael's "I said nothing":

- I remember.
- With shame?
- No.
- With remorse?
- No.
- With sadness?

- Not that either. With nothing at all. It's a memory that is associated with no emotion.

I leaned forward slightly:

- What did you feel?

- Nothing.

The muscles in my face were tightening:

- Outside, children were dying of thirst: what did you feel?

- Nothing.

- Outside, men turned away their eyes to avoid seeing their children writhing in pain: what did you feel?

- Nothing.

A silence, then:

- Absolutely nothing. My wife was crying in the kitchen. Not me. She was sad and depressed. Not me. (*Ville,* 180–81)

Michael discovers that his purpose in returning to his hometown was to confront the witness. This turns out to entail an element of self-confrontation, since the "nothing" of the witness is an uncanny reflection of Michael's "I said nothing." And this may also reflect the moral neutrality of literature, which Michael's ethical conversion at the end of the novel attempts to mute, but which reemerges through the excess of meaning in the text. The witness here is not the survivor-witness of Wiesel's nonfictional writings, on whom it is incumbent to preserve and transmit memories of atrocity. He is, on the contrary, an entirely indifferent figure, characterized by negation, signaling the temptation of indifference by which Wiesel's fiction is fascinated, even while it attempts to elude or condemn it. Wiesel's committed literature—like that of his prominent literary forebears in the French tradition, Malraux, Sartre, and Camus—can perhaps be characterized by the tension between the desire for an art freed from moral constraints and the need to resist such a desire. The witness rejects the moral concerns of Wiesel's text; so, in staging the confrontation between Michael and the witness, *La Ville de la chance* also confronts and gives voice to the obverse of its own ethical imperative:

The witness eludes us completely. He sees without being seen. He is there without being conspicuous. The lights protect him. He does not applaud, does not protest: his presence is evasive, it commits him less than his absence. He says neither yes nor no, nor perhaps. He says nothing [*Il ne dit rien*]. He is there, but he acts as if he weren't there. Worse: he acts as if we weren't there. (*Ville,* 175)

Wiesel's text pursues a prolonged and partly concealed meditation on the "nothing" of the witness as it discloses and explores his ambiguous, uncommitted stance. Ambiguity is depicted as both fascinating and dangerous: a thematic illustration of this is provided by the establishment and disruption of barriers and oppositions in the novel. As a child, Michael is intrigued by the bond between his father, a rationalist and humanist, and Moishe the Madman: "The young boy had never fully understood the bond between these two men, one of whom believed only in the power of reason, whilst the other refused all clarity" (*Ville*, 23). This bond between opposites is reflected in the marriage of Michael's parents:

> They are strange, my parents: my mother is a fervent follower of the Hassidic movement. Her actions and thoughts are devoted to God. My father is a worshipper of reason. He spends his time putting everything into question. (*Ville*, 36)

Michael observes a link between clearly differentiated positions: madness and reason, religion and skepticism. The boundaries appear distinct, but Michael is put in an intermediary position, simultaneously drawn to both poles of the opposition as those poles are also drawn to one another. Michael's role is to reconcile opposites and to become the living embodiment of the bond between conflicting positions. He mediates between the inclinations of his parents in his choice of a future course of study: "To make peace between them, I promised them that I would study both philosophy and religion" (*Ville*, 36). On a more theological level God is also characterized by Michael's father as the paradoxical mediation between opposites: "God is God because he is a link [*trait d'union*]: between things and beings, between the heart and the soul, between good and evil, between the past and the future" (*Ville*, 55). The keyword here is *entre* (between), repeated four times in the sentence: God is between, he is defined by his in-betweenness. If Michael is to succeed in his role as mediator, he must—like God—become the "link" that makes possible the union of opposites.

Opposites, however, remain separate despite the bond that keeps them together. The importance of separation is foregrounded in the theme of the wall, which is acknowledged in the English translation of Wiesel's novel as *The Town Beyond the Wall*. *Mur* (wall) and related words— *muraille, clôture, rempart, rideau*—appear frequently in *La Ville de la chance* with a variety of literal and nonliteral senses. *Mur* refers to the wall by which Michael stands while being tortured (*Ville*, 16, 148), the wall that separates the vision of the madman from that of the sane (*Ville*, 23), the barrier between man and God (*Ville*, 157), a barrier between men (*Ville*, 199). *Muraille* has this latter sense (*Ville*, 54, 95), and it also refers to the boundary between madness and sanity (*Ville*, 102). *Remparts* must be overcome for mankind to liberate its free will and conquer death (*Ville*, 43); and Western and Eastern Europe are separated by a *rideau de fer* (iron curtain) (*Ville*, 190). The barrier separates, but also marks the proximity of what is kept apart. And the barrier invites transgression. Michael crosses the iron curtain illegally in order to return to Hungary; he is tempted to cross the boundary between sanity and madness; and he attempts to break down the wall between himself and *le Silencieux*.

This transgression of boundaries also involves disobedience. As a boy, Michael becomes intrigued by Vàrady, an ancient neighbor toward whom Michael's parents exhibit an unexplained hostility. They refuse to answer the boy's questions concerning the old man, and the prohibition that they set up ("What is the meaning of this prohibition, of this mystery?" *Ville*, 32) is described as a protective wall: "the wall that his parents raised to protect him from the old man" (*Ville*, 37). The prohibition is compounded by the literal *clôture* that separates Vàrady's garden from that of Michael's parents:

> Vàrady lived in the next house. The two gardens were separated by a wooden fence [*clôture*]. Vàrady's property was declared a "forbidden zone" for the young boy. (*Ville*, 32)

Obedience to the parents would involve respect for barriers, both literal and metaphorical; Michael's disobedience involves the breaking of the fence that separates the forbidden garden from his own. Michael sees the old man "through the gap in the dividing fence" (*Ville*, 32), and Wiesel's text emphasizes the relationship between crime, destruction, and the crossing of boundaries: "His heart beating like a thief, he removed the nails from a plank, forced an opening and slid through to the other side of the fence [*de l'autre côté de la clôture*]" (*Ville*, 33). The phrase "de l'autre côté de la clôture" has resonances that exceed its literal meaning in the context of Michael's crossing into the forbidden garden. Michael is acting out a version of the Talmudic story, frequently mentioned in Wiesel's writing, of the four sages who enter the garden of esoteric knowledge. Only one of the sages leaves the garden with his faith intact; and Michael, through his conversations with Vàrady, is reminded of Elisha ben Avuya, who lost faith in the garden, and whose name recalls that of the narrator of *L'Aube*.[10]

The encounter with Vàrady entails, then, at least three transgressions: Michael disobeys his parents, breaks through the *clôture* into the forbidden garden, and faces a trial in which the desire for knowledge endangers both faith and reason. Vàrady, however, does not sanction these transgressions; on the contrary, he alerts Michael to the dangers involved in the confusion of what should be separate. Vàrady's use of the phrase "de l'autre côté de la clôture" (which was first used to describe Michael's entry into the garden [*Ville*, 33]) underlines its symbolic significance; and Vàrady denies the viability of Michael's desire to make peace between his mother's faith and his father's doubt:

> - It's dangerous, the old man repeated. To swear loyalty to light and to darkness, that's cheating. There are not several paths that lead to the truth. For each man, there is only one. In this sense, the atheist is like the mystic: both go right to their goal without turning aside. Of course, at the end they come together. But if their paths cross in the middle, they risk destroying each other. You can't be both inside and outside. Man is too weak, his imagination is too poor to enter the garden and remain at the same time on the other side of the fence [*de l'autre côté de la clôture*]. I know what I'm talking about . . . (*Ville*, 36)

According to Vàrady, Michael cannot be both *dedans* (inside) and *dehors* (outside); there is no deconstructed position outside the binary opposition. The *clôture* can be crossed or transgressed, but not abolished; and the transgression of barriers involves danger, not erasure.

Michael occupies an intermediary position between religion and doubt, faith and reason, past and present, madness and sanity; but this in-betweenness is qualified by Vàrady as untenable, even dangerous. Michael must occupy one pole of the opposition or the other, there is no third option; so his in-betweenness is manifested as instability, a continual changing of positions, rather than the consistent espousal of a fixed third position. The desire to reconcile opposites falters, as the young Michael studies Kabbalistic mysticism in defiance of his father's authority: "Michael had to overcome strong opposition from his father in order to join the disciples of Kalman" (*Ville*, 54). One option triumphs over another, but only temporarily. The German occupation of Hungary puts an end to Michael's mystical endeavor: "Michael left his master"

(*Ville*, 59). This also saves him for the first time from the path of madness in that he does not follow the same route as his two fellow students. (The text comments, somewhat ironically, "The Germans saved him," *Ville*, 59.) Nevertheless, the temptation of madness remains, and the text adopts an array of shifting attitudes. Confronted with the madwoman Martha, Michael feels the draw of madness: "There is no reason not to follow her into madness" (*Ville*, 102). After the death of Yankel, he is tempted but refuses to succumb: "I resisted, I said no" (*Ville*, 111).

In prison he begins to lose his sanity: "Michael could feel his reason dying away" (*Ville*, 189). He seems inclined to give in to madness: "Go mad: why not?" (*Ville*, 195). He recovers his lucidity through his attempts to save *le Silencieux*, but the end of the novel leaves him, perhaps, on the point of succumbing again to the temptation of madness: "Michael was reaching the limit of his strength" (*Ville*, 204).

The alternations of temptation and resistance are accompanied by shifting views of the relationship between madness and freedom. At one moment madness appears as the negation of freedom: "A free act that destroys freedom" (*Ville*, 111–12); but later it appears as a route to freedom: "For Michael, madness always represented a doorway into a forest, into freedom where everything is allowed and possible" (*Ville*, 194). This view is in turn contradicted shortly afterward: "It is wrong to see freedom only in madness: liberation, yes; freedom, no" (*Ville*, 198). *La Ville de la chance* constantly adopts different positions; and if at the end of the novel Michael seems to choose reason over madness, there is no ground for thinking that this choice could or should be definitive. The conclusiveness of the ending is made precarious by the unease and instability that have characterized the text up to this point. The desire, at the final moment, to arrive at firm conclusions is resisted by the constant fluctuations in the preceding narrative and, as I argue, by the persistence of ambiguity in the final pages of the novel.

The madness/reason opposition has a particular importance in respect to the necessity of choosing between contradictory positions. Madness is not simply the radical alternative to reason, because—once its attraction has been felt—it threatens to invade reason and undermine the certainties of the rational subject. Madness is the extreme pole of an opposition that threatens to negate the very existence of its opposite; it confounds the categories upon which reason relies. So, the fear of the spread of madness comes to haunt Wiesel's novel, taking the form of an anxiety over the limits of madness and the possibility of distinguishing with confidence where madness begins and ends. (I discuss this further in chapter 4.) The anxiety is first expressed when it occurs to Michael that Moishe the Madman may not be mad:

> That's his secret, Michael thought. He isn't mad. But in that case, the others are. And what about me, then? Who am I: Moishe or the others? (*Ville,* 27)

Someone who believed himself to be rational could not know that he was mad; hence, the crucial question: "- Are you sure that you are not already mad?" (*Ville,* 190). And once this doubt has been raised, nothing is preserved from the spread of madness:

> I have the impression that the whole universe has gone mad. Here and everywhere. (*Ville,* 197)

Vàrady expresses the necessity of choosing between opposites, of being either inside or outside, but not both. Madness, however, confuses oppositions and distinctions, and thereby threatens the possibility of choice. It also endangers the values that *La Ville de la chance* attempts to establish. Moishe insists that nothing is genuine; madness corrodes value as it proclaims the falsehood of everything, including itself. There is only falsehood, with no reassuring polar opposite:

> - I am not happy, he exclaimed in fury as he threw the bottle against the wall. Wine brings no joy to my heart. What is written in books is false! Just like wine! Wine is also false! Just like the heart! The heart is false as well!
> Suddenly, tears began to flow and disappeared into his dense beard.
> - You, he said, you, you know nothing. You are too small. Too young. Me, I know. I am mad and in this low world only the mad know. They know that everything is false. Wine is false, the heart is false, tears are false. And perhaps the mad are also false. (*Ville,* 24–25)

Madness confuses and confounds; the madman describes a universal falsehood that sits uneasily with those aspects of Wiesel's novel that attempt to establish positive values and the possibility of meaningful ethical conversion. The text resists madness, as does Michael. Moishe is described as someone who "refused all clarity" (*Ville,* 23), whereas, in his hometown, Michael experiences a revelation that seems to make sense of his return: "Everything became clear, laid bare" (*Ville,* 171). Nevertheless, *La Ville de la chance* does not entirely cast off the temptation of madness. The form of the novel is itself influenced by the instability and confusion that endanger the rationalist's desire for clear boundaries.

The deliberate strategies of confusion adopted on the opening page of the novel continue as the text shifts between different time periods in a way that is calculated to disorientate. Indeed, readers are warned from the beginning of the novel of the effect that this is likely to have:

> How many hours have already passed? These leaps from one world to another have killed all notion of time. No longer any reference point [*point de repère*]. (*Ville*, 16)

The novel exploits this disorientation and ultimately tries to overcome it by a gesture of regrounding: the foundation of ethical action "on the fragile terrain of the human" (*Ville*, 197). However, it is no coincidence that Moishe includes the written text in his account of universal falsehood: "What is written in books is false" (*Ville*, 24). *La Ville de la chance* is haunted (but perhaps also made possible) by the knowledge that literature belongs to the realm of the inauthentic; neither *témoignage*, nor history, it discloses the emptiness of its language by qualifying its own statements as "nothing": "I said nothing." The text is drawn to and horrified by madness, which represents the freedom to say anything, but also the knowledge that nothing will be taken as true. This madness endangers the ability of Wiesel's text to make even straightforward affirmations:

> Is Yankel still there? Yes. Has he left? Yes. He is there and he is not there. (*Ville*, 66)

La Ville de la chance is, then, a crucial novel for Wiesel: the tensions inherent in his earlier writing emerge with an insistence that cannot be overlooked. From the coherent narrative of experiences that undermine coherence in *La Nuit*, *L'Aube*, and *Le Jour*, Wiesel comes closer to a mode of writing that matches his subject: the collapse of the intelligible world narrated in an ambiguous text. Wiesel withdraws from the full consequences of this by giving his novel a "conclusion" that appears to resolve some of the preceding confusions. But Wiesel is now approaching his mature aesthetic, as the thematic failure of understanding is mimicked by an ambiguous practice of writing that exposes the reader more directly to the incoherences of the text.

FOUR

Crises of Narration (Later Fiction)

THE BROKEN PROMISE: *LES PORTES DE LA FORÊT*

As a novelist Wiesel is not limited to or committed to describing only what he has seen and experienced; on the contrary, he acknowledges that writing may represent a way of avoiding confrontation with his own experience: "sometimes it seems to me that I speak of other things in the sole aim of keeping silent about the essential [*taire l'essentiel*]: lived experience" (*Paroles*, 12). Although Wiesel is not talking specifically about his fiction, the need to "taire l'essentiel" has a direct relevance to the practice of literature, and particularly to the aesthetics developed by Wiesel after the publication of *La Ville de la Chance*. In this chapter I examine some of the ways in which crises of meaning influence the theme and practice of storytelling in Wiesel's fiction: primarily four of the later novels, *Les Portes de la forêt* (1964), *Le Serment de Kolvillàg* (1973), *Le Mendiant de Jérusalem* (1968), and *Le Crépuscule, au loin* (1987).

The opening words of Wiesel's first books suggest a faith in language and its referential capabilities, even if such faith turns out to be misplaced: "He was called Moché the Beadle" (*N*, 13); "Somewhere a child began to cry" (*A*, 9); "The accident happened one July evening, in the very heart of New York" (*J*, 9); "Outside dusk has fallen onto the town" (*Ville*, 11). The first paragraphs of *Les Portes de la forêt*, published one year after *La Ville de la Chance*, seem confusing by contrast:

> He [*Il*] didn't have a name, so he [*il*] gave him [*lui*] his [*le sien*]. As a pledge, as a gift [*En gage, en cadeau*], what's the difference? In time of war all words are of equal value. You only possess what you give away.
> Grégor loved and hated [*aimait et haïssait*] his laugh, which resembled no other, which did not even resemble itself. (*Portes*, 11)

The opening sentence disorientates the reader, as we are thrown from *He* to *he*, *him* to *his*, without any indication of the identities that lie behind these pronouns. The differences between *gage* (pledge) and *cadeau* (gift) are erased, *aimer* (to love) and *haïr* (to hate) coexist; and we are left wondering what exactly it means to describe "his laugh, [. . .] which did not even resemble itself." The desire to explain such enigmas is itself mocked by the metalinguistic skepticism implied in "all words are of equal value," which might just as well imply that all words are equally valueless. The words do not matter because they are meaningless; *Il* cannot be confused with *il* because there are no referents; it does not matter whether you say pledge or gift because nothing is being pledged or given away, nothing is being described or asserted.

The third paragraph of the novel continues the disruption of any realist presumption by its exhortations to the reader: "Imagine a struggle to death between two angels [. . .] imagine that both succeed in their aims [. . .] imagine the laughter that would rise above their corpses" (*Portes*, 11). The fourth paragraph is hardly of any greater help, consisting as it does of a single sentence without a predicate: "The laughter of the man who has saved his life" (*Portes*, 11). Not until the fifth paragraph of the novel are we given anything like a sober descriptive statement: "It was a night without moon" (*Portes*, 11); but even this is interpreted in the second half of the paragraph in a way that distracts from the factual content of the description. The clouds that hide the moon are, it seems, not real clouds at all: "they were not properly speaking clouds; but Jews who, chased from their houses, had been transformed into clouds; in this disguise they could return to their homes occupied by strangers" (*Portes*, 11).

"Printemps," the opening section of *Les Portes de la forêt*, sets an ambiguous scene for the rest of the novel. Grégor, introduced in the second paragraph, is not really called "Grégor" as we discover when he is questioned by the mysterious stranger who joins him in the forest:

> - What's your name?
> Grégor hesitated, then said:
> - Grégor, my name is Grégor.
> He was lying, the other noticed:
> - That's not a Jew's name. (*Portes*, 20)

Grégor is lying when he tells the stranger that his name is Grégor; and the text encourages any confusion the reader may feel, as it continues to use a name it acknowledges as false. Later, in justification of the opening sentence of the novel, Grégor gives his real name to the stranger as a gift:

> - Listen, I've got an idea. My name, I don't use it anymore. I'll give it to you, it's yours. Take it, Gavriel. (*Portes*, 23)

Gavriel has become Grégor, and the nameless stranger has become Gavriel. These names will be used throughout the novel, even after Grégor reclaims his "real" name:

> - What's your name? asks the boy.
> - Grégor.
> He blushes and corrects himself:
> - Gavriel. My name is Gavriel. Grégor is not a Jewish name, you know. (*Portes*, 235)

The exchange of names causes confusion, to which the text itself seems to succumb at one point. Grégor offends Gavriel in an angry outburst, and the text "forgets" for a moment to distinguish between "Gavriel" (i.e., the name given to the character with no name) and "Grégor" (i.e., the character called Gavriel):

> The smile froze on Gavriel's face. His companion had never seen him overwhelmed by such sadness. Now, Gavriel regretted his words. Too late. (*Portes*, 51)

Les Portes de la forêt opens in the midst of a situation of crisis (marked by the exchange of names), which concerns not only the thematic question of Grégor's survival, but also the descriptive competence of the text.[1] The crisis of narration is associated with the abandonment of the narrator by his father. The novel begins at the point when the father has broken a promise made to his son:

> His father had promised him that he would return in three days. Grégor had counted three days, then three more. Since then he had stopped counting. Father has departed and taken the numbers with him. For ever. (*Portes*, 12)

The father's broken promise is a deeply significant event, the originating event of the whole narrative. Grégor had believed his father to be "all-powerful" and "unshakable" (*Portes*, 13), and he had associated him with unerring truth:

He was the personification of precision. Incapable of lying or of being mistaken [. . .] He spoke little, but what he said had the sound and the force of truth. He would say: "Tomorrow the sun will shine"; the sun obeyed him. He would say: "Whoever travels toward the source becomes the source"; so, you traveled. But he had also said: "I will come back in three days." And he is elsewhere. (*Portes*, 13)

The broken promise and the absence of the father are presented as an interruption in the moral and epistemological order that Grégor had known. Grégor feels tempted to disobey his father's instructions: "And Grégor felt the need to disobey his father" (*Portes*, 13); and his decision to start smoking may be directly related to the fact that "his father had forbidden him to do it" (*Portes*, 16).

In the absence of his father, Grégor is joined in the forest by Gavriel; and in a sense Gavriel replaces the father as Grégor's companion. This does not, however, entail the replacement of paternal authority by the authority of a friend. Gavriel does not restore the order that had been endangered by the father's absence; on the contrary, he consolidates its demise. The father's broken promise represents the collapse of the truth/falsehood paradigm: the man associated with truth ("incapable of lying or of being mistaken") is revealed to have been in error. Gavriel represents a new order in which it is impossible to decide between truth and falsehood:

His voice concealed a trace of unspeakable irony. It seemed to affirm and to deny the same conclusion: everything is true *and* everything is false. (*Portes*, 16)

The arrival of Gavriel signals the fall into ambiguity, becoming now a theme of the text, in the same way it had been put into practice in the opening paragraphs. Through Gavriel, Grégor discovers the disjunction between words and meaning in a world that is losing its coherence:

He could understand the words, but not the meaning they contained. What he heard sounded sad and beautiful, but without coherent significance. (*Portes*, 17)

And Gavriel's irritating and persistent laughter gives another indication of the fundamental ambiguity of the character. In his thorough study of laughter in Wiesel's works, Joë Friedemann has shown how its polyvalent and multiple associations cannot be unified in any single interpretation; so, laughter becomes an ambiguous signifier as it represents an order opposed to the father's regime of truth and falsehood.[2] Laughter functions as a signal of the absence of unequivocal meanings. As seen in the second paragraph of the novel, laughter confuses the distinction between emotions that seem to contradict one another, and it confounds the urge for description or comparison (see *Portes*, 11). It is indescribable; and when Grégor first hears it, he perceives its relation to madness, another of the ambiguous values of Wiesel's writing characterized by its indifference to the conventional logic of truth and falsehood: "Grégor wanted to block his ears: the other wanted to drive him mad" (*Portes*, 14). Gavriel's laughter defies understanding because it represents that which cannot be understood:

> And he began to laugh. Grégor shrugged his shoulders and gave up any attempt to understand.
> There was nothing to understand. Whether Gavriel was mad or gifted with exceptional intelligence, what was the difference? (*Portes*, 44)

Gavriel is also, importantly, a storyteller; and his stories are particularly concerned with the coming of the Messiah. In *The Sense of an Ending* Frank Kermode describes how the story of Apocalypse is a historically potent version of an end-directed plot, in which the final event confers significance on preceding incidents;[3] it is by reference to an end that history, and fiction, make sense. Faith in the coming of the Messiah offers a way of making history part of a meaningful, end-directed narrative. In *Le Crépuscule, au loin* the Messiah is referred to as "the conclusion [*dénouement*] of history" (*Crépuscule*, 219). Wiesel's texts on Hassidism emphasize its Messianic aspects, implicitly contradicting Gershom Scholem's contention that the movement "neutralizes" the Messianic element of Judaism, in as far as it lacks the belief that the coming of the Messiah may be imminent.[4] In *Les Portes de la forêt* Grégor recalls his grandfather, described as "a fervent Hassid of the Rabbi of Witzsnitz" (*Portes*, 19); his grandfather represents "messianic nostalgia," and he owned an expensive suit that he never wore, keeping it in reserve for the day when the Messiah would come (see *Portes*, 26).

In the grandfather's "messianic nostalgia" we can see the traces of the coherent, end-directed narrative that has not been entirely overcome in Wiesel's writing. But the belief system upon which it relies is, if not collapsed, at least in the process of collapse. Gavriel does not abandon the messianic story, but his stories emphasize the lack of assurance that it will end as expected. A medieval Kabbalist succeeds in capturing Satan, thus allowing the release of the Messiah, but at the last moment he feels pity for Satan and his endeavor fails (see *Portes*, 25–26). What is lacking here is the sense-giving ending, and indeed the story is understood by Grégor as endangering sense itself: "Grégor did not dare question him, did not dare enter into that closed world where things and events must have a secret meaning [*un sens secret*], a secret bond, escaping under-standing, a sick meaning [*un sens malade*], a sick bond" (*Portes*, 26). Despite Grégor's hesitation, the text pushes on into this sickness of meaning, the domain of "un sens malade." Gavriel shows how the Great Narrative, the story of the coming of the Messiah, is susceptible to variation and contradiction: according to the Talmud the Messiah is "seated at the entrance to Rome," whereas the Kabbalists believed him to be "locked away in the most holy of inaccessible sanctuaries" (*Portes*, 39). Gavriel then recounts a conversation with the prophet Elie (Elijah), Wiesel's namesake and surrogate, who insists that "the Messiah will not come, the Messiah will no longer come, he has already come" (*Portes*, 41). There have always existed different versions of the Messianic story, and indeed there are different ways of understanding the significance of the Messianic coming; what is important here is Gavriel's pessimistic treatment of the variety of available stories. The unity of the narrative has been shattered, and it has lost its end-directed, sense-giving linearity. In his final version of the story he describes his encounter with the Messiah, who passively awaits his own murder at the hands of the Nazis. Gavriel reverses the creed of Maimonides, "ANI MAAMIN BEVIAT HA-MASHIAH, I believe in the coming of the Messiah" (quoted in *Un Juif*, 207), as he makes the impotence of the Great Narrative into the linchpin of an interpretation of history:

> I'm telling you, Grégor, that I no longer believe in the coming of the Messiah: he has already come and nothing has changed; he got lost on the way, he laid down his arms, without a fight, he got taken prisoner, he will never know freedom again. I'm telling you then, Grégor, that hope is no longer possible or allowed: the Messiah came and the executioner continues his work. The Messiah came and the world has remained what it was: a vast abattoir. (*Portes*, 56)

Les Portes de la forêt begins with the father's broken promise. That broken promise is reflected at a different level in Gavriel's versions of the

Messianic narrative, which disrupt both its coherence and its meaning; the promise of the end-directed story is not fulfilled when the end (the coming of the Messiah) has already happened and nothing has changed. Gavriel is described as "a messenger in search of a message" (*Portes*, 19); later, Grégor understands that Gavriel's message is purely negative:

> He had just understood the message of the messenger: father will not come again. No one will come again. (*Portes*, 25)

This negative lesson is echoed in the words of the prophet Elie to Gavriel ("the Messiah will not come again," *Portes*, 41) and in the novel as a whole. Whatever happens, nothing will happen; or rather, a great deal will happen, but there will be no return of authority (the father, the Messiah), no End to justify events and give them meaning.

The "Printemps" section of *Les Portes de la forêt* is played out in a context of crisis that inevitably has consequences on the form of the text itself. Wiesel's novel is not end-directed; if anything, it is the opposite. The four sections of the novel, "Printemps" (Spring), "Eté" (Summer), "Automne" (Autumn) and "Hiver" (Winter), indicate a cyclical return to the beginning (if the novel had a fifth section it would presumably be entitled "Printemps") rather than a forward progression. And what matters here is less the end, Grégor's reciting of the Kaddish (prayer for the dead), than the beginning, the broken promise (suggesting the broken covenant between man and God), which sends shock waves throughout the rest of the novel. In the "Eté" and "Automne" sections, the novel attempts to break away from the discursive stagnation of the first section, but even the action of the novel becomes to a large extent tied to the effort to explain and understand the mystery of Grégor's encounter with Gavriel. Leib sets in motion the main action of the "Automne" section through his desire to question Gavriel for himself:

> - Listen, said the leader, Gavriel knows things that we do not know. In consequence, we should try to free him. (*Portes*, 140)

And the "Hiver" section can be read as a commentary on the earlier sections of the novel. The description of Gavriel as "a messenger in search of a message" (*Portes*, 19) becomes a figure of the text itself, coming into existence through a catastrophe of meaning and finding only negative messages: the father will not return, the Messiah will not come, there will be no ultimate arrival of meaning to assuage the hermeneutic anxieties of protagonists and readers.

The father's broken promise, related as it is to the collapse of a truth-centered system of belief, must also have consequences on the act of narration itself. As in all Wiesel's fiction, the *theme* of narration has a direct bearing on his own *practice* of writing. The opening paragraphs of *Les Portes de la forêt* frustrate the expectation of any referential relationship to something existing outside the text. This divorce from communicative clarity does not signal the *end* of narrative, but on the contrary a vertiginous *explosion* of narrative; storytelling proliferates precisely at that moment when the storyteller has nothing more to say. Gavriel's different versions of the Messiah's story fragment and subvert the end-directed narrative that gives meaning to history. The function of storytelling is to mask this absence of meaning, the terrible silence, which the collapse of belief leaves behind. When Grégor arrives at Maria's village, he speaks because she will not:

> So it was he, the fugitive, who in the drunkenness of exhaustion began to recount anything in any way about anyone, fighting against silence like a drowned man fights against the force that keeps him conscious. The past became present, the self changed persona, everything was getting mixed up. People lost their identity, objects lost their weight. (*Portes*, 67)

The "Eté" section of the novel is almost wholly devoted to storytelling, as the villagers reveal their secrets to Grégor, believing him to be mute and retarded. In the "Automne" section Leib, Grégor, and Clara attempt to discover the whereabouts of Gavriel so that they can test the truthfulness of the stories he recounted in the first section of the novel; and in the final section, "Hiver," Grégor meets a man he believes to be Gavriel who listens to his stories with amusement but not understanding:

> - I don't know what you want from me, said Gavriel, half mocking half cruel. I don't understand a word of your stories.
> - So why do you listen to them?
> - I like stories. (*Portes*, 220)

Acts of narration have come to dominate the text; but there is no jubilation here in the liberation of storytelling from referential concerns.

The status of the story is a subject for anxiety precisely because it is problematic and ambiguous. The truth-content of the novel's proliferating stories may be in doubt and indeed may be ultimately undecidable, but that does not bring with it a pseudo-Nietzschean indifference to the question of truth. The most complex illustration of this, and indeed one of the most interesting representations of storytelling to be found anywhere in Wiesel's writing, occurs toward the end of the "Automne" section of *Les Portes de la forêt*. After Grégor's return to the forest, he must explain to his companions how their leader, Leib, came to be captured. The first version of the story is recounted with some confidence:

> As he spoke, his voice strengthened, became clear, free of tiredness: the voice of the perfect witness. The story followed a coherent, chronological line. The meetings with the guard, the meals, the laughter, the lies. Nothing was omitted. Beyond the pain, a certain pride began to glimmer within him. For these men, he represented someone who was returning from a wild country where monsters and dragons swarm; for these men he was someone who had seen destiny at work. Each of his phrases conveyed a part of an infinite evil, of a murderous truth. (*Portes*, 172–73)

After telling his story Grégor can claim: "All is said" (*Portes*, 173), everything has been recounted, there is nothing to add. However, it must be underlined that this first account, although the most immediate, is not necessarily the most truthful. Grégor is already blinded by his prestige as storyteller; he believes himself to be a "perfect witness" whose language is capable of communicating the truth, even if that truth is qualified as "a murderous truth." But he is borrowing narrative forms—"The story followed a coherent, chronological line"—that are possibly inappropriate to the story he has to tell; and the claims that "Nothing was omitted" and "All is said" rely on a fallacy of completeness that is hardly supported by the rather summary list of incidents given in the text: "The meetings with the guard, the meals, the laughter, the lies." The reference to Grégor's "pride" indicates, perhaps, that factors are at play here that bring into question his credibility as an objective, factual witness.

Leib's followers are not wrong, then, to insist that Grégor tell his story a second time. And the retelling brings new difficulties. Already the storyteller is beginning to feel alienated from his narrative; he is losing his sense of the truth of his story:

He retraced the route taken yesterday, the day before yesterday, trying this time to correct certain errors without succeeding. His mind could not follow his voice; on the contrary, it took the opposite direction: I did not meet Jànos, I did not ask him to find a Jew who changed name and existence and who laughed. (*Portes*, 174)

As it is narrated for a second time, life tends toward fiction: it is a story that could end differently. When Grégor tells his story for a third time, his alienation is complete. The repeated act of narration has succeeded in blurring the crucial distinctions between memory and imagination, fact and fiction; and the narrator can no longer identify himself as the protagonist of his own story:

> Once again Grégor spoke and became other. He rediscovered the other in himself. He listened to his own voice and now found that it sounded artificial, mendacious. He thought: what you are saying is not true, you are not saying what is true. The repetition of truth betrays it. The more I speak, the more I am emptied of truth, of infinity. (*Portes*, 175)

When Grégor tells his story for the fourth time, he emphasizes its fictional nature: "Since you insist on not understanding, I am going to tell you a story" (*Portes*, 178). The scene has been transformed: the partisan reporting to his companions has become a storyteller addressing his audience (and this shift from témoignage to fiction perhaps parallels Wiesel's own development from the autobiographical *La Nuit* to his later novels). The story is the same, but also utterly different:

> The narrative was similar to the preceding ones in every detail, and yet it was new with a supply of revelations and implications unknown up to that point. Everyone listened in fascination, as if they were hearing these things for the first time. (*Portes*, 178)

Finally, Grégor gives his audience what he believes it wants. In his fifth telling of the story he subjects it to a new interpretation:

> Without a moment's hesitation, Grégor began again and for the final time to recount his meal with Jànos, now giving it a grotesque interpretation: it was a dinner of accomplices. Jànos was an old friend of his father's, he often came to the house; Grégor had denounced Leib and in exchange Jànos had promised to have his father released. What

could be more simple? What could be more logical? Fair's fair. In taking the path of lies in this way, Grégor discovered that they contained their own truth. It was enough to proclaim himself guilty in order for the enigmas to be explained. (*Portes,* 182–83)

While retaining elements of the original episode, the story has now been fictionalized and its meaning transformed; and the false account of events commands more belief than the true accounts because it makes better sense of mysterious data. What seemed to be bad luck in the first version (the capture of Leib) is explained in the final version as the result of Grégor's wrongdoing. The final version actuates the arbitrary and excludes chance from the narrative. The partisans are inevitably more disposed to believe this final account. Where the truth meets with suspicion, lies are greeted as true. However, even as he fabricates his false account of events, Grégor knows that Clara is present in the audience and that she can prove this final version of events to be false. Eventually she intervenes: "Briefly, Clara revealed the facts and brought forward the proof of Grégor's innocence" (*Portes,* 186).

In his final version Grégor lies and is disproved; and this gives credence to his original account of the event, which initially had met with hostility. So, it may be that Grégor lies in order to be disbelieved, so that in the end the truth is reestablished. But a final twist is also possible. In the passage quoted above Grégor discovers that lies contain "their own truth," though this phrase is not entirely explained by what follows. It requires further explanation. It is possible that, although it is *factually* untrue (Grégor did not betray Leib), Grégor's final account of events does contain an element of truth: he may have desired the death of Leib even if consciously he did nothing to bring it about. Grégor may have envied and resented Leib's strength, authority, and prestige, as well as his relationship with Clara. (Leib's death does in fact make the way for Grégor to marry Clara after the war and thereby to become the surrogate of her former lover.) This has the consequence that at least some of what Grégor says when he is "lying" may be true: "- To tell you the truth, I must stress here that I never much liked Leib the Lion; basically, I envied him his strength, his calm, his superiority over his comrades; he was always the leader" (*Portes,* 184). The final twist in this confusing spiral of alienation through storytelling is that Grégor may be most honest when his story is furthest removed from factual truth; but he protects his honesty from being understood by clothing it within a factual narrative that can easily be disproved. On the one hand he lies so that when Clara disproves his story the truth will finally be accepted. On the other hand, and at the same time, he tells the truth with the purpose of being disbelieved. Because the final version of events will be revealed as being untrue, the partisans will also discount any detail of the story that does not correspond to the first version, now credited as "true." So Grégor's assertions of resentment toward Leib meet with disbelief. In the fictionalization of his life Grégor discovers a way of confessing something that could not be admitted in a totally "truthful" narrative. Fiction provides a way of expressing the inadmissible.

This in turn may allow an insight into Wiesel's impulse to turn to literature. His writing frequently evinces hostility toward fiction because of its lack of grounding in truth; but Wiesel not only writes fiction, he actively cultivates those ambiguous or self-reflexive moments that constantly remind the reader that this is fiction, and no more than fiction. Rather than inviting us to suspend disbelief, he positively encourages an awareness of the artifice of literature: this is mere fiction, it is not true, it did not happen. Wiesel chooses literature *because of* its ambiguity, not in spite of it. At the same time Grégor discovers that "the path of lies" may lead to knowledge of a different truth (see *Portes*, 183); Wiesel suggests the same thing in his response to the Rabbi who accuses him of writing lies:

> - All that, Rabbi, is not as simple as you seem to think. You see, certain events have taken place but are not true; others, on the contrary, are true but have not taken place. (*EDS*, 11)

The disclosure of the falsehood of fiction allows Wiesel to explore territories of pain, imagination, fantasy, and desire from which he can, while in the very act of exploration, dissociate himself. Here again, the voice of Gavriel imposes itself as the figure of fictional language, with its disruptive trace of "unspeakable irony," affirming and denying at the same time: "everything is true *and* everything is false" (*Portes*, 16). Fiction for Wiesel occupies a limbo between truth and falsehood; and this limbo offers what is perhaps the only possible margin of freedom, a minimal degree of salutary distance, from the trauma that his writing describes.

HESITATIONS: *LE SERMENT DE KOLVILLÀG*

In *Les Portes de la forêt* storytelling proliferates at the expense of any secure relationship between story and event. Wiesel foregrounds the autoreferential aspects of storytelling, and in particular the distortions brought about in the very act of narration; in this way he draws attention to the inadequacy of the story as a vehicle for the direct expression of experience. Despite its importance as a theme in Wiesel's fiction, témoignage is precisely what does not take place, as fictional narrators describe fictional events that have no direct relationship to historical realities. This raises the question about the ethics of storytelling that forms the motive force behind Wiesel's *Le Serment de Kolvillàg*. The whole novel is written in contradiction of its opening sentences:

> I will not speak, said the old man. What I have to say, I do not want to say it. (*Serment*, 9)

Azriel's refusal to speak soon becomes a refusal to narrate:

> I will not recount, said the old man. Kolvillàg cannot be recounted. (*Serment*, 11)

But the story of Kolvillàg will be narrated: "so be it, I will recount, said the old man" (*Serment*, 178). And from the very beginning the novel's second narrator, the young man saved from suicide, undertakes a history of the town that combines scholarship with the most traditional narrative forms:

> Once upon a time, a long time ago, there was a small town with a mysterious past, a black speck under a purple sky, which was called Kolvillàg in Hungarian, Klausberg in German, Virgirsk in Russian. (*Serment*, 9)

The novel hesitates, then, between silence ("I will not speak"), storytelling ("Once upon a time") and témoignage (although the pogrom depicted in the novel is not historically real, it can clearly serve to represent any number of such events, even the Holocaust itself). This hesitation is represented thematically in the conflict between Azriel's father (the scribe of the Jewish community in Kolvillàg) and the mystical Moshe. The conflict culminates in the meeting between Moshe and the father in prison, after Moshe has assumed responsibility for the disappearance of a local Christian boy. Azriel's father is convinced of the value of bearing witness:

My duty is to note everything, to transmit everything. Even what surpasses my understanding [. . .] Are we not the people of memory? Is not forgetting the worst of curses? An act that is transmitted is a victory over death. (*Serment*, 171–72)

Moshe, on the other hand, denies the value of verbal transmission and prefers the plenitude of mystical silence: "Me, I love silence, transmitted only between the initiated, like a secret tradition that refuses language" (*Serment*, 172–73). Azriel, observing this encounter, internalizes this conflict of values and finds himself torn between his father's commitment to language and Moshe's faith in silence:

Memory, insisted my father, everything is in memory. Silence, Moshe corrected him, everything is in silence. (*Serment*, 254)

Le Serment de Kolvillàg is a novel in dialogue with itself, as it gives expression to a range of differing and even contradictory attitudes to language. At least four can be identified.

1. Certain experiences lie beyond the capability of language; to narrate them is to falsify them: "Kolvillàg cannot be recounted" (*Serment*, 11); "I had never felt such powerlessness: how can one speak of what negates speech? how can one express what must remain unspoken?" (*Serment*, 41).
2. The word replaces what it names, it always names an absence: "The word names things and then replaces them. Whoever says tomorrow negates it" (*Serment*, 14); "I no longer say light to name it, but to replace it; I say love not because it is present, but because it isn't" (*Serment*, 77).
3. At the same time the word summons what it names: "The word foretells what it names, it provokes what it describes, didn't you know?" (*Serment*, 184; see also 216–18). This idea explains the oath taken by the Jews of Kolvillàg: if they recount the pogrom, they might provoke more pogroms.
4. On the other hand language has a mystical function as an all-powerful link between mankind and God: "By convincing my peers, by guiding them, I managed to persuade myself that, linking man to his creator, language was all-powerful" (*Serment*, 51).

Language appears as both lie and truth, as ineffective and as dangerously powerful. These conflicting attitudes lie behind the debate within the novel over the value of narration. Here again, a variety of convictions can be distinguished, which recall what I called in chapter 1 *le raisonnement du silence*.

1. Some experiences cannot and should not be described: "I am afraid of losing my reason by expressing the inexpressible, by naming the unnameable. I am afraid of saying what should be kept silent, what cannot be said" (*Serment*, 80).
2. Narration can be an act of betrayal. In order to tell the story of Kolvillàg Azriel must break his oath of silence and thereby make himself subject to Moshe's curse: "Never will he be pardoned, never will his fault be expiated" (*Serment*, 221).
3. On the other hand narrating is a mode of survival and even of salvation: "You don't kill yourself in the middle of a sentence. You don't kill yourself whilst speaking or listening" (*Serment*, 19); "so, recount [. . .] It's our only chance" (*Serment*, 83); "I will break my oath not to save you, but to save me as well" (*Serment*, 86).
4. Narration is also a duty for anyone who has a message to transmit: "You transmit your experience to him and he, in turn, will be obliged to do the same thing. In his turn he will become a messenger. And the messenger, he is obliged to remain alive as long as he has not transmitted his message" (*Serment*, 34).

Azriel's situation, then, presents the dilemma of the survivor-witness in particularly paradoxical form: he *must* tell a story that *cannot* be told; he must break the oath of silence that enshrines his debt to the dead in order to save the living. The witness damns himself in the very act of giving testimony ("his damnation will be eternal," *Serment*, 221); and Azriel's hesitations reflect the unease in Wiesel's writing over the act of narration itself:

> - The story that I have to tell you, I was forbidden to tell it. Tell me what I am supposed to do. I would like to be able to speak without going back on my oath, without lying. I would like to be able to live without reproaching myself for it. I would like to be able to be silent without making even of silence a lie or a betrayal. (*Serment*, 42)

Azriel, it seems, must choose between his father and Moshe, between the responsibility of témoignage and the temptation of silence, the faith in language and the abnegation of language; but *Le Serment de Kolvillàg* also indicates that both silence and language have positive and negative aspects. The word can be affirmation or destruction, silence can be plenitude or lie, a higher truth or a form of dishonesty. By entitling the final section of the novel "Le Fou *et* le livre" (The Madman *and* the Book) rather than "Le Fou *ou* le livre" (The Madman *or* the Book) (my emphases) Wiesel implies that the choice between the mystical silence of Moshe the Madman and the commitment to the written word has not been made, and indeed that his writing consists in the refusal or inability to make that choice. *Le Serment de Kolvillàg* is a novel in conflict with itself: a novel about silence but also the description of a pogrom, a rejection of the book but also an account of the transmission of the book, as Azriel's father ensures the survival of memory by entrusting the records of Kolvillàg to his son.

One might argue that *Le Serment de Kolvillàg* does, nevertheless, overcome its hesitations when Azriel decides to bear witness to the pogrom: between silence and témoignage he ultimately chooses témoignage. However, it is crucial to remember that témoignage and storytelling are not identical. The former depends on experience and memory, and it requires belief from its audience; the latter may be pure fiction. Storytelling is not silence, but neither is it subject to factual legitimation; and indeed in as far as it discloses its fictionality it positively invites its audience to disregard questions of belief or disbelief. Storytelling can be a way of not bearing witness, of hiding rather than showing. Forbidden to describe the destruction of the Jewish community of Kolvillàg, Azriel makes up stories in order not to tell of what he has seen: "I recounted all sorts of stories except my own: in inventing them, I gave free rein to my imagination" (*Serment,* 51). It is possible to see this as an illustration of Wiesel's own procedure in writing *Le Serment de Kolvillàg,* telling the fictional story of Kolvillàg in order not to tell the true story of Sighet, describing an imaginary pogrom in order not to describe the Holocaust.

Even when Azriel resolves to talk about the pogrom, it is not certain whether he is describing an event or telling a story, whether it brings an end to the text's hesitations or whether those hesitations persist in the account of the event itself. Early in the novel the story of Kolvillàg is described as "a very old fable" (*Serment,* 92). Even as it prepares to narrate the night of the pogrom, the text hesitates. The account of the assault on the Jews is delayed by a series of "extracts from the Book of the holy community of Kolvillàg" (see *Serment*, 232–39). This has two functions: it indicates a reticence to recount even within the narrative, and at the same time it inscribes what is to follow within a long history of anti-Semitism. The event, then, is preinterpreted as part of a pattern of events repeated throughout history. Before the pogrom has even taken place its meaning is established:

> Gloucester, 1168. Fulda, 1235. Lincoln, 1255. Pforzheim, 1267. Stupidity knows no frontiers; it transcends the centuries. The stories follow one another and resemble one another. A Christian boy disappears and the Jews are massacred. Trent, 1475. Tyrnau, 1494. Bazin, 1529. (*Serment*, 187)

Throughout the description of the pogrom the implication is that this is simply the reenactment and retelling of a familiar story: "The ancient images of pogrom had arisen again" (*Serment*, 244); "-Well done, the crowd roared, excited by the prospect of a spectacle that was new and so ancient" (*Serment*, 249); "The town, as it was consumed, recounted an eternal story for the last time and there was no one to listen to it" (*Serment*, 254).

Recognized before it begins, the pogrom belongs to the domain of the already-interpreted, which is also the already-narrated. History has been assimilated in a succession of repeated stories, and the story of Kolvillàg is itself made to represent all pogroms, and ultimately the Holocaust ("I had just glimpsed the future," *Serment*, 254). The story has lost its uniqueness as it repeats and represents other stories. In a sense, then, Azriel's insistence that "Kolvillàg cannot be recounted" (*Serment*, 11) has not been contradicted by his subsequent narrative. He cannot talk of Kolvillàg without turning it into a story, with a preestablished development and a ready-made meaning. When *Le Serment de Kolvillàg* finally overcomes its hesitations and begins to narrate what it had initially refused to narrate, it nevertheless finds fictionalizing tendencies within its own "factual" narrative; storytelling plays a crucial role in the interpretation of experience and endangers its objectivity. Azriel ends his account of the pogrom by suggesting that he has after all kept his promise to Moshe:

> Every story has an end as every end has a story. Yet, yet . . . In the case of this city reduced to ashes, the two stories are joined together in

one *and it will remain secret:* such was the will of my mad friend called Moshe, last prophet and first messiah of a humanity that is no more. (*Serment*, 254; my emphasis)

The narrative ends by suggesting that there is more to tell, that the true story of Kolvillàg has not been told; but we are given no clue to the secrets of that true story, we cannot even guess what it might be. The fictionalized témoignage brings its own authority into question by suggesting that what we have heard is ultimately only a story, the truth remains untold. This can be taken as representative of the situation of the Holocaust novelist, painfully aware that the story of the Holocaust must be and has been told, but that, because the Holocaust cannot be narrated as a *story*, the truth also remains unspoken and unwritten. As I demonstrate in the next section, at least part of Wiesel's ambivalent preoccupation with madness can be explained by the desire to find an access to truth beyond the falsifications of conventional narrative or the categories of discursive knowledge.

NARRATIVE DELIRIUM

Madmen, and sometimes madwomen, appear throughout Wiesel's fiction. More than most modern writers, in fact, Wiesel seems to be attempting to give madness a place of respect in literature, and to fulfill the program prescribed by Shoshana Felman in her book *La Folie et la chose littéraire*: "our historical task is to let madness speak, to restore its language." However, Felman immediately acknowledges that "it is impossible for us to articulate this language."[5] If, following Foucault, madness is characterized as the absence of language, then the attempt to give language to that which stands outside intelligible discourse will necessarily be paradoxical. Wiesel is inevitably caught by this paradox: his madmen are seen through sane eyes with a mixture of fascination and anxiety; they are befriended but not emulated (though the temptation to emulate them persists). In an essay on Moshe the Madman, Wiesel's narrator (Wiesel himself?) describes the "admiring fright [*frayeur admirative*]" (*Chant*, 101) he felt for the madman; and Raphael in *Le Crépuscule, au loin* shares this mixture of respect and fear: "As a child, Raphael Lipkin loved the mad and dreaded madness" (*Crépuscule*, 11). Like silence and laughter, madness is an ambiguous value in Wiesel's writing;

both tempting and terrifying, it represents mystical plenitude and mental debility, knowledge of God and an escape from reality. In this section I examine the theme of madness in *Le Mendiant de Jérusalem* and *Le Crépuscule, au loin*, with particular regard to its relevance for the theme and practice of storytelling.

Wiesel distinguishes between "the clinically mad [*les fous cliniques*]" and "the mad mystics [*les fous mystiques*]" (*Qui êtes-vous?* 64).[6] The former may be, he says, "touching," but it is the latter in whom he is primarily interested because they "disturb the order, disrupt, incite to excess" (*Qui êtes-vous?* 64). In the Jewish tradition to which Wiesel belongs, the mad beggar is accorded a particular respect. His madness may be holy, his insanity may represent an access to truth beyond the constraints of ordinary discourse. So, he will remain unintelligible to even the most brilliant psychiatrist, who looks to the madman for illness rather than insight (see *Qui êtes-vous?* 64–65). The privilege of madness indicates that truth is not to be found in the sanities of the rational world; more bleakly, Wiesel frequently implies that our rationality is itself insane, so that madness is a sane reaction to a world in which all decency has been overturned. After Auschwitz, he suggests, you have to be mad not to go mad (*Qui êtes-vous?* 67). This is reflected in *Le Mendiant de Jérusalem* by the man who believes he has lost his reason because he can no longer see the Jews who filled his town before the war (*Mendiant,* 26–33); it is better to believe you are mad than to think such things could be true.

Madness, then, appears as a response to an unacceptable or unintelligible reality; it represents both an acknowledgment that the world of our experience does not make sense and the attempt to explore an alternative discourse in which truth might be located. It consistently serves in Wiesel's texts to signify the failure of conventional reason. *Le Mendiant de Jérusalem* begins with a reflection on the Six-Day War in 1967. The author calls for time "to delimit the meaning and the import of the event" (*Mendiant,* 9); but he also acknowledges that there remains "an element of mystery" in the Israeli victory: "There was something else and I do not know what" (*Mendiant,* 11). The ensuing text, then, is offered as a response to this acknowledgment of a need for "something else" to explain the events of history. The text turns to madness in search of a solution that it cannot find in its own rational reflections; and the mad beggars of Jerusalem appear to offer commentary and explanation of historical action in terms that exceed the conventional limits of historical analysis. The madman claims a degree of certainty that contrasts with the characteristic self-doubt of Wiesel's sane characters: "It's a beggar who is telling you this, he knows what he's talking about" (*Mendiant*, 13); and Wiesel's texts never entirely dismiss the implication that the madman may have access to an order of experience and truth from which the sane are precluded by their very sanity.

In *Le Mendiant de Jérusalem* and *Le Crépuscule, au loin*, then, Wiesel presents madness not as an illness to be diagnosed and cured (and thereby suppressed), but as a language to which we might listen and from which we might learn. Much of *Le Crépuscule, au loin* takes place in an asylum and consists of the monologues of its inmates. Psychiatry, as it is presented in the novel, aims to socialize the madman by returning him to "normality." The psychiatrist claims to possess a body of knowledge external to but effective on madness:

> - Ultimately, everything falls within the scope of psychiatry, said Doctor Benedictus. Its task consists precisely in returning the patient to the golden mean by giving him back his balance. (*Crépuscule*, 44)

There is no exchange between psychiatrist and patient, the latter needs the former but there is no reciprocity in the relationship: "In other words: mystics may need the psychiatrist, but the psychiatrist does not need mystics" (*Crépuscule*, 44). In Raphael's view, however, psychiatry can never offer complete knowledge of madness because it is indifferent to the truth that madness may contain ("How can you be sure that their truth does not reside in what we call their madness?" *Crépuscule*, 91) and it remains strictly and necessarily external to its subject ("Psychiatry will surely remain an approximative domain because the practitioner will never manage to put himself in the place of the patient," *Crépuscule*, 90). Raphael endeavors to *listen to* the madmen rather than to find ways of assimilating their experiences to the preexisting body of psychiatric knowledge. This can be interpreted as a representation of what Wiesel attempts to do when he writes about the mad, particularly in *Le Mendiant de Jérusalem* and *Le Crépuscule, au loin*, which more than the other novels allow the madmen to recount their own stories. Because the novelist or poet does not aim to understand the mad in the light of a preexistent theoretical model, Raphael suggests that he or she may actually have a greater insight into human behavior than the trained psychiatrist (see *Crépuscule*, 223).

Raphael's attention to the madmen involves a suspension of disbelief and recognition of the internal logic of their stories:

> Without realizing it, he has accepted the rules of the game; he is "going along"; he accepts the logic of the narrative. Am I mad like he is? wonders Raphael. Could he have passed on to me the seed of his madness? His delirious narrative, I listen to it as if it were a real experience. (*Crépuscule*, 141)

The approach here is Laingian: Raphael accepts the stories of the madmen on their own terms, rather than simply decrying them as nonsense.[7] By doing this he discovers that the stories contain their own coherence:

> Once more, Raphael is surprised by the logic that characterizes certain forms of madness. Not at all incoherent, the words of this patient seem to him to be perfectly reasonable. (*Crépuscule*, 219)

Le Mendiant de Jérusalem and *Le Crépuscule, au loin* invite us, then, to listen to the stories of the madmen without regard for any conventionally verifiable truth. The young officer who asks if Itzik has, as his story suggests, "really been to war" (*Mendiant*, 48) has simply misunderstood the rules of the game; he is still bound to an inappropriate logic of truth and falsehood.

To hear the stories of the madmen is not, however, to understand them in any conventional sense. Psychiatrists' knowledge of madness is limited because they do not enter into the delirium of the patient; but to enter into delirium is also to suspend presumptions of intelligibility. The stories of the madmen are models of enigmatic narrative: they are fully indifferent to rational notions of truth, consistency, verisimilitude, or intelligibility. They make sense only in as far as listeners accept the madman's own terms, without wishing to impose their own. Madness is the domain of the essentially enigmatic: "Since it is a question of madness, everything is mystery" (*Crépuscule*, 63). Indeed, madness sometimes appears as synonymous with misunderstanding; Pedro tells Raphael at one point that "the misunderstood writer is a mad writer" (*Crépuscule*, 48). And *Le Mendiant de Jérusalem* begins with a reflection on the mystery of history, which then prompts the narrator's exploration of the world of the beggars and madmen in search of an explanation not afforded by rational thought. Madness explains what reason cannot; but at the same time, it remains essentially mysterious, it cannot itself be "understood." So the explanation the novel finally offers us for the Israeli victory in the Six-Day War makes sense only on its own terms; it "explains," but excludes any possibility of verification:

> Israel defeated its enemies, do you know why? I am going to let you know: Israel won because its army, its people, contained an extra six million names. (*Mendiant*, 180)

There is something intuitively persuasive in the implication of a connection between the six million Jewish victims of the Holocaust and the Israeli victory of 1967; at the same time it is not empirically justifiable, it self-consciously eludes ordinary criteria of argument and evidence. Like the tales of the madmen, the explanation seems to require either acceptance on its own terms or rejection because it cannot be proved.

In order to enter into the world of the madmen, Raphael realizes that he must share their delirium. But this brings with it its own danger. By attempting to share the madness of the patients, Raphael risks becoming mad himself: "If I put myself in the place of Adam, even for the slightest moment, I condemn myself to stay there" (*Crépuscule*, 90). This danger is reflected in *Le Mendiant de Jérusalem* by the experience of the pilot who listens to the stories of the beggars. Initially, he adheres to conventional logic when he asks whether Itzik has *really* experienced what he describes (*Mendiant*, 48): what matters is the truth of the story. He becomes increasingly disconcerted: "The pilot feels uncomfortable, but, rather than admitting it, he decides to play the game [. . .] No longer knowing what to think, he seems ill at ease, irritated" (*Mendiant*, 49). He tries to leave but is held back; and gradually he is drawn into the world of the mad beggars:

> He is adrift. He feels his reason give way. [He is] caught in the mechanism. (*Mendiant*, 53)

And eventually he reaches the point where, like most of Wiesel's principal characters, he doubts his own sanity: "The pilot wipes his forehead,

thinks that he will go mad, and wonders if he is not already mad"
(*Mendiant*, 56).

In *La Folie et la chose littéraire* Shoshana Felman describes how the
search to understand madness may turn against the inquirers, as it
confronts them with fundamental questions about knowledge: "Beyond all caricature, we can begin to see that, if the question of madness
goes together so insistently with the current overturning of the very
status of knowledge, it is because it effectively poses, and in more than
one way, the question of which we have not yet fully understood the
importance—and the meaning—and which, from now on, can no
longer be taken for granted: not 'who "knows" and who does not
"know," ' but *what does it mean 'to know'?*"[8] In Wiesel's texts also,
madness brings knowledge itself into question. The theme of madness
indicates a mystical nostalgia that the author has never fully overcome; at the same time it is associated with an anxiety about knowledge that endangers "sane" epistemology. When Raphael is preparing
to leave the clinic in *Le Crépuscule, au loin,* he admits he is frightened
by its inmates:

> Your patients frighten me. They give me a glimpse of a universe
> outside my own, a world next to my own, a possibility of being alien to
> my own, a way of thinking as valid as my own. So there is a place that,
> for me, will remain impenetrable. Forbidden. (*Crépuscule,* 257)

The more Raphael enters into the world of the madmen, the less he
knows: "This stay at the Clinic has eaten away at my knowledge: each
day I knew less, ever less" (*Crépuscule,* 257). Madness gives a glimpse of
a separate world in which the categories and strategies of rational
knowledge have no purchase. To understand it you must enter into it, but
if you enter into it you can no longer understand it. Madness endangers
rationality and threatens to engulf the sane subject. The anxiety of the
pilot who finds himself wondering if he is himself mad (see *Mendiant,*
56; quoted above) haunts Wiesel's narrators. There is a spread of madness
in Wiesel's writing, to the point where sanity can never be taken for
granted: Raphael, in *Le Crépuscule, au loin,* constantly repeats his fear of
going mad; he considers the possibility that Pedro may be mad (see
Crépuscule, 48); and he suggests that not only the patients, but everyone
connected with the clinic may be mad: "In a lunatic asylum, everyone is
mad" (*Crépuscule,* 256).[9]

Wiesel gives voice to the mad, but this also leads to a disruption of the boundaries between madness and sanity. The madman encountered by David at the beginning of *Le Mendiant de Jérusalem* is in fact horribly sane: he sees the town as it is, devoid of its Jewish community, but prefers to disbelieve his own perceptions. On the other hand, one can never be certain of one's own sanity, as Raphael learns in a conversation with a waiter:

> - Are you going to the Clinic?
> - Yes.
> - Are you crazy or what?
> - I don't think so.
> - That's what they all say. (*Crépuscule*, 66)

Only others can know you are mad, since to recognize oneself as mad is to accept a logic that madness itself refuses; hence the anxious interrogation that never receives a confident reply:

> What is essential in the personality of a sick person? Who is a sick person? (*Crépuscule*, 47)

Naming madness is a way of excluding it, keeping it at arm's length; listening to madness restores its place on the inside of society, but also brings dangers with it. Wiesel's texts maintain an uneasy relationship with madness because of its fascination and danger. Raphael is prepared to enter into the world of the mad, but only conditionally: "I don't mind entering into madness, under the condition that I can get out of it unharmed" (*Crépuscule*, 86). This accurately represents the attitude implicit in Wiesel's use of madness as a theme in his writing. Madness exercises a fascination that must be resisted. Both *Le Mendiant de Jérusalem* and *Le Crépuscule, au loin* attempt to establish an encounter with madness, but also to remain immune to its danger; both texts oscillate between the delirious stories of the madmen and the narration of events more firmly rooted in the real—the Six-Day War in *Le Mendiant de Jérusalem* and the early stages of the Holocaust in *Le Crépuscule, au loin*. Both texts attempt to maintain themselves in a dangerous proximity to madness without ever being fully drawn into it: fascinated by the delirious narratives of the madmen, but able to preserve their foundation in history.

However, the madmen of Wiesel's novels are captivating storytellers, and as such they serve to represent the storytelling impulse of the novelist himself. The stories of the madmen cannot easily be assimilated to conventional ethics or epistemology; and madness is the thematic trace of the irresponsibility of the storyteller that Wiesel both desires and resists. As madness represents a threat to sanity that Wiesel's characters at least partly seek, so it also represents a threat to the rational and historical foundation of the texts themselves. From *La Nuit* onward, Wiesel's characters repeatedly suggest both that "this is true" and "this cannot be true." As David narrates the capture of Jerusalem in *Le Mendiant de Jérusalem*, he also undermines his own ability to bear witness:

> It was delirium [. . .] - Have we all gone mad? [. . .] However the impression of living a dream had not yet left me [. . .] By singing, I will become mad; so what, I will dream [. . .] But I also know that I am dreaming [. . .] All that, you didn't see it that day! Very well. So what? I saw it another day, a week, a month later. Time doesn't matter much. (*Mendiant*, 172–80)

Another sign of the pervasiveness of madness can be seen in the breakdown of the mimetic illusion, as the texts allow an element of fantasy to circulate within and disrupt the predominantly realist narrative. As a child, Raphael witnesses an execution; he recognizes the victim as an old madman he has befriended, but later he is addressed by that same madman. Raphael cannot yet abandon the realist presumption of consistency: "It was not the old man with extinguished eyes that the Germans had just executed, it can't have been him, because the old madman was there beside him" (*Crépuscule*, 39). Wiesel's novel, on the other hand, disregards Raphael's common sense and permits the madman to flout temporal and spatial barriers. In the previous section I suggested that reality is only accessible when mediated through stories; the theme of madness in Wiesel's writing goes further in undermining the representation of reality by privileging the story for its own sake, without reference to its historical truth or moral import. The trace of madness as it pervades Wiesel's writing is in the double gesture by which the texts deny the reality of the real and affirm the truth of that which cannot be assimilated by conventional logic; this gesture creates the space in which storytelling proliferates:

- I'm going to tell you a story.
- Is it about fear?
- Yes, if you like.
- Is it true at least?
- Of course. All our stories are true.
- Good. Start. (*Mendiant*, 53)

In his essay on Moshe the Madman, Wiesel recounts how he had the idea of using fiction in order to neutralize the fascination exercised by the madman:

> One day I thought I had found the answer: I imprisoned him in a novel. With a roof above his head, an address, a home, surrounded by people who show him affection, I hoped that he would at last leave me in peace. It was only later, when I had finished working, that I realized the trick he had played on me: unknown to me, he had crept, like a thief, into the other characters, without distinguishing between age, sex or religion. In turn he said I, you, he. Two characters spoke: he was both at once. They were torturing one another: he was the cause and the expression of their suffering. Driven crazy [*affolé*], I reread my previous stories: he was in command of all of them. There again, he was ahead of me. More seriously: he granted himself the status of temporary resident, appearing and disappearing at will. Hardly revealed, already he was disappearing, more wild than ever, heading toward new adventures to which he dragged me by force.
>
> Sometimes I have the idea that I myself am only an error, a misunderstanding: I think I am living my life, while in truth I am only translating his. (*Chant*, 102)

Literature appears here as a way of imprisoning madness and hence contributing to its exclusion; but the madman invades and inhabits the text, and ultimately even the author of the text regards himself as possessed by what he had attempted to control through writing. Fiction releases madness even as it endeavors to restrict its danger. And the ultimate fascination of madness is that it becomes, for Wiesel, a figure of fiction itself, the narrative delirium of stories freed from truth or moral responsibility, the frightening and fascinating liberation of language for the benefit of storytelling but to the detriment of truth:

Raphael did not understand, but that was only natural. The old man was mad, and the mad hardly need to make others understand them. They can say anything, the mad; and do anything, undo anything, without having to explain themselves. Happy are the mad, they are free. It is because they are free, liberated, that they are mad. Is that why Raphael felt such an attachment to the old man? (*Crépuscule*, 12)

FIVE

Victims and Executioners

> We all play a role in crime, even when we fight it: there is no way out of the trap. The guilt of the assassin rebounds onto his victims. That is what constitutes the madness of our generation: the complicity between executioners and victims, which is imposed on the latter without their knowing.
>
> (*Portes*, 139)

I SUGGESTED in chapter 1 that it is impossible to read Wiesel's fiction as a straightforward expression of the moral attitudes put forward with such power in the essays collected in *Les Juifs du silence* (1966), *Un Juif, aujourd'hui* (1977), *Paroles d'étranger* (1982), *Signes d'exode* (1985), and *Silences et mémoire d'hommes* (1989). In this chapter I examine this assertion more carefully, outlining the nature and ethical foundations of Wiesel's human rights work and indicating some of the tensions that exist between his essays and his fiction. In particular, the theme of terrorist struggle in *L'Aube* (1960) and *L'Oublié* (1989) cannot easily be reconciled with the unconditional respect for others that forms the basis of Wiesel's ethical stance. It should be said at the outset that such discrepancies do not in any way diminish the importance of Wiesel's commitment to human rights, nor do they detract from the value of his admirable and outspoken interventions on behalf of Jews (in the former USSR, or the Ethiopian Falashas) and non-Jews (in Biafra, Bangladesh, Cambodia, Ethiopia, and South Africa). My intention here is to show the specific interactions of literary texts with the ethical criteria underpinning Wiesel's nonliterary texts.

Wiesel's writing derives its authority from two important sources: Judaism and the experience of the Holocaust. Wiesel interrogates and elucidates Jewish tradition, for example in his texts on biblical interpretation and Hassidism, frequently underlining the universalist and humanist aspect of Jewish ethics as well as the continuing relevance of traditional stories for the modern world. At the same time, his texts are concerned with the traumas of the present day (the nuclear threat, apartheid and other forms of political suppression); they make constant reference to the Holocaust, which Wiesel links to subsequent ills while being careful to insist that no simple comparison can be made. The Holocaust puts survivors in a privileged position to recognize crimes against morality, and also obliges them to speak out in protest.

Jewish tradition and the first-hand experience of Nazi persecution, then, provide the ethical foundations for Wiesel's writing and his involvement in human rights. A problem arises (and this is indeed one of the central problem of Wiesel's work) when the two are in conflict. A simple but important illustration of this is given in *Le Cinquième Fils*. In the ghetto of Davarowsk, Reuven, the narrator's father, and his friend Simha take an oath to kill Richard Lander, the man responsible for the death of Simha's wife and other Jews; the rabbi opposes the oath on the grounds that Jewish tradition and law forbid murder (see *Fils*, 159–60). After the war Reuven and Simha are given the opportunity to be present at the assassination of Lander, and Reuven readily accepts:

> - My answer is yes. We took an oath. By what right could I betray it? (*Fils*, 163)

Reuven must choose between breaking his oath or breaking Jewish law; he cannot keep both. Subsequently, after the attempted assassination, which they wrongly believe to have been successful, Reuven and Simha are haunted by guilt. Their discussions of biblical texts and current affairs involve the attempt to find definitive grounds on which to justify or to condemn their actions once and for all. Reuven's categorical rejection of violence leads him to condemn his own former involvement in a violent act (see *Fils*, 147–49). Yet at the time he had no hesitation, and indeed he felt obliged by his oath to condone the assassination. Moreover, the depiction of atrocities committed by Richard Lander may lead at least some readers to disagree with Reuven's later self-condemnation.

A formal system of rules governing right and wrong behavior is challenged by circumstances for which such rules seem inadequate. As a character says in Wiesel's short play "Il était une fois," describing a Jewish uprising in an unnamed ghetto, "the Talmud did not predict the ghetto" (*EDS*, 239); in other words, there are situations in which traditional imperatives may be suspended and ethical behavior has to be rethought on new bases. The difficulty lies in deciding when such situations arise and what actions they authorize; this difficulty tends to be elided in Wiesel's essays, with the consequence that its prominence in some of his fictional texts is all the more striking. I return to Wiesel's fiction in the final part of this chapter; first, I discuss the ethical basis of Wiesel's essays.

ETHICAL POSITIONS

In 1965 Wiesel visited the USSR for the first time. On his return he wrote about the situation of the Soviet Jews in a series of passionate articles collected in 1966 as *Les Juifs du silence*. Subsequently he wrote a play, *Zalmen ou la folie de Dieu* (1968), that was intended to give a dramatic and more popular form to some of the questions dealt with in the earlier articles. *Les Juifs du silence* gives evidence of Wiesel's increasing involvement in human rights issues, and it marks a new stage in his writing. This can be shown by the new emphasis he places on the term *témoin* (witness).[1] In *La Ville de la chance,* published three years before his visit to the Soviet Union, *le Témoin* was a character who watched the deportation of the Jews in indifference; he witnessed but did not react or feel involved. In *Les Juifs du silence* the role of the witness is fundamentally different. At the beginning of the text Wiesel insists that his text should be read as a témoignage:

> These pages are only an eye-witness account [*témoignage*] [. . .] So, the author is keen to underline that he has not attempted to make this into a work of literature or of synthesis. He has only wanted to transmit a few impressions. And the elements of fear that emerge from them. In doing that, he is only accomplishing his role and his duty as witness [*son rôle et son devoir de témoin*]. (*JS, 5*)

La Nuit was also described as a témoignage, but that text was written more out of inner need than a sense of moral compunction (though this is not for a moment to deny that the work has immense moral power). The important shift here is to be found in the phrase *son devoir de témoin.* Bearing witness now involves a positive moral obligation; the witness cannot remain neutral to what he has seen, he is both empowered and required by a sense of duty to recount his experiences. And Wiesel insists that his book should not be understood as political in a narrow sense. He does not intend to become engaged in anti-Communist propaganda because, he suggests, bearing witness responds to an ethical injunction that transcends politics (see *JS*, 5).

The role of the *témoin* does not consist in analyzing, theorizing, or even understanding. Throughout *Les Juifs du silence* Wiesel insists that the courage and endurance of the Soviet Jews, and the persistence of their faith despite unremitting fear, will be unintelligible to outsiders: "As for us, it is our role to look, to listen, that is all; it is not our role to understand" (*JS*, 26; see also *JS*, 28, 34, 36, 58, 98). Wiesel draws attention to the gulf that separates them and us, just as elsewhere he refers to the unbridgeable gap between Holocaust survivors and those who did not experience the death camps. He repeatedly discloses the incommunicablity of the experience of individuals or isolated groups; there are no analogies in our own experience that can make it possible for us to understand them. However—and this is the crux of Wiesel's moral stance—this does not absolve us from responsibility. The witness sees but does not understand; at the same time he becomes responsible for the suffering he has observed. His debt to what he has seen entails the preservation of its mystery, revealed without being assimilated to familiar, intelligible structures of experience. The experience of others must be retained as *other*; our responsibility toward it requires respect for its alterity.

Les Juifs du silence is a deeply committed work. Wiesel is uncompromising in his criticism of the West, in particular of Western Jews, for not protesting against abuses of human rights in the Soviet Union: "In this respect, the guilt lies on the shoulders of us, the Western Jews, rather than on those of the Soviet authorities [. . .] And we are all guilty" (*JS*, 82, 85). Wiesel comments that the refusal of Jews and Christians to react to the suffering of the Soviet Jews "will never be forgiven them" (*JS*, 108). The cautiously impersonal construction does not specify who may be in the position to judge and pardon; and his later reference to "the judgment that history will make on us [*nous*]" (*JS*, 109–10) is equally noncommittal in its attribution of judgmental authority. The use of *nous* here implicates the author in the guilt he describes; importantly, however, this does not impair his judgmental attitude. In writing *Les Juifs du silence* he distances himself from those who do not bear witness and speak out, and from those who hide behind "theories and the usual alibis" (*JS*, 98). Wiesel's self-judgments form part of his polemical assault on the reader's comfortable indifference; he both identifies with and dissociates himself from his reader: we are all guilty, but I who protest against oppression am at least not guilty of silence. In the last sentence of Wiesel's final essay he plays upon the title of his collection in order to condemn the silence of his readers in the Western world: "But what torments me most are not the Jews of silence that I met there, but rather the silence of the Jews amongst whom I live today" (*JS*, 110).

The articles collected in *Les Juifs du silence* make a powerful rhetorical appeal to the reader. The strategies of persuasion that Wiesel adopts in his subsequent essays on human rights are already in place here. The Holocaust provides a crucial point of reference, one that Wiesel uses with caution. Consistent with his view that the Holocaust constitutes a unique event in the history of mankind, he refuses to make direct comparisons:

> Any analogy of this sort would be unjust, indeed loathsome. The situation of the Russian Jews is not the same as that known during the war by the Jews in occupied Europe. (*JS*, 82)

Nevertheless, the Holocaust illuminates all subsequent experience, be it individual or collective. The Soviet Jews and the victims of the Holocaust share "the same feeling of solitude" (*JS*, 82), and the reaction of the outside world is also thrown into relief by its reaction during the war: "For the second time in the same generation, they are committing the error and the sin of silence and indifference" (*JS*, 108). Wiesel condemns comparisons as nefarious, but draws on the Holocaust both as a source of his own authority and to highlight the potential consequences of indifference. In his later writings he extends this strategy in his texts on non-Jewish issues, constantly suggesting that a new Holocaust is always possible. He suggests, for example, that apartheid and the "final solution" are strictly incomparable, but similar in important respects: "Without comparing apartheid to Nazism and its 'final solution'—the latter defies all comparisons—it is impossible not to classify the two so-called legal systems in the same camp" (*Silences*, 147). In the destruction of native tribesmen in Paraguay he finds "very familiar reference points" (*Un Juif*, 46); and the starving of Ethiopia remind him of the deprivation of food in the death camps (*Signes*, 187). In this essay on the Ethiopians, Wiesel makes explicit that, while nothing can be compared to the Holocaust, everything is linked to it:

> Of course I am not comparing. But I do not have the right not to take the past as a term of reference. To be more clear: It is because one people have been marked out for extinction that others have been marked out

for slavery. Because the final solution was envisaged against the Jews, other solutions have been envisaged against other groups. At a certain level, all human dramas are linked. (*Signes*, 187)

The ethics of bearing witness depend upon an epistemology in which all individual and historical dramas are linked to one another, though evidently not, for Wiesel, according to a straightforward logic of cause and effect. Wiesel is more concerned with causality in a purely moral sphere. The Holocaust appears in his essays as an absolute moral nadir, a unique event that inaugurates a historical era in which it may be repeated in different forms: because the Holocaust took place, other atrocities became possible. For this reason the survivor is obliged to speak out against what he sees to be unjust (see *Paroles*, 89); or, as Wiesel puts it somewhat programmatically, "it is enough for us to evoke Auschwitz in order to combat future Hiroshimas" (*Paroles*, 107). In this formulation, and in Wiesel's writing as a whole, it is important that the specifically Jewish experience (Wiesel rarely considers the non-Jewish victims of Nazism) has consequences for the non-Jewish world. Jewish suffering is both unique and universal, not comparable to the suffering of others yet somehow paradigmatic for it. This requires some explanation. Wiesel does not regard Jewish suffering as inherently more important than atrocities committed against non-Jews; it is unique only in the sense that all suffering is unique, yet its specificity should never be denied. At the same time it is of universal significance precisely because everything human is linked; the treatment of the Jews serves as a barometer of the prevailing moral climate. Because the world turns its back on the persecution of Jews today, tomorrow it will turn its back on the suffering of non-Jews:

> You start by killing others [*les autres*], you end by killing your own kind [*les siens*]. Without Auschwitz, Hiroshima would not have taken place. The extermination of one people inevitably leads to the extermination of humanity. (*Un Juif*, 51; see also *Paroles*, 133)

This concern with general moral issues and the attribution of universal significance to individual instances of suffering lie behind Wiesel's consistent claims to be uninterested in and ignorant about politics: "I distrust politics—moreover I don't understand anything about it" (*Un Juif*, 127); "politics is not my field" (*Qui êtes-vous?* 122). He insists that his campaigning is ethical rather than political, and this perhaps helps to explain the uncontroversial nature of many of his interventions, at least for a Western readership. Because the position from which he speaks cannot easily be identified as, say, left- or right-wing, then both left- and right-wing readers and activists can find reason to support him: he criticizes Communist and Fascist regimes, champions the cause of the oppressed and the rights of the individual, opposes state violence and individual acts of terrorism, and attacks Western indifference as a whole without singling out particular nations, leaders, or parties. In short, it is easy to find oneself in agreement with him.

Israel is the only country that escapes his uncompromising moral stance, as he generally refuses to criticize Israel overtly and publicly over such issues as its treatment of Palestinians. A passage from his novel *L'Oublié* indicates his awareness of a degree of inconsistency on this point. Malkiel attempts to dissuade Tamar from publishing an article that accuses Israel of repression and torture; she insists that she must reveal the truth, he argues that nothing can justify endangering the Jewish state (*O*, 301–5). When the article is published, Elhanan says, "I do not understand [*Je ne comprends pas*]" (*O*, 305), the phrase normally used in Wiesel's writing to indicate the reaction of those faced with evidence of crimes committed *against* the Jews; and in this instance it is left unclear whether Elhanan's sorrow and incomprehension are caused by Tamar's disloyalty in publishing the article or by the acts that the article accuses Israel of committing.

Malkiel's attempt to suppress the article on Israel (and to a lesser extent Wiesel's reluctance to criticize Israel) contravenes one of the guiding principles of Wiesel's essays, namely that silence is tantamount to complicity. This first emerges at the beginning of *Les Juifs du silence*, when Wiesel insists that to protest against the treatment of the Jews should be regarded as "a moral obligation that no free man can shirk" (*JS*, 11). Wiesel constantly reiterates the point in his later essays. The main target of his polemic is indifference, and he reserves his most forthright rhetoric for this attack:

> Indifference is a crime. To do nothing is to allow death to do what it wants [. . .] Today we know: evil is in indifference. One might even say that indifference to evil allows it to grow, to spread out and take root [. . .] If nuclear war breaks out one day, it will be because of our apathy. (*Paroles*, 104, 106)

> But silence here would signify acquiescence. Therefore, complicity. (*Paroles*, 81)

Children who have been tortured, bloodied, mutilated, denatured, assassinated, should haunt us.

And call out to us. To make us aware of our complicity, which is silent. And shameful. (*Signes*, 175)

Someone who knew Wiesel's writing only through his fictional works would, I think, be most surprised here by the moral confidence and certainty Wiesel shows; the narrators of his novels seldom approach such certainty. In the above extracts Wiesel employs his most persuasive rhetorical devices: the blunt aphorisms, short paragraphs, and staccato phrases. The very style leaves little space for doubt or equivocation, as Wiesel cuts through political complexities and replaces them with a relatively simple moral causality: indifference is evil, silence is complicity, apathy may lead to nuclear war.

So far, I have discussed some of the most important elements in Wiesel's essays on human rights: the use of the Holocaust as a point of reference, the appeal to moral justice independent of political factors, the attack on indifference. All this is sustained by a fundamental sense of responsibility for the suffering of others. The language of moral obligation pervades the essays. We have obligations toward others even if, as *Les Juifs du silence* and other texts make clear, they are unintelligible to us. Our obligation toward them entails respect for their alterity. In his essay "L'Étranger de la bible" Wiesel describes how Judaism, traditionally, does not seek converts, but seeks instead to maintain respect for the authentic identity of other religions and races (*Paroles*, 145). The *étranger* (outsider, foreigner, stranger) should be regarded as a brother (*Paroles*, 148). The refusal to negate the alterity of the other is replicated in Wiesel's texts on human rights. He does not assimilate disparate events by making them conform to an identical structure; at the same time all are linked by a causality that is moral rather than logical. Wiesel's ethical stance entails a fundamental paradox: on the one hand, the suffering of others is radically unknowable, alien to us and incommensurable with our own experience; on the other hand, in the moral sphere everything is interrelated and we are responsible for the suffering of others even though it is alien to us. It is crucial to Wiesel that this paradox should not be diminished, so that both the absolute difference of others and our absolute obligation toward them should be maintained. Individuals and isolated groups, however unique, occupy a moral continuum in which each person shares responsibility for all others.

To expect Wiesel to provide a philosophical justification for this primordial responsibility would be wrong. His concern in his essays is with situations requiring urgent attention rather than theoretical arguments. Nevertheless, it is possible to make some suggestions concerning the sources of Wiesel's ethics. The initial difficulty lies in the fact that his attitudes seem to rely neither on categorical moral principles nor on utilitarian calculations. He does not have recourse to Kantian imperatives founded on reason and valid for all situations.[2] On the other hand he does suggest that certain things (torture, starvation, humiliation) are absolute moral evils that cannot be justified in any circumstances by even the most sophisticated ethics of situation. Jewish religious law cannot provide the necessary foundation, since it is binding for Jews only, whereas Wiesel's moral pronouncements are universal in their scope. However, if Jewish law is restricted in its applications, Jewish ethics may not be. The Talmud reports how Rabbi Hillel reduced all Jewish teaching to a simple ethical principle: "Whatever is hateful to you, do not to your neighbour. That is the whole Torah: the rest is commentary."[3] Nicholas de Lange comments that "the whole of Jewish teaching, it could be said, is grounded in a passionate concern for justice and compassion in human relations."[4] When the law conflicts with ethics, then the latter takes precedence, as Wiesel illustrates in his essay "Kaddish en Cambodge," published in *Paroles d'étranger*. Wiesel recounts how he was in Cambodia on the anniversary of his father's death when, according to Talmudic law, he should have gone to the synagogue to recite Kaddish for his father; yet, he insists, he went to Cambodia *as a Jew*, his experience as a Jew obliged him to go to the aid of the Cambodians (*Paroles*, 89). Wiesel frequently repeats that, although Judaism does not seek to convert the world, it does offer it a lesson in human values. The commitment to justice and compassion at the base of Jewish ethics creates an obligation to Jews and non-Jews alike: "The more the Jew is a Jew, the more he serves those around him who are not Jews" (*Paroles*, 132).

Morality, then, is based on a fundamental relationship of responsibility to others rather than on inflexible imperatives or pragmatic calculations. In the opening chapter of *Les Juifs du silence* Wiesel suggests this in narrative rather than theoretical form. The title of the chapter, "Première rencontre" (First Encounter), is already rich with overtones. In particular the word *rencontre* (encounter) is loaded, suggesting in Wiesel's writing an apparently chance encounter that will later seem to have been providential. "Première rencontre" tells of the first, and in a sense originary, encounter. Wiesel recounts how, on his first evening in Moscow, he was accosted in a synagogue by an anonymous Jew. He could not clearly see the face of the man:

> I could not make out his features. So I would be unable to say whether the first Jew I was given to meet on Russian territory was young or old, intrepid or despondent. (*JS*, 13)

Wiesel does not interpret the man's desire for anonymity in the obvious sense—as fear of getting into trouble—but as the sign that he is both no one and everyman: "He had chosen darkness so that I would not discover his secret: that he does not have a face of his own, that he does not have a name or a destiny of his own, that he could have been any Jew in any town in this vast country" (*JS*, 13). Consistent with this interpretation, Wiesel claims that he saw the man many times during his stay in the Soviet Union, "even though he looked different at every new meeting" (*JS*, 14). The encounter with the anonymous Jew thus becomes paradigmatic for all subsequent encounters; so the message transmitted by the man is of particular importance:

> You are lucky to live far away from us, but do you know what is happening here? Look and remember. Listen and forget nothing. Return to your country and recount. Time is pressing, we can't take it any longer. Don't get stuck on details. Don't ask for explanations. Understand. We may be being watched. This conversation, I may have to pay a high price for it. At least, don't forget it. (*JS*, 13)

A page later, Wiesel says that the same message was repeated by the man in all his subsequent guises: "Everywhere he had only one message to transmit: you must forget nothing, you must recount everything" (*JS*, 14). On this first encounter as in its later repetitions, the stranger issues instructions. His first short speech contains ten imperatives (an echo of the Ten Commandments, perhaps), summarized later as an absolute injunction: forget nothing, recount everything. The passage illustrates how Wiesel's témoignage cannot be understood simply as a factual narration of events, since the individual experience becomes suffused with a significance that surpasses it. Here, the meeting with the anonymous stranger becomes paradigmatic for the encounter with the other and the obligation that is at the foundation of that encounter.

Like Lévinas, who describes responsibility as "the essential, primary, fundamental structure of subjectivity," Wiesel regards the relationship with others as necessarily ethical in nature.[5] And ethics, concerned with the relationship with others, takes precedence even over theology, concerned with the relationship with God. Wiesel makes this clear in the course of his interviews with Philippe-Michaël de Saint-Cheron. After death, he reports, the first question asked of the dead after their souls are taken from the tomb is, "Have you been honest in your dealings with others?" (*ME*, 228), and the second question is, "Did you await the coming of the Messiah?" (*ME*, 228). Wiesel concludes that the order of these questions illustrates the primacy of the ethical over the theological: "This text teaches us once again that human relations have priority over all others" (*ME*, 228).

Wiesel's sense of responsibility for others entails a resolute opposition to violence. In his letter "A un jeune palestinien arabe" he shows admiration for the survivors of the death camps who did not seek vengeance on their former persecutors (*Un Juif*, 131–32); and he uses this to criticize Palestinians who take the suffering of their people as justification for acts of violence (*Un Juif*, 132). In his *Discours d'Oslo*, delivered when he received the Nobel Peace Prize, he reiterates this view; referring to the Palestinians, he says, "I am sorry for their suffering, but I deplore their methods when they lead to violence" (*Discours*, 15). He goes on to explain this, typically, by recourse to aphorism: "Violence is not an answer, terrorism is the most dreadful of answers" (*Discours*, 15). This does not mean that Wiesel is a pacifist. In "Le Juif et la guerre," written shortly after the Yom Kippur War in 1973 and published in *Paroles d'étranger*, he discusses the view of war in the Jewish tradition. The tradition, he argues, is opposed to war: everything possible must be done to prevent it; idolatry and lies are permitted if peace may be preserved; an offensive war and even a war fought to preempt aggression are forbidden; it is better to allow enemies to escape rather than to kill them. However, in extreme circumstances, when the survival of the nation is at stake, war is permitted; and Wiesel declares his support for the Yom Kippur War: "I am against war and for humanism, but, as a Jew, belonging to the traumatized generation that is ours, I fully support what is happening in Israel. I am with Israel; and what Israel does, Israel does in my name also" (*Paroles*, 132).

Wiesel can argue, of course, that a war fought for the survival of a nation is fundamentally different from other forms of hostility. However, a passage from one of Wiesel's novels, *Le Cinquième Fils*, undermines this distinction. A rabbi tells the narrator that Jewish law allows killing when committed in self-defense, but only when we are certain that the potential aggressor intends to kill us. This raises difficulties:

But how do you acquire such certainty? Suppose he tells you he is
going to kill you, how can you be sure that his threats are not purely
verbal and psychological? In other words, the biblical verse forbids all
murder: it can never, in fact, be justified. (*Fils*, 195)

According to this view, we can never be sure that we are acting in
self-defense because we cannot know that the enemy intends to kill us
until he has actually done so. In consequence, the law that apparently
permits killing under some circumstances actually forbids it categori-
cally. And the same principle could be extended to war: the stated desire
of the enemies of Israel to destroy it does not necessarily correspond to
their real intentions. I do not want to defend this view, merely to point
out that it is *suggested* and *permitted* by the above passage from *Le
Cinquième Fils*, but it does not receive attention in Wiesel's essays. In
other words, the literary text raises and examines a possibility that
threatens to undermine the positions explicitly endorsed by Wiesel in his
nonliterary texts.

Throughout his essays Wiesel relies on aphorisms that provide unambiguous rulings on moral duty. However, his fiction appears less
self-confident; it explores the ambiguities of moral choice, and Wiesel's
fictional characters discover that certainty in such matters is at best
precarious. In the discussions between Reuven and Simha in *Le Cinquième Fils*, the two characters discuss the case of Moses, who killed in
order to save the life of a Jew and later became the most important
legislator in Jewish history (see *Fils*, 54–56). This seems to suggest that
killing is permissible in some circumstances; yet Moses killed before the
revelation of the Law at Sinai, he is anyway not comparable to other men,
and moreover God did not fully forgive him because he was not permitted to enter the Promised Land. The case proves to be problematic as soon
as it is examined in detail; the principles governing the actions of Moses
cannot easily be applied to other situations. In exceptional circumstances
laws that are normally binding no longer apply; but it is not possible to
know with certainty when such circumstances occur. Even the criterion
of self-defense requires an interpretation that will always be open to
dispute. It is important that doubt over this issue is raised in *Le Cinquième Fils*, one of Wiesel's fictional texts, rather than in his essays.
Some of the issues left unresolved in Wiesel's ethical writings are
explored in his fiction, particularly in those texts, such as *L'Aube* and
L'Oublié, that deal explicitly with the ethics of violence.

MORAL CONFUSIONS

Wiesel's fiction reflects his political and ethical commitments. All his novels deal with the victims and survivors of Nazi persecution; and other specifically Jewish issues receive extended treatment: persecution and pogroms before the Holocaust (*Le Serment de Kolvillàg*), the problems of Soviet Jews (*Zalmen ou la folie de Dieu, Le Testament d'un poète juif assassiné*), the struggle for the foundation and defense of Israel (*L'Aube, L'Oublié, Le Mendiant de Jérusalem*), problems encountered by the children of survivors of the death camps (*Le Cinquième Fils*). Non-Jewish issues also play an important role: both Michael in *La Ville de la chance* and Paltiel in *Le Testament d'un poète juif assassiné* are victims of Communist totalitarianism in Eastern Europe; in *L'Oublié* Malkiel visits Cambodia, as Wiesel had done, and sees the consequences of atrocities committed by the Khmer Rouge. The prominence of these aspects of Wiesel's fiction indicates that the need to bear witness influences his novels as much as it does his nonfictional texts. The moral urgency is no less; however, the tone is significantly different. The confident polemic of the essays is matched by the doubts and self-doubts of the fiction; if Wiesel, in his essays, seems to have a firm sense of right and wrong, his fictional characters speak with less conviction. Moreover, the fictional texts confront moral dilemmas that are virtually absent from the nonfictional texts. In this section I discuss the question of terrorism as it appears in Wiesel's first novel, *L'Aube* (1960) and in his 1989 novel, *L'Oublié*. In *Un Juif* Wiesel condemns Palestinian terrorism and suggests that terrorism can never be justified: "Suffering is often unjust, but it never justifies murder" (*Un Juif*, 132). However, in *Silences et mémoire d'hommes* Wiesel reports that he attempted to join a clandestine organization in the late forties (*Silences*, 14); and the experiences of Elisha and Malkiel, in *L'Aube* and *L'Oublié* respectively, illustrate that clandestine struggle cannot be as easily dismissed as Wiesel's condemnation of the Palestinians suggests.

Maurice Friedman reports a disagreement he had with a friend over whether *L'Aube* proves Wiesel to be in sympathy with the Jewish terrorists.[6] Part of the difficulty in resolving such a dispute stems from the exclusive use of first-person narration, which makes it impossible to decide where identification gives way to irony. This difficulty is made all the more acute in the case of *L'Aube* by the biographical similarities between Elisha and Wiesel (both are survivors of the death camps, both studied philosophy in Paris after the war) and by the similarity of their names (Elisha is not the same as Elie, but, again, the two are nevertheless connected: Elisha was the disciple of Elijah). Elisha himself feels ambivalent about his terrorist activities; enthusiasm mingles with a sense of self-disgust ("I was horrified at myself," *A*, 41) which is exacerbated when he is called upon to commit a cold-blooded murder. It is impossible, then, to rule confidently that the novel either entirely supports or totally rejects terrorism; indeed, most of the evidence provided by the text tends to undercut the grounds upon which a straightforward judgment of right or wrong on this issue might be made.

While in Paris, Elisha is initially persuaded to join the clandestine movement by Gad's romantic vision of a free Jewish state in Palestine. In the course of their first meeting, it is repeatedly suggested that Elisha is enticed by the messianic overtones of Gad's words. This allows him to conflate the religious and the political senses of Zionism and in turn justifies violent political struggle in the cause of a messianic ideal that gives meaning to that struggle. In other words, he has been converted to the view that the end justifies the means. The consequences of his conversion are made clear once he is in Palestine and enrolled in a "course in terrorism" (*A*, 38) presided over by Gad. The confusion between religious and political Zionism that provoked Elisha's conversion to terrorism and that continues to sustain his commitment once in Palestine ("I was entering a messianic world," *A*, 41) now puts him into conflict with Jewish law. The sixth commandment ("THOU SHALT NOT KILL," *A*, 40) must be suspended in order for the Zionist ideal to be realized

> The objective of the movement was: to kill the largest number of soldiers. It was as simple as that. (*A*, 38)

The Jewish homeland can be established only if Jewish law is broken. Gad explains the thinking behind the actions of the terrorists:

> I know very well. It's unjust. It's inhuman. It's cruel. But we don't have any choice. For generations we wanted to be better, more pure, than those who were persecuting us. You know the result: Hitler, the extermination camps in Germany. Well we have had enough of being more just than those who purported to speak in the name of justice [. . .] If we must become unjust and inhuman to get rid of those who are unjust and inhuman toward us, we will do it [. . .] We will be like

everyone else. Death will be, not our trade, but our duty. During the days, weeks, months to come, you will think only of this: killing those who make us murderers . . . Kill them so that we can become men again . . . (*A*, 39–40)

One of the most interesting aspects of this passage lies in the fact that it seems to be in open opposition to one of the principles central to Wiesel's essays: Gad justifies killing by referring to the injustices of which the Jews have been victims, whereas Wiesel asserts that suffering never justifies violence (see *Un Juif*, 132). Gad also uses language in a different way from Wiesel. In Wiesel's essays words such as *justice* and *duty* have rigid, inflexible meanings; in Gad's speech they become fluid to the point that clear distinctions between opposites are lost. The terrorists must be *inhuman* in order to *become men again*, they must be *unjust* and *cruel* in order to establish justice; the unjust will be defeated only if the just act unjustly; evil becomes the tool of good. The need to keep moral opposites rigorously separate is endangered when they appear in such disconcerting proximity to one another.

In some quarters the terrible logic and persuasive poetry of Gad's discourse may win consent in preference to the possibly ineffectual moral purity of Wiesel's own stated view; his literary text thereby perhaps unwittingly obscures the moral clarity of his essays. The exploration of terrorist ethics in *L'Aube* can be contrasted with the views set out in Wiesel's essay "Contre l'indifférence," published in *Silences et mémoire d'hommes*. Wiesel makes a connection between the current sense of indifference as lack of concern and its etymological sense as the inability to make clear distinctions between, for example, "good and evil, joy and sadness, friend and enemy, day and night" (*Silences*, 171). The two senses are related in that the failure to make adequate and clear distinctions leads to moral neutrality, which Wiesel also equates with the chaos that preceded creation (*Silences*, 171). Some of the examples Wiesel gives of clear distinctions are significant in the context of *L'Aube*: in that novel, good (the foundation of Israel) depends upon evil (terrorism); toward the end of the novel Elisha seems on the point of befriending his enemy when he goes to talk to John Dawson; and the moment of dawn, the crucial moment of the novel referred to in the title, and a time of vast importance throughout Wiesel's writing, is neither day nor night but the point at which the two meet.[7] Perhaps it could be said that the essay expresses a desire and the novel exposes a fear: the essay insists on the need for distinctions, whereas the novel blurs those distinctions.

As in Camus's play *Les Justes*, the attempt to achieve ultimate justice through the use of violence threatens to compromise the moral aims of the terrorists. The central dilemma of *L'Aube* concerns the relationship between ends and means. Elisha accepts his involvement in terrorism and the execution of John Dawson, but is fully and painfully aware of the implications of his actions. If killing is a duty for the Jews, the victims have become executioners and are no better than their persecutors:

> I imagined myself in uniform, in a dark grey uniform, in the uniform of the SS [. . .] No, it wasn't easy to become God; particularly when it required you to wear a dark grey uniform, the uniform of the SS. (*A*, 41–42, 45)

The Jews, Gad concedes in that passage, have relinquished their ethical superiority and become like everyone else.

The phrase "That's war [*C'est la guerre*]" is repeated throughout *L'Aube* in justification for the exceptional measures taken by the terrorists. The phrase suggests that in times of war ordinary ethical codes are suspended and actions ordinarily forbidden are provisionally permitted. Elisha, however, is tormented by his uncertainty over whether the state of conflict can justify the disregard for moral laws. He finds his actions in conflict with his feelings, with the consequence that he obeys the instructions of his commanders but never escapes self-disgust. The novel can be understood as dramatizing a confrontation between Jewish tradition (represented by the figures from Elisha's past, including his past self, who appear before him in the course of the novel) and political expediency, between the Law (THOU SHALT NOT KILL) and Zionist aspirations, and between the competing demands of moral purity and practical action. There is no resolution or reconciliation; and the question of whether the novel supports or condemns terrorism is ultimately unanswerable. From the standpoint of fidelity to the past, terrorism is condemned; from the standpoint of present effectiveness, it is necessary. The novel reflects the existentialist debates of the forties and fifties as it offers a stark scenario in which the only choice available is between the role of victim or executioner: the Jews must either retain their sense of moral purity but remain victims, or take effective action thereby becoming executioners and violating their own moral tradition. The distinction between victim and executioner turns out not to be absolute; each is dependent on the other and, in the context of compromised morality that dominates Wiesel's novel, the roles are reversible. Elisha blames this on a state of affairs in which a clear moral conscience is impossible, and for which God is finally responsible:

> It is He who made the universe and made it in such a way that justice should be obtained by injustices, that the happiness of a people should be acquired at the cost of tears, that the freedom of a nation—like that of men—should be a statue raised on the bodies of those condemned to death . . . (*A*, 99–100)

L'Aube neither fully sanctions nor totally condemns violence; the novel does not permit the easy conscience on which unambiguous moral postures might be sustained. *L'Oublié* picks up the themes of Wiesel's earlier novel when Elhanan joins a clandestine movement in the struggle for the foundation of Israel; indeed, the novel contains a discrete allusion to *L'Aube* ("The English authorities are threatening to execute 'terrorists'? These same terrorists take officers as hostages: an eye for an eye, a life for a life," *O*, 210). The theme of the morality of violence is central to *L'Oublié*, particularly in the episodes set during World War II, when Elhanan was engaged in armed conflict as a partisan. *L'Oublié* is a more reflective text than *L'Aube*, more explicitly concerned with the justification and limits of terrorism. Yet it is also a more reticent text: it repeatedly threatens to undermine a secure moral stance that is then reasserted. In this respect it is not openly in contradiction with Wiesel's apparent views on terrorism, as *L'Aube* seems to be; but it reveals weaknesses, tensions, and simplifications within those views, and finally it also exhibits a troubling fascination with the reenactment of violence.

Elhanan and Itzik join the Jewish partisans when it becomes clear that the Hungarian army, for which they are working, regards them as expendable slaves who may be summarily executed or worked to death. Initially their escape and partisan action can be justified within Jewish law on grounds of self-defense and unavoidable warfare. From the beginning, however, the behavior of Itzik seems to go beyond the limits of acceptable violence. His sobriquet rapidly changes from Itzik the Tall to Itzik the Avenger. The Jewish children who refuse to take vengeance by murdering their Nazi persecutors (see *O*, 166) give him a lesson in morality that goes unheeded. The text suggests here that cold-blooded murder exceeds the bounds of permitted violence. Elhanan, who attempts to preserve moral probity within exceptional, violent circumstances, vaguely and increasingly disapproves of his friend's excesses. The myth of friendship transcending all other relationships, which frequently recurs in Wiesel's fiction, is seen in this novel to be fragile. Friendship is not unconditional and cannot survive the immoral behavior of one friend or the disapproval of the other. Itzik's desire for revenge strains and eventually destroys his friendship with Elhanan.

The text suggests, then, that there is a necessary distinction between vengeance and legitimate warfare. On one occasion even Elhanan gives way to the desire for revenge (see *O*, 180). Itzik approves of this lapse, but Elhanan is unable to celebrate. Elhanan's momentary desire to increase the suffering of his enemies may be understandable; but, as his own sense of regret indicates, it cannot be condoned. However, a revealing discussion between Elhanan and his lover Lianka raises important difficulties concerning the condemnation of Itzik's actions. Lianka tries to prevent Elhanan from becoming like Itzik, and Elhanan asks if she is judging his friend:

> - Are you judging him?
> - No. By what right could I judge him? But I am not sure that vengeance is the right response.
> - Why shouldn't it be? Why not punish the killers? Why not make their accomplices tremble in fear?
> - I don't know, Elhanan. Your questions are good; they are even pertinent. How can I reply? I don't have a response; perhaps I am too young. But I know enough about it to distrust avengers.
> - And justice, Lianka? You don't think that justice should be done?
> - Yes, I do.
> - Well? Isn't the avenger an agent of justice?
> - Yes, but . . .
> - . . . but what?
> - I don't know . . . I only know that I wouldn't be capable of killing a man in cold blood . . .
> - Even if he were a killer?
> Disconcerted, harassed, Lianka pleads:
> - I cannot imagine myself in the role of someone who kills . . . who kills an unarmed man . . . Don't force me, I beg you, Elhanan. Don't force me . . .
> Moved, Elhanan interrupts the discussion. (*O*, 176)

The dialogic, self-interrogating nature of Wiesel's fiction can be seen here, in distinction to the polemical assurance that often informs his essays. The tentative tone of the passage is striking. Lianka disapproves, but denies her right to judge; she can barely support her views: "I am not sure [. . .] I do not know [. . .] I have no answer." In the end her rejection of vengeance may be attributable to nothing more than a failure of the imagination ("I cannot imagine myself in the role of someone who kills . . ."). Elhanan, here, plays devil's advocate; he defends actions of which he also basically disapproves. But the objections he makes to Lianka's views have a force that threatens and for a while silences his own moral stance. He suggests that the *avenger* may also be an *agent of justice*, hence that vengeance may be conflated with justice; and this connection invalidates the condemnation of Itzik by providing a moral justification for his actions. In the end the disagreement between Elhanan and Lianka remains unresolved, the discussion is interrupted rather than terminated and the text does not offer the reader a single authoritative view.

The use of dialogue in the above passage is particularly effective in giving voice to a moral dilemma that remains unresolved: the text does not adopt a position of unambiguous judgment; indeed it brings into question the grounds upon which such a judgment might be made. In the end, however, the text is not prepared to confront the full implications of this potential self-subversion. The discussion is curtailed, and the moral certainties of the text, briefly endangered here, are confidently reasserted. This is made possible by the narrative when Itzik goes too far and places himself outside the possible justification sketched by Elhanan in the passage quoted above. Elhanan comes across Itzik in the act of raping the wife of a prominent anti-Semite. Itzik's self-justification carries no force, and in this instance Elhanan has no hesitation in judging and condemning unambiguously:

> "You are judging me," says Itzik.
> "- You shouldn't have done it," Elhanan replies. He repeats: "You shouldn't have done it." (*O*, 191)

Few readers will disagree with Elhanan's response; and by making Itzik into a rapist Wiesel's novel effectively simplifies its own moral position and resolves the uncertainties that surface in the discussion between Elhanan and Lianka. The text raises a disruptive possibility and then retreats from it. The same pattern is repeated when, some years later, Elhanan meets Itzik again during the struggle for the foundation of Israel. Elhanan rediscovers his former outrage; then, surprisingly, he begins to question his right to judge his former friend:

> And, faced with his silence, I am surprised to find myself taking his defense. In my thoughts, of course. Doesn't the Talmud teach man that

he should not judge his peer before putting himself in his place. Only in this way can he understand his true motives. (O, 228)

This moment of self-doubt is interrupted by Itzik, and Elhanan reiterates his former condemnation. The doubt is not openly expressed, only the condemnation is made explicit; and the text partly occludes its self-subversive moments by reaffirming clear moral judgments.

The second episode relevant to the question of violence in _L'Oublié_ concerns Elhanan's hesitations and ultimate decision to become involved with the terrorist struggle in Palestine. As in the discussion of vengeance with Lianka, the novel uses dialogue between characters to reveal the difficulties in establishing a position of moral purity. Talia, Elhanan's wife, protests against the execution of Jewish terrorists:

> "It must stop, it must," said Talia. I agreed: I was opposed to terrorism as a means of action. Talia and I discussed it frequently. "And you're not opposed to the English oppression that produces this sort of means of action?" Yes, I was. "So you're opposed to everyone?" said Talia. Yes. I was opposed to everyone in this world, which was too violent for my liking. (O, 212)

The passage begins with a misunderstanding: Elhanan's agreement with Talia seems to be based on the belief that the phrase "It must stop" refers to terrorism, whereas (presumably) she is talking about the execution of terrorists. The subsequent report of discussions between the couple shows that Elhanan's misunderstanding derives from an unwillingness to confront the issues raised by terrorism. Just as earlier Elhanan's persistent questioning had shown up Lianka's inability to justify her rejection of vengeance, here Talia's questions expose the weakness of Elhanan's position. He opposes terrorism, but also opposes that which the terrorists are combatting. By his rejection of terrorist tactics, he implicitly supports the perpetuation of the status quo. His moral purity entails paralysis at the level of practical action. Elhanan wants to remain aloof from the stark choices that _L'Aube_ suggests are the condition of effective change and that Talia, unbeknownst to Elhanan, has already made.

Subsequently, Elhanan does decide to join a clandestine organization. After the United Nations vote of 29 November 1947, which lay the way for the establishment of an independent Jewish nation,[8] Elhanan realizes that "war was inevitable, not to take part in it would be dishonorable" (O, 216). Elhanan's statement that not to take part would be dishonorable is curiously unhelpful in explaining the complex conversion that has taken place; nevertheless he seems to be in line with Jewish law, which, as Wiesel explains in "Le Juif et la guerre," permits war when it cannot be avoided. In the episodes relating both to World War II and to the foundation of Israel, the novel attempts to maintain parameters on the legitimate use of force. The friendship of Elhanan and Itzik turns into hostility as the two illustrate, respectively, restraint and excess in their use of violence. The text at moments reveals uncertainties that disrupt this opposition between Elhanan and Itzik, between armed force as a last resort and unrestrained vengeance; but ultimately it reasserts its adherence to such distinctions, and it avoids the difficult choices made by the terrorists in *L'Aube*.

Toward the end of the novel, however, the moral self-confidence of the text is challenged once again. If, as I suggested, the rape committed by Itzik allows a simplification of the moral issues raised by the war, as Itzik can now be unambiguously condemned, it also prepares one of the most tense and startling scenes to be found anywhere in Wiesel's fiction. Many years after the war, Malkiel, Elhanan's son, returns to his father's hometown. Eventually, toward the end of the novel he manages to track down the woman raped by Itzik, and for reasons that he does not fully understand (and that are never adequately explained) he decides to visit her. At first, despite Malkiel's insistent and strangely aggressive questioning, the woman cannot recall the occasion on which she was raped. As she begins to remember, Malkiel is struck by a terrifying possibility:

> He thinks he knows, he knows what the old lady is going to say to him. She is going to reveal to him the awful, abject face of the knight [i.e., Elhanan, his father]. "Ha, you see him as a noble man, rushing to the aid of a poor defeated woman, you are really naive, sir. In war all men are animals. They think only of doing evil, humiliating, possessing! Your knight, well, let me tell you what he did, him, the savior with the pure soul: he waited for his friend to finish so he could take his place! And you thought that . . . Ha, you make me laugh, sir . . ." That's what she is going to say, the old lady. To take revenge because he has disturbed her rest? So that truth may triumph? But then, what is the meaning of his quest? Where is hope, is redemption still possible? (*O*, 297)

The possibility raised here has devastating implications: the father's prestige will be lost, Elhanan will be no better than Itzik, war will be seen to reduce all men to an equal level, and meaning, hope, and redemption will be forfeit. As previously in this novel, disruptive ideas are introduced in order to be negated; once again the text rapidly withdraws from the possibilities that Malkiel has glimpsed:

> The old woman will not follow his scenario. The glory of the knight will remain radiant and comforting [*réconfortante*]. (*O*, 298)

The use of the word *comforting* is revealing here. The text retreats from the terror of moral chaos into the comfort of simple oppositions between wicked rapists and heroic knights on white chargers. Elhanan's prestige is reestablished and enhanced, as the woman recalls his attempts to comfort her:

> - Thanks to him, I can still believe that not all men are bad. I am convinced that he was decent and charitable. (*O*, 298)

However, this resolution seems to be a little too rapid. The extraordinary tension in this passage from *L'Oublié* derives from the possibility that the whole moral framework that sustains the rest of the novel might collapse. The reassurance ultimately offered by the old woman is unable entirely to neutralize the danger that has been given expression. The reassertion of Elhanan's moral ascendancy is too absolute, too evidently close to wish fulfillment, to carry full assent. The anxious idealization that occurs in the passage can be seen clearly in the discrepancy between the original account of Elhanan's intervention in the rape and the version of that same intervention offered in the later passage. The original account is sober and undramatic:

> Elhanan takes a step toward his friend, wants to touch his arm, changes his mind: "Itzik, my friend . . . Come . . . I beg you . . . Stop . . . what you are doing is not good . . ." Itzik rebuffs him: "You want to be a saint? Well go to the synagogue . . . And leave us in peace." Itzik continues to violate the woman who, gagged again, begs Elhanan with her troubled and troubling eyes as if he were her savior, as if he were all-powerful . . . But he is not. He leaves the room backward. In the street, he leans against a wall and vomits. (*O*, 190)

By contrast, Malkiel's description of his father's actions is rhetorical and emotional:

He speaks to your torturer, in Yiddish, he tries to reason with him; the other is deaf. He begs him not to be a fool; he raises his voice and cries to him that what he is doing is cruel, immoral, inhuman, he yells with all his force, but it serves no purpose . . . So, he weeps, this other man . . . He sobs . . . Your gazes meet . . . You remember, madame. (*O*, 297)

Malkiel supplies details not given in the original account; his use of enumeration ("cruel, immoral, inhuman") and the carefully contrived repetition and escalation ("He speaks [. . .] he tries to reason [. . .] He begs [. . .] he raises his voice and cries [. . .] he yells with all his force [. . .] he weeps [. . .] he sobs") give the account a rhetorical construction and dramatic structure that were previously lacking. The rather surprising absence of a question mark at the end of the final sentence makes it a statement, indeed almost an instruction; it is as if Malkiel were trying to create a memory as much as to reawaken one, to give the past a meaning that, for the old woman, it may not have had. Subsequently, the woman gives him what he wants, perhaps responding to his urgent needs rather than to the voice of reawakened memory. She seems coerced rather than spontaneously cooperative. "Who gives you the authority to force [*forcer*] my memory?" she asks Malkiel (*O*, 298), and the ambiguity of her phrase potentially subverts the comfort that she is about to offer him. Her memory may be being forced in the sense that she is being obliged to recall things that she had long forgotten; but the phrase may also suggest that her memory is forced in the sense of brutally falsified; and the verb *forcer* has, perhaps unfortunately, sexual overtones that may suggest that her earlier rape is being repeated as it is being recalled. In this context, then, her words to Malkiel fail to resolve the tensions of the passage precisely because they are too close to what he desperately wants to hear.

A curious misunderstanding at the end of the episode serves to draw attention to the ambiguity of Malkiel's role in the passage. The woman does not properly understand Malkiel's interest in her rape; when Malkiel finally tells her, "It was my father" (*O*, 299), he realizes from her horrified reaction that she thinks he is referring to the rapist rather than the man who attempted to defend her. For a moment, then, she suspects, and he seems to admit, that he is related to the man who raped her. Although the identification of Malkiel with the rapist is factually incorrect, this momentary confusion does go some way to explaining Malkiel's behavior in the encounter with the old woman. Forcing her to recall the rape also obliges her to reexperience the degradation she felt at the time ("Why are you so keen that I should see myself again soiled, bruised, repudiated in my flesh as in my soul?" *O*, 298), and is thus in a sense tantamount to a repetition of the rape.[9] Throughout the episode there are hints that Malkiel is using unnecessary aggression in his interrogation of the old lady. Metaphors of violence are used to describe the manner in which he asks his questions:

> In a sharp, staccato tone, Malkiel deals her blow upon blow [*Malkiel lui assène coup après coup*]. In order to hurt her? (*O*, 291)

Once he has begun, he cannot stop his questioning ("Why? A question of instinct; he knows that he must" [*O*, 293]), even though he knows he is causing the old woman distress. His behavior is menacing:

> - Try to forgive me, madame, he says as he leans toward her. I am going to hurt you, but I have my reasons . . . They are valid; I think that they are even honorable . . .
> - That's what everyone says, observes Lidia [the translator]. You can always find honorable reasons for hurting people. (*O*, 295)

Malkiel claims that the suffering he is causing is justified by his honorable motives. Lidia's comment undermines his self-righteousness. As Malkiel's behavior becomes increasingly more aggressive, Lidia tries to stop him, but he refuses to give way. He does not believe the old woman's claims that she cannot remember the events to which he is referring:

> Malkiel doesn't believe her; he tells her in a rather harsh voice.
> - Stop, says Lidia. Can't you see that she is suffering, that she is suffering because of you?
> - I haven't done anything to her, says Malkiel, stubborn. It was someone else who made her suffer; not me. Me, I'm part of her present, not her past.
> - But it's in the present that you're making her suffer, says Lidia.
> - No. Because of me she is remembering past suffering, it's not the same thing.
> - I don't remember, says the old woman in a flat voice. (*O*, 296)

Malkiel disowns responsibility ("I haven't done anything to her"), just as Gad did in *L'Aube* when referring to terrorist violence ("we don't have any choice," *O*, 39); but the woman's inability to remember the past emphasizes that her distress is real and present rather than a distant recollection, caused by Malkiel rather than Itzik. Malkiel cannot stop his relentless enquiry:

> Inflexible, Malkiel is incapable of stopping in mid route. His enquiry, he must push it to its conclusion, and well beyond. (*O*, 296)

The parallels between this scene and the original rape are remarkable. The victim is the same; the aggressor speaks a language that the victim does not understand (Itzik spoke Yiddish; Malkiel's English has to be translated by Lidia); and in each case there is a third, more sympathetic character who attempts to intervene. Lidia's "Stop [*Arrêtez*]" (*O*, 296) echoes Elhanan's "Stop [*Arrête*]" (*O*, 190); and her exclamation "That's enough [*Ça suffit*]" (*O*, 296) recalls the words of the victim's aunt when Elhanan returns to the scene of the crime: "That's enough, sir, that's enough . . . [*Ça suffit, monsieur, ça suffit*]" (*O*, 190). Given these disturbing parallels, it is perhaps not surprising that the old woman confuses Malkiel with her original tormentor: "The old woman, panting, looks at him now, as if it were he who had violated her" (*O*, 296); and later she admits, "A moment ago, I wondered if you were the man . . ." (*O*, 299). The initial rape is repeated here in two senses: first, because the woman is forced to bring it back to mind as it is described by Malkiel; and second, because the situation of the original rape is reproduced in the later scene, with Malkiel playing the role of Itzik and Lidia the role of Elhanan. Malkiel, Elhanan's surrogate here, takes the role of Itzik, and thus (the representative of) the compassionate man becomes the tormentor. This interchangeability of roles has disruptive consequences on the stable oppositions (Elhanan/Itzik, kindness/cruelty, victim/tormentor) that underpin the ethical scheme of the novel.

No less than in *L'Aube*—though less openly—the roles of victim and persecutor are revealed as interchangeable, and this insight cannot be fully neutralized by the hasty reassertion of Elhanan's prestige at the end of the episode. The text reconstructs the original rape scene and raises doubts about the confused motives of Malkiel and perhaps by extension of Elhanan. In this context, and despite the attempt to eliminate such doubts at the end of the scene, it is perhaps significant that the episode is immediately followed by the passage in which Malkiel attempts to persuade Tamar to suppress an article criticizing Israel. In this passage, once again, Malkiel's moral integrity seems to be in question. The text hesitates between constructing and deconstructing secure ethical positions. The initial rape allows the reader to reject Itzik and his call for vengeance; the later repetition of the rape scene reopens some of the issues that were apparently resolved by the original episode; it then attempts to resolve those issues once again, but can do so only precariously.

L'Oublié is a more complex and accomplished text than *L'Aube*. It is more subtle, but also more evasive, in its treatment of the ethics of violence; and at moments it also gives evidence of a need to simplify issues that are threatening to undermine necessary moral certainties, so it withdraws from the most dangerous and most damaging implications of the narrative. Neither novel adopts unambiguous or stable positions on the question of violence, as is shown by the dispute over whether *L'Aube* supports or condemns terrorism. It is in this ambiguity, the impossibility of excluding competing possibilities of interpretation, that Wiesel's fiction is most unlike his nonfiction. His essays lack almost entirely the tension and moral doubt that pervades his fiction. Barthes's distinction between the *écrivain* and the *écrivant* helps to explain this discrepancy. The écrivant, according to Barthes, uses language as a tool to communicate thoughts and ideas to the public: "Écrivants are 'transitive' men; they posit an end (bearing witness [*témoigner*], explaining, teaching) for which the word is only a means; for them, the word supports an action, it does not constitute it [. . .] the function of the écrivant is to say on every occasion and without delay what he thinks."[10] For the écrivain, on the other hand, writing is intransitive and self-absorbed, although Barthes also insists that such writing continually puts the world in question. Two uses of language are forbidden to the écrivain: doctrine and testimony (témoignage). Doctrine becomes ambiguous as it is transformed into a spectacle to be appreciated rather than a message to be received, and témoignage is impossible because the écrivain works on language rather than experience. One of the crucial differences between the écrivant and the écrivain lies in the ambiguity that characterizes the texts of the latter:

> [The écrivant] thinks that his language can put an end to the ambiguity of the world, institute an irreversible explanation (even if he concedes that it is provisional), or some incontestable information (even if he sees himself as a modest teacher); whereas for the écrivain, we have seen, it's quite the opposite: he knows full well that his

language, intransitive by choice and design, inaugurates ambiguity, even if it presents itself as peremptory, he knows that it is given paradoxically as a monumental silence to be deciphered, that it can have no other motto than the deep saying of Jacques Rigaut: And even when I affirm, I am still questioning.[11]

Barthes's distinction helps explain why Wiesel's essays appear so assertive and dogmatic, even when they repeatedly draw attention to the unintelligibility of their subject, and why on the other hand his fiction remains ambiguous and open to interpretation even when it seems to be most assertive. Wiesel appears as both écrivain and écrivant at different moments: the essayist-écrivant expresses his views clearly and the novel-ist-écrivain produces provocative and ambiguous texts. This is not an instance of Barthes's hybrid écrivain-écrivant (of which Barthes himself is surely the most obvious example), because the two functions are largely confined to separate texts.[12] Nevertheless, the écrivain and the écrivant are dependent on one another: Wiesel always works on fictional and nonfictional projects simultaneously, suggesting perhaps that the two are linked by their very differences. One provides a necessary corrective to the other, and the oscillation between the roles of écrivain and écrivant provides a means of negotiating the paradoxes that constitute the dilemma of the survivor-moralist: the need for moral guidelines in a world that has lost its coherence; the duty to speak coupled with a sense of the impossibility of meaningful communication; the desire for sense and the knowledge of failure.

Wiesel's fictional and nonfictional texts illustrate the two poles of his ethical thinking: on the one hand, in the essays, the desire for clearly articulated principles that govern fundamental duties and responsibilities; on the other hand, in the fictional texts, the complexities and brutal choices to be made in concrete situations. It may appear paradoxical that the *fictional* works seem most sensitive to the dilemmas of *real* situations, whereas the essays sometimes seem to simplify contemporary issues by their confident taking of sides. However, the self-doubts and self-subversions of the fiction are in a sense a luxury the activist cannot afford. In a novel no one's life is actually at stake; and fiction can act as a testing ground where it is possible to be undecided, troubled to the point of speechlessness and effective paralysis by the horrible conflicts of recent history. The essays, on the other hand, cannot make too much allowance for their own self-questioning, or they might be undermined past the point of being useful. In this context, their polemical assurance may be seen as a necessary tactic that Wiesel (consciously or unconsciously) accepts as the price of real influence.

Wiesel's fiction has the quality of a parable that always partially eludes its interpreters. In consequence, it cannot be dominated by any interpretative discourse, and Wiesel's own ethical discourse is no exception. The excess of implication in the text means that it may solicit interpretations that endanger and even overturn the moral positions that Wiesel adopts elsewhere. But this is the risk that Wiesel accepts when he writes fiction; and it may even permit a kind of honesty that is not possible in nonfiction, because it reveals a moral perplexity that might impede effective militancy. And in its boldest moments, Wiesel's fiction approaches an insight that, I think, he could not express in his nonfictional texts: the struggle for morality may need to be more than metaphorical, and, as the terrorists of *L'Aube* see with fearful clarity, the price of success may be that you make yourself no better than your enemy. This is, I suggest, the dreadful knowledge that Wiesel's texts—fictional and nonfictional—simultaneously disclose and strain to evade.

SIX

Impaired Meaning

Our mourning is hard to bear, our distress infinite.
(*Crépuscule*, 26)

Mourning is no longer in season.
(*Crépuscule*, 149)

I SUGGESTED in chapter 4 that the father's broken promise to his son at the beginning of *Les Portes de la forêt* is of vital importance to the development of that novel. The father's departure and unfulfilled promise of return are perceived as a desertion that justifies Grégor's acts of disobedience; at the same time it constitutes the originary act that inaugurates a new order of meaning, in which ambiguity replaces paternal authority. In this chapter I argue that the father-son relationship is crucial not only for an understanding of *Les Portes de la forêt*, but for Wiesel's fiction in general. The first section of the chapter discusses the role of the father in Wiesel's writing, beginning with *La Nuit* and then turning to the later fictional works, in particular *Le Testament d'un poète juif assassiné* (1980), *Le Cinquième Fils* (1983), *Le Crépuscule, au loin* (1987), and *L'Oublié* (1989). *La Nuit* describes the traumatic experiences that dominate Wiesel's writing; and as I suggest, the loss of the father as narrated in that text is associated with a crisis of meaning and intelligibility that has direct consequences on the poetics of Wiesel's later fiction. Wiesel's attempt to come to terms with the past through storytelling involves a practice of writing that exploits the potential for ambiguity offered by literary form; and in the first section I establish the link between the process of mourning, of which successive fictional versions of the father-son relationship give evidence, and the impairment of meaning in Wiesel's fiction. The second section of this chapter, concentrating on the form of traditional biblical commentary known as Midrash, offers a more general discussion of the problem of ambiguity in Wiesel's writing.

THE DEATH OF THE FATHER

Wiesel's experience of the concentration camps is inseparable from his memory of the death of his father. *La Nuit* recounts the stages of the father's decline and demise in autobiographical form, and thereby provides the grid against which the later fictionalized versions of the same events may be measured. As I argued in chapter 3, the narrative of events in *La Nuit* is always influenced and mediated by the narrator's understanding of them, so that there is no raw depiction of uninterpreted reality. With respect to the death of Eliezer's father I briefly highlight five elements that will dominate the later fictional versions of the relationship with the father.

1. Ambivalence. Eliezer's filial loyalty is tested in the course of *La Nuit* as his father becomes an increasing burden on him. The obligation to help a sick and enfeebled man diminishes his own chances of survival. The desire to be rid of his father is emphasized by the stories of filial disloyalty that Eliezer recounts in the course of the book, and that he perceives as having important similarities to his own situation (see chapter 3). Finally, after his father's death, Eliezer confesses to a sense of liberation: "And, within myself, if I had searched the depths of my enfeebled mind, I would perhaps have found something like: free at last! . . ." (*N*, 118).

2. Guilt. This ambivalence results in a sense of guilt. The term "survival guilt" has been used to describe the feeling common to many Holocaust survivors that their own survival is in some sense culpable.[1] This is intensified in the case of Eliezer by the fear that survival was bought at the price of rejection of the father. In *La Nuit* Eliezer underscores his sense of guilt by emphasizing his increasing disloyalty to his father: "I had not stood the test any more than the son of Rabi Eliahou" (*N*, 114).

3. Reversal of roles. In the concentration camps Eliezer begins to take over his father's dominant role. He issues instructions and brings food for his increasingly childlike father: "He had become like a child: weak, fearful, vulnerable" (*N*, 112). As his father becomes more like a

child, Eliezer assumes a more adult role. Indeed, *La Nuit* could be read as the narrative of Eliezer's coming to adulthood, a process that corresponds to the usurping of the father's authority. After the liberation of Buchenwald Eliezer classes himself among the "free men" of the camp (see *N*, 121); he has now become a man.

4. Impaired mourning. This is signaled in *La Nuit* and the later fiction by the absence of tears (see for example *Ville*, 106). Mourning, according to Freud, is essential if the bereaved person is to come to terms with loss; it forms part of the process of recovery.[2] For Eliezer this process is arrested before it has begun: "I did not cry, and it hurt me that I could not cry. But I had no tears left" (*N*, 118). By failing to remove trauma through mourning, by not accomplishing the rituals that traditionally mark the decease of a loved one ("There were no prayers over his tomb. No candle lit in his memory," *N*, 118), Eliezer impedes his own recovery and so remains locked within the trauma of loss: Wiesel will be condemned to reenact his father's death in his fiction because of Eliezer's failure to undertake the work of mourning.

5. Loss of authority. At the beginning of *La Nuit* the father is represented as having authority over language and as being, in particular, "a good storyteller [*un bon conteur*]" (*N*, 22). In the course of the book that authority is diminished and lost; but in the process of role reversal, the son does not simply *replace* the father and assume his authority. With the death of the father authority seems to be lost definitively, and the son is unable to establish an adequately secure position from which to assume paternal power for himself. This has consequences on the nature of the narrative: *La Nuit* is hardly the "good story [*bonne histoire*]" that his father might have narrated (see *N*, 22). And the loss of paternal authority also has consequences on intelligibility. At the end of *La Nuit* Eliezer's father can no longer deliver the judgments, instructions, and interdictions upon which his authority was founded. After he has pronounced Eliezer's name for the final time, he produces only unintelligible mutterings: "When I returned after the roll call, I could still see his lips murmuring something as they trembled" (*N*, 118). Eliezer can never know what his father's final message might have been; the father's ultimate legacy is an incomprehensible murmur. Although this is given relatively little prominence in *La Nuit*, the fact that Wiesel returns to it in later texts indicates its importance. *La Ville de la chance* refers to the father's "unintelligible words [*mots inintelligibles*]" that the son

must, but cannot, interpret (see *Ville,* 91: "His lips were murmuring unintelligible words and you were trying to pick them up, to decipher them with your eyes"). And the problem of understanding the father's final message occupies a crucial position in Wiesel's essay "La Mort de mon père," published in *Le Chant des morts:*

His dried out lips were moving imperceptibly. Incoherent murmurs [*Murmures incohérents*], I could just hear the sounds but not the words. Probably he was fulfilling his duty as a father by passing on his last wishes, perhaps also he was telling me his definitive views on history, knowledge, the abjection of the world, his life, mine. I will never know. (*Chant,* 11)

Here, the failure to understand the father's message represents more than the disappointment of a son who does not hear his father's dying words, since it is associated with broader intellectual questions: "history, knowledge, the abjection of the world, his life, mine." In Wiesel's essay, the absence of interpretable meaning in the sounds made by the father seems linked to the senselessness of his death, the unintelligibility of the Holocaust, and the inadequacy of language to communicate the experience of the death camps. The father's mutterings, then, are the sign of a more general intellectual and linguistic failure that forms the background to all Wiesel's texts.

Before examining how these five factors are treated in Wiesel's later novels, particularly *Le Testament d'un poète juif assassiné* and *Le Cinquième Fils,* I look briefly at his first retelling of the death of the father, given in *L'Aube.* Elisha, the protagonist of Wiesel's *récit,* is clearly related, if only by his name, to Eliezer from *La Nuit. L'Aube,* however, is an overtly fictional work, and therefore not subject to the same criteria of factual truthfulness as the earlier *témoignage.* Indeed, Wiesel himself highlights the fictional nature of the text by describing it as a way of experiencing through the imagination what could not be experienced in reality: "It is because I could not, at that time, join the clandestine Jewish struggle in Palestine that I wrote a novel about it later" (*Silences,* 14). It is important that *L'Aube,* unlike *La Nuit,* be read as fiction. This is of particular importance for the transposed and disguised account of the father's death given in the fictional work.

Elisha has been ordered to kill a British officer in retaliation for the execution of one of his comrades in arms.[3] The connection between this murder and the death of the father is suggested in the title of *L'Aube*. In *La Nuit* the body of Eliezer's father is removed "before dawn [*avant l'aube*]" (*N*, 118); the father's death is presumed to take place, then, some time before dawn, and it is at dawn that the British officer (called significantly John *Dawson*) is due to be killed. Dawson's role as father figure is further indicated by his references to his own son, who is compared and contrasted with Elisha:

> - I have a son of your age, he began. He is your age but he is not like you. (*A*, 121)

Before being shot, Dawson writes a letter for his son, just as Paltiel in *Le Testament d'un poète juif assassiné* and the father in *Le Cinquième Fils* write to their respective sons; and Dawson's letter is confided to Elisha, who thereby becomes the surrogate of his enemy's son. When Elisha shoots Dawson he interrupts a story that the latter is about to recount; this recalls the father's interrupted story at the beginning of *La Nuit*. Dawson's smile shortly before his death ("John Dawson began to smile," *A*, 139) is reminiscent of the father's mysterious smile in *La Nuit* ("Then he smiled. / I will always remember that smile," *N*, 98). But the most telling evidence for the view that the murder of Dawson is a transposed version of the death of the father is given by verbal echoes between *La Nuit* and *L'Aube*. Before his words become unintelligible, Eliezer's father pronounces the name of his son twice; before he is shot, Dawson twice addresses Elisha by name. The following comments of Eliezer and Elisha strongly resemble one another:

> My father made one last sound—and it was my name: "Eliezer." (*N*, 118)

> It was a dead man who, his lips still warm, had pronounced my name: Elisha . . . (*A*, 140)

After the death of his father Eliezer feels that he also has died; when he looks in a mirror, he comments that "a corpse looked back [at him]" (*N*, 121). After he has shot Dawson, Elisha has the feeling that he has in fact killed himself: "It's done. I've killed. I've killed Elisha" (*A*, 140).

In *L'Aube* the son's sense of guilt over the father's death receives its most extreme and (perhaps because it is so extreme) its most disguised treatment. The son not only colludes in his father's demise, but even pulls the trigger that brings it about. Survivors of the Holocaust or

Hiroshima have often been found to have a sense of responsibility for the death of those who did not survive; and as Ellen Fine (drawing on the work of Robert Jay Lifton) has shown, "I am responsible for his death" can easily be translated in the mind as "I killed him."[4] Dawson's murder represents, then, a heightened but repressed (in as far as it is disguised and presented as fiction) sense of responsibility for the father's death. But the episode may also indicate the ambivalence that characterizes many love relationships. Murdering Dawson is perhaps both a sign of guilt and of parricidal desire. Elisha can kill the displaced representation of his father in fiction in a way that we do not (normally) in reality; and through the detours and disguises of fiction it is possible to realize the desire to murder the father, which in an autobiographical text such as *La Nuit* cannot openly be expressed.

Nevertheless, this should not be understood as indicating an imminent successful conclusion to the work of mourning. This is excluded by the sense shared by Eliezer and Elisha that their own demise is linked with that of their father or father-surrogate. The realization of the desire to kill the father is necessarily accompanied by an increase in the sense of guilt; so, the act of dissociation from the father binds the subject to the past all the more effectively, because it condemns him to live with the guilt that accompanies parricidal desire, while also effecting an impoverishment of his own identity. The son dies with the father. The act that might have ended the work of mourning has the result of impeding its completion; the past retains its hold over the present, the lost object retains its power over the living (but half dead) subject. Eliezer's feeling in *La Nuit* that the death of his father makes him "free at last" (*N*, 118) is illusory, and it is belied by the very existence of the text in which it is expressed. Eliezer is free from his father, but tied to a perpetual recollection and reenactment of the events that led to that freedom; he is irredeemably bound to the past by the very event that seems to liberate him from it. Further evidence of this is given in *La Ville de la chance*, published two years after *L'Aube* and seventeen years after the liberation of Buchenwald. This novel presents another survivor subject to guilt because of his failure to cry over his father's death:

> - Tell me, Yankel, what was I doing whilst my father was dying?
> - I've just told you. Nothing. You did nothing. You watched.
> - I didn't cry.
> - No, you didn't cry.
> - Did you wonder why I didn't cry whilst my father was dying.

- No.
- You're lying! I know that you're lying. (*Ville*, 91–92)

The increased prominence of the theme of paternity in Wiesel's later fiction may in part be explained by the fact that he became a father in 1972; the return of the theme to the center of his writing also marks a greater degree of reconciliation with the past. Like *La Nuit*, *Le Testament d'un poète juif assassiné* recounts the life and death of a father figure, Paltiel. That this is at least in some sense related to the earlier narrative is indicated once again by the time of day of Paltiel's execution. The body of Eliezer's father is removed "before dawn [*avant l'aube*]" (*N*, 118); this same phrase is used in the order to execute Paltiel: "The Jewish poet Paltiel Gershonovitch Kossover must be executed before dawn [*avant l'aube*]" (*Testament*, 283); as if to reinforce the point, the phrase is repeated a few lines later: "- I said: before dawn [*avant l'aube*]" (*Testament*, 283). *Le Testament d'un poète juif assassiné* and *Le Cinquième Fils* are, however, novels of reconciliation; they indicate, if not the eradication, then at least the control of ambivalence and hostility toward the father figure. They deal with continuity and reintegration within the Jewish community, rather than emphasizing revolt or the desire to break with or annihilate the past. (The desire to annihilate the past by not recounting it is one of the elements, though not in the end the dominant factor, in Wiesel's preceding novel, *Le Serment de Kolvillàg*).

Le Testament d'un poète juif assassiné deals with three generations of the Kossover family, represented by the three men Gershon, Paltiel, and Grisha. Continuity is emphasized by the use of the same names: Paltiel gives his father's name to his son (Grisha is a diminutive form of Gershon). The novel can be read as an account of how this continuity comes to be established. Paltiel revolts against his father and the community he represents; he leaves home, neglects his religion, becomes involved with communist groups in Berlin, Paris, and Spain, writes articles interpreted as hostile by the Jewish press, settles in the Soviet Union, and joins the Communist Party. At the same time he never entirely forgets his origins; he continues to receive letters from his father, and he thinks particularly of his father during a brief trip to Palestine. After settling in the Soviet Union he becomes a victim of anti-Semitic persecution, which strengthens his sense of being a Jew; he returns to live in the town in which he was born, has a son, who is circumcised and given the name of Paltiel's father. The birth of the son in particular consolidates his return to origins: "I recounted stories to him in Yiddish, I sang to him the lullabies that my mother had sung to me" (*Testament*, 277); he begins to regard his son as a representative and continuation of his father: "I thought of my father and my son *at the same time*. The same thought covered both of them" (*Testament*, 278–79; emphasis in original). The Jewish newspapers that had once condemned him now take his side (see *Testament*, 146–47); and he writes a testament for his son, who completes the process of reintegration with the Jewish community by emigrating to Israel when he is an adult. The father in *Le Cinquième Fils* follows a parallel evolution. He rebels against, but does not entirely reject, the values and religion of his parents in order to pursue an academic career; subsequently he returns to his community and becomes its leader during the Nazi persecutions.

Paternity, in these two novels, seems to bring both reconciliation with the past and a prospect of continuity with the future. Grisha, Paltiel's son, considers having a child in order to preserve the family line: "a son who will be like me, who will be like my father . . ." (*Testament*, 106). The identification of father and son seems stronger than ever. In *Le Cinquième Fils* the son acknowledges the resentment he has felt toward his father: "Certainly, I sometimes bore a grudge against him" (*Fils*, 21); but he also emphasizes his resemblance to his father: "- I am like you despite everything" (*Fils*, 30). (In his account of his early life the father also acknowledges his desire to resemble his father: "I had only one desire: to be like my father, a simple and upright man, with flawless integrity," *Fils*, 34). The son both resembles the father ("for we are like one another," *Fils*, 42) and becomes confused with him ("I don't know if it is me or my father who is traveling in this train," *Fils*, 191). Lisa, the son's girlfriend, offers the son a way of establishing a relationship with the father: "I think that I love Lisa because my father loves her as well" (*Fils*, 199); and Lisa herself identifies father and son with one another: "and my father, for her, is me" (*Fils*, 200). The son travels to Germany in order to confront the SS commander responsible for the death of his brother, and thereby to succeed in gaining vengeance where earlier his father had failed ("to complete my father's work," *Fils*, 203). And throughout the novel, the son reiterates his undiminished love for his father:

> My father, I love him [. . .] Despite everything and because of everything, I love my father [. . .] Now, more than before, my love for my father is complete. (*Fils*, 15, 176, 230)

The final sentence quoted here goes on to add that the son loves the father "as if he were [his] son" (*Fils*, 230): the desire to reverse roles and usurp paternal authority has not been abandoned, but it has become benign. The father becomes the object of love and filial protection rather than hostility and resentment.

In *La Nuit* and *L'Aube* the son destroys himself by destroying (or wishing the destruction of) the father figure; now, the need to destroy has been overcome, and the son preserves selfhood and self-respect by affirming respect for the father. The process of mourning makes it possible for the bereaved subject to become detached from the lost object while preserving fond memories of it. This is what, in Wiesel's earlier texts, seemed impossible for his principal characters: they attempted to dissociate themselves from the past by violent, parricidal desires that could only ever be partly successful, because they also resulted in guilt and self-violence. Now, Wiesel's characters seem more capable of achieving a balance of dissociation and respect, which is shown in the son's severe but entire love for his father in *Le Cinquième Fils:*

> And yet I love him. I love him severely. And entirely. (*Fils*, 132)

Le Testament d'un poète juif assassiné and *Le Cinquième Fils* mark, then, a distinct advance in the work of mourning. In *Le Testament d'un poète juif assassiné* in particular this is precipitated by Paltiel's own paternity; his son shares the name of his father and helps reconcile him with his father's memory and with his community. In *La Nuit* and *La Ville de la chance* the son is unable to cry at his father's death; in *Le Testament d'un poète juif assassiné* Paltiel begins to cry when his son is circumcised, an event that marks his own reintegration into the Jewish tradition as well as a belated acceptance of the work of mourning:

> I managed to find—I won't say where or how—a *Mohel;* he circumcised my son. As I recited the prayer of the alliance, I had tears in my eyes. My son, in my arms looked at me in silence; and, in silence, I made the wish that he would know joy. When the *Mohel* pronounced the name of my father, I began to sob. (*Testament*, 276–77)

Wiesel, like Paltiel, gave the name of his father to his son; and the emphasis on return, community, and reconciliation in *Le Testament d'un poète juif assassiné* attests that he is accomplishing, through the writing of the novel, the work of mourning (detachment without violence, preserving fidelity and respect), which is signaled by Paltiel's belated tears.[5]

L'Oublié, published in 1989, represents a further stage in the liquidation of ambivalence toward the father figure. The son's hostility toward the father is presented as little more than ordinary adolescent revolt. The guilt-laden parricidal ambivalence of *La Nuit* and *L'Aube* are defused and transformed into an insignificant family squabble:

> Like other adolescents, Malkiel had discussions, arguments and misunderstandings with his father. He wanted to go out more often, Elhanan tried to dissuade him [. . .] Malkiel wanted to go to every baseball match in the season, Elhanan argued that that was too much. (*O*, 132)

Malkiel regrets his former attitude, which in any case has long since been superseded. Now, his love for his father is faultless: "He loved his old father with a total, all-embracing love. No one was so close to him" (*O*, 74). The novel revolves around the father's attempt to transmit his memory to his son, who will then replace him and speak in his place. Filial disloyalty lies in the distant past, and the text concentrates instead on the drama of continuity.

The differences between the various versions of the father-son relationship are as important as the similarities. Wiesel returns compulsively to the theme, but repetition incorporates significant variations. In *Le Testament d'un poète juif assassiné* both the father figures (Gershon and Paltiel) die, whereas in *Le Cinquième Fils* the father survives. Moreover, in *Le Testament d'un poète juif assassiné* the paternal role is divided among a number of literal and surrogate fathers. David Aboulesia constantly reminds Paltiel of his Jewish background, and is even confused with his father: "David Aboulesia—or is it really my father?—looks at me as if in a dream" (*Testament*, 280–81; see also 196). Viktor Zupanev, the scribe, assumes some of Paltiel's functions in respect to his son Grisha; he records the father's words and ensures that his testament is transmitted to the son; and his role as father surrogate is made explicit: "Grisha needed a father, and Zupanev needed a son" (*Testament*, 79). Dr Mozliak, the lover of Grisha's mother, also takes on some paternal functions; contrasted with Paltiel ("He [Mozliak] speaks well [. . .] Your father spoke little," *Testament*, 45), he becomes the object of Grisha's resentment and jealousy, largely because he takes his mother away from

him in a way that his real father, being dead, does not. Mozliak represents, then, the bad father, whereas Paltiel represents the good father; one
is the focus of hostility, the other is the focus of love and fidelity. These
different paternal functions, split between different characters in *Le
Testament d'un poète juif assassiné*, are reunited in one figure in *Le
Cinquième Fils*. Reuven Tamiroff becomes the focus of polarized attitudes, he is both the good father and the bad father. On the one hand he
is idealized: before the war he seems destined for a brilliant academic
career (see *Fils*, 35), he plays a heroic role in the war (see *Fils*, 66–67), and
as leader of the Jewish council under the German occupation he wins the
admiration of all ("He is strong, your father, and I admire him, and we all
admire him," *Fils*, 121). On the other hand, he hardly communicates
with his son and appears as a pitiable, pathetic figure:

> My father, I say to myself. He is capable of spoiling everything, as
> he has spoilt everything so far. I feel sorry for him: that is the feeling
> that, suddenly, dominates all others. And I pity him . . . How can
> anyone be so clumsy? (*Fils*, 172)

In *Le Testament d'un poète juif assassiné* ambivalence toward the
father is focused on two distinct characters, Paltiel and Dr Mozliak; in *Le
Cinquième Fils* ambivalence is focused on a single figure who gives rise to
contradictory emotions. *Le Testament d'un poète juif assassiné* recounts
the death of the father; *Le Cinquième Fils* recounts his survival. At the
same time *Le Cinquième Fils* represents a reversal of the basic narrative
given in *La Nuit* and reflected in later texts. In *La Nuit* the father dies and
the son survives; in *Le Cinquième Fils* the father survives and Ariel, the
father's first son, dies. *Le Cinquième Fils* also represents a significant
variation on the situation at the end of *L'Aube:* there, the son murders
the surrogate father; in the later novel the father collaborates in the
attempted murder of the man responsible for the death of his first son. *Le
Testament d'un poète juif assassiné* and *Le Cinquième Fils* indicate that
the work of mourning enacted through Wiesel's fiction has reached a
stage where ambivalence toward the father has been abolished or at least
controlled; and this corresponds with an increased awareness that the
narrative of the death of the father can be modified, as in the case of *Le
Cinquième Fils*, in ways totally at variance with the original autobiographical account in *La Nuit*. Rewriting becomes, for Wiesel, the agency
through which mourning may succeed in achieving the necessary combi-

nation of dissociation and fidelity. In other words, coming to terms with the death of the father seems inseparable from the arrogation of the right to change and reinterpret the stories to which the father gives rise.

Further evidence of this is given in *Le Crépuscule, au loin*. At the beginning of this novel, Raphael's father appears as an idealized figure:

> Raphael has a lot more questions; he asks them in order to hear his father speak. He loves to hear him speak. It's his job, his vocation. A teacher, he spends his life with children. He teaches them to read and to write, to sing, to dream, to grow up, to conduct themselves as good Jews. (*Crépuscule*, 20)

But Raphael is not the only son with a father in the novel; and it is remarkable how many of the stories of the biblically named madmen, recounted episodically throughout the book, also focus on the question of relationships between sons and fathers, reflecting and refracting Raphael's own life and at the same time introducing new variations on Wiesel's central, obsessive theme. Adam breaks with his parents in order to pursue his dialogue with God, the father of mankind (see *Crépuscule*, 44–47). Caïn claims to have killed his brother because his gift to his father was rejected, and his story revolves around his father's lack of love and understanding for him (see *Crépuscule*, 60–65). Abraham, who reminds Raphael of his own father ("his father walked like that," *Crépuscule*, 118), feels responsible for the death of his son (see *Crépuscule*, 116–22; there are echoes here of *Le Cinquième Fils*). Nadav is named after "the son of Aharon the high priest" (i.e., Aaron, the brother of Moses; see *Crépuscule*, 140), and Aharon is also the name of Raphael's father; Nadav admires his father, and is present when he disappears (see *Crépuscule*, 139–44). Moshe (whose name is the Hebrew version of Moses) believes he will be saved if he can remember his father's name (see *Crépuscule*, 164–78). Joseph believes that his father is his mortal enemy, that he hates his son and has sent him to his death; and again Raphael is led to think of his own father (see *Crépuscule*, 210–13). Later, Raphael meets the Messiah (or at least one of them), who, it seems, has too many fathers: he is the "[son] of a protestant pastor," but also "son of Joseph" and the son of God (see *Crépuscule*, 218–22). And ultimately, Raphael meets the madman who thinks he is God, the father of mankind, who seems eager to avoid responsibility for the actions of his "children" (see *Crépuscule*, 261–79).

In this explosion of narratives concerning the father there are echoes of the original narrative of *La Nuit*. Nadav observes the disappearance of his father just as Eliezer had watched his own father in the process of dying; Joseph's father is heard murmuring "incoherent words [*des mots incohérents*]" (*Crépuscule*, 211), which perhaps recall the unintelligible mutterings of Eliezer's father. But the basic story as told in *La Nuit* has now become subject to so much variation as to be unrecognizable; the proliferation of stories around the father figure has now overcome and obscured whatever autobiographical truth may originally have been in the story. And this fictionalization, the evacuation of literal, historical truth from the narrative, accompanies the overcoming of trauma that Wiesel's later texts record. The displacement of reality into fiction, the telling of stories without recognizable autobiographical reference, seems essential to the work of mourning and the process of healing. Consequently the fictionality of the story, its unverifiability, is crucial to its therapeutic value. The role of fiction, for Wiesel, is not to tell the truth of experience, but to displace, distort, and mask experience, and in the process to move toward an eradication of biographical trauma.

The father in Wiesel's fiction is a producer of texts in two senses: his story, and its displacements, provide the material for fiction; and the father himself appears as an author of written texts. Before his murder John Dawson writes a letter for his son; Paltiel receives letters from his father and, in prison, begins to compose one for his own son; and Reuven Tamiroff writes letters to his dead son Ariel. Paltiel in *Le Testament d'un poète juif assassiné* is of special interest in this respect since he is the only one of Wiesel's main characters who is an author of literary texts. The importance of the father's judgment on the son's work is indicated when Paltiel receives a letter from his father who has read extracts from his polemical writings, believing them to have been written by someone bearing the same name as his son: "Of all the reactions to my article, only his caused me pain" (*Testament*, 146). But the father's influence on writing is not only shown in the author's fear of paternal judgment. Paltiel is principally the author of two texts: the collection of poems, *J'ai vu mon père en songe* (I saw my father in a dream), and the testament, which comprises the major part of Wiesel's novel. The title of the first foregrounds the relationship with the father; the second, containing Paltiel's unfinished *Lettre à Grisha* (Letter to Grisha), is at least in part addressed to his son.

It is worth looking for a moment at what we are told about Paltiel's collection of poems. Critical reaction is mixed:

My collection appeared at the end of 1946. It received a mixed reception. Some critics expressed their admiration, others tore it to shreds, not having understood a word. I must say that I had done everything possible to confuse them. The volume was entitled: *I saw my father in a dream*—and no poem referred to my father. (*Testament*, 269)

Hostile reaction to the collection is attributed to the critics' lack of understanding; yet it is hardly their fault that they have not understood, since the title of the collection does not correspond to its content. The title *J'ai vu mon père en songe* draws attention to the importance of the father, but the father does not appear in the collection itself. Paltiel goes on to say that he has suppressed the one poem that refers to the father, and that would have made sense of the rest of the collection:

At the last moment I had decided to cut out a sort of lyrical, mystical vision in which I described a procession led by my father; I ask him where he is going and he does not answer me; I ask him where he is coming from and he does not answer me; I wait for the procession to pass and I follow it at a distance—we walk, we walk in silence, but I hear someone speaking to me and I don't know who it is, he speaks to me and I know that it is forbidden to know who it is; I look in front of me and I can't see anyone, I lower my eyes and I see a small boy who is growing, who is growing; he signals to me, I recognize him; he questions me without saying a word—and I understand that it is his silence that spoke to me a moment ago—he questions me without looking at me: "What have you done to me?" And behind him my father appears, signalling to me and asking: "What have you done to me?" I tell him, and my reply is the collection. (*Testament*, 269)

Here, then, is an account of the poem that explains the rest of the collection; however, the poem itself appears to be more of an enigma than an explanation, reminiscent of the parable recounted by Katriel (see chapter 2). The son asks questions of the father, which remain unanswered, and these unanswered questions reflect the way in which the enigmas of the text remain unexplained: where is the father going, where is he coming from, what is the nature of the procession, why is it forbidden for the poet to know who is speaking to him, who is the boy, why does the poet respond to the question of the father but not to that of the boy? The text foregrounds enigma, and the poet's response to the questions asked of him produces a further text: "and my reply is the collection of poems." Paltiel's poems are a response to the father's question "What have you done with me?" The collection is therefore both a reply to the father and a transformation of the father through and into writing. The text is (a substitute for) the father, which also marks his absence; Paltiel admits that "no poem referred to [his] father." The father, then, is the principle of explanation that is absent from the text; his presence would elucidate (even if it would also raise new questions), but his absence makes the text unintelligible. The critics who did not understand Paltiel's poems were in this sense correct in their response: in suppressing the father from the collection, Paltiel ensures its unintelligibility.

The father is transformed into a book, from which the father is nevertheless absent. This indeed is what happens to Paltiel himself. When Grisha discovers Paltiel's poems, he identifies the book with his father and regards its existence as a guarantee that in a sense his father is not dead: "My father is a book and books do not die" (*Testament*, 27). The text, then, offers a mode of survival: it is, as Wiesel himself indicates, a tombstone erected in memory of the dead (see *Chant*, 15). It preserves the identity of the father but transforms it into something unrecognizable, which may subsequently be identified as the author himself (it is obviously both possible and tempting to regard the boy in Paltiel's dream who also asks "What have you done to me?" as the poet's younger self). Paltiel turns his father into a book, and is at the same time turned into a book for his son. The process of transforming life into text is performed on a larger scale in Paltiel's testament. Paltiel associates his own survival with that of his text: "While I write, as long as I blacken sheets of paper, Death will be powerless against me" (*Testament*, 19). As it happens, he is wrong: he is killed before he has finished his text, and the fact that his text remains incomplete is itself important. Paltiel is killed, and his testament ends, at a point when he is promising to reveal to his son an important secret:

> Tomorrow I will start my *Letter to Grisha* again, I will add more nuance, I will make it into a real testament—in which past experiences will serve as signs for the future.
> I will tell him what I have not yet told anyone; I will tell him that . . . (*Testament*, 281–82)

Paltiel fails to give the final message that will make the work "a real testament" and will bind together the past and the future into a coherent, intelligible whole. Throughout the novel Paltiel records his experiences as a child, and later in Berlin, Paris, Spain, and the Soviet Union. His account seeks, but never achieves, an overview of history. Finally, he dies at precisely the moment when he seems about to reveal something that might provide a key to such an overview; and the withholding of the secret marks the failure of the book to give totalizing significance to the individual's experience of history. The Testament resembles *J'ai vu mon père en songe* in that both texts require, but lack, a principle of explanation. It is reminiscent of the unfinished stories of the father in *La Nuit* and John Dawson in *L'Aube;* and it is reflected by the end of *Le Testament d'un poète juif assassiné*, of which the final sentence is ungrammatical and unfinished: "it is necessary, for otherwise" (*Testament*, 290).

It is of crucial importance that the failure to make sense appears as a direct consequence, in *J'ai vu mon père en songe* and Paltiel's testament, of the absence or death of the father. The father produces texts, both as object of the son's discourse and as subject of his own; but the texts he produces are unreadable. This is literally the case with Reuven Tamiroff's letters to his dead son in *Le Cinquième Fils:* "That night, you came to say to me (illegible words) [. . .] Then I say to her (illegible words)" (*Fils*, 39–40). In both these extracts an important message is anticipated but withheld. This unreadability is reproduced in the son's texts about the father: the long portrait of the father at the beginning of *Le Cinquième Fils* emphasizes his enigmatic and secretive sides (see *Fils*, 13–23). He is a man who "detested explanations" (*Fils*, 13); he "understands without understanding that there is nothing to understand" (*Fils*, 14); even when he seems to be listening to you "in the middle of a phrase you observe that he has disappeared" (*Fils*, 17). In *Le Testament d'un poète juif assassiné* Paltiel describes how he had contrived to "dérouter" (disconcert) his critics (see *Testament*, 269); this word recurs, significantly, in the son's description of the father in *Le Cinquième Fils:*

> I know: what I say about my father disconcerts [*déroute*] you; what I am going to say will perhaps disconcert [*déroutera*] you more. Am I old-fashioned? My father, I love him. I love him even to his lacunae [*jusque dans ses lacunes*]. (*Fils*, 15)

In Wiesel's fiction the father produces and gives rise to, and indeed seems to be conceived as, a lacunary, unreadable text.

The problem of understanding the father's final mutterings, the "something [*quelque chose*]" of *La Nuit* (118), the "incoherent mur-

murs [*murmures incohérents*]" of "La Mort de mon père" (*Chant*, 11),
the "unintelligible words [*mots inintelligibles*]" of *La Ville de la chance*
(91), has now expanded to become a more general problem of reading in
Wiesel's texts. The son aims to supplant the father and assume his
authority; but the death of the father, and the particular circumstances in
which it occurred in Wiesel's life, bring a collapse of the structure of
authority and the impossibility of its reestablishment; the son can
replace, but not reproduce, the father's authority. Paltiel's unexpected
death prevents him from finishing his testament and condemns his text
to definitive incompleteness. This is reflected also by the end of *L'Oublié*,
which makes even more evident the relationship between the death of the
father and the collapse of coherence, and importantly also indicates the
withdrawal of God as a guarantor of meaning; like *Le Testament d'un
poète juif assassiné*, the novel ends promising an explanation ("for
[*car*]") that is not given. Faith in God is reaffirmed, but the answers He
should provide are not forthcoming:

> God cannot be so cruel that he would erase everything for ever. If he
> were, he would not be our father, and nothing would have any
> meaning any more.
> And I who am speaking to you, I would no longer be able to speak,
> for (*O*, 318; no punctuation in text)

*Le Testament d'un poète juif assassiné, Le Cinquième Fils, Le
Crépuscule, au loin*, and *L'Oublié* indicate a greater reconciliation
with the loss of the father. That reconciliation is inseparable from and,
I think, dependent upon, the greater ambiguity of Wiesel's later
writing. The death of the father brings with it a loss of stable and
established meaning; and this loss ensures that the story of the
father's death can be rewritten, displaced, and made unrecognizable,
to the point that in *Le Cinquième Fils* the facts of the story are
reversed and the father actually survives. Mourning goes together
with the fictionalization, and the overcoming through fiction, of
experience. And fiction, together with the assumption of fictional
personae, allows Wiesel to explore a variety of attitudes and subject
positions: the position of father and son, or, as in the case of Paltiel,
both at once; love and hate for the father, rejection and reconciliation,
vengeance and forgiveness. This also results in a sense of loss. The
unnamed narrator of *Le Cinquième Fils* assumes the voices of his
living father and his dead brother:

> I have tried to live their lives by assuming them. I have said "I" in
> their place. By turns I have taken myself for one and for another. (*Fils*,
> 230)

The self is dispersed and diminished through the roles that it espouses:
"but when, yes, when will I begin at last to live my own life?" (*Fils*, 230).
Writing, for Wiesel, begins with and reenacts the death of the father and
the associated loss of meaning. The compulsion to retell is taken to the
point where recognizable autobiographical content is lost or even wilfully
obscured; and fiction comes to occupy—but only ever in the mode of
ambiguity—the space left by the death of the father, the collapse of
authority, the impoverishment of the self and the absence of stable
meanings.

MIDRASH

The previous section established a connection between paternity, writing,
and ambiguity; in this section I develop the relationship between storytelling and the loss of meaning in Wiesel's texts by focusing on his
discussions and adaptations of biblical stories. By way of introduction, it
will be useful to distinguish the Hebraic understanding of textual authority from the Hellenic tradition, particularly as the latter appears in the
influential presentation of Jacques Derrida. In "La Pharmacie de Platon"
Derrida describes a condemnation of writing considered by him to be
characteristic of the Western metaphysical tradition: speech is privileged
over writing because it is guaranteed by the living presence of the
speaker. In his discussion of Plato he associates this privileging of speech
with paternal authority, as he describes "a platonic scheme which assigns
the origin and the power of speech, of the *logos* precisely, to the paternal
position."[6] Writing disturbs this scheme, marking an interruption in the
authority of the father and the orphaning of the *logos*; as Socrates
comments, writing is like a child without a father, "being unable to
defend or help itself." Derrida glosses this by describing the connection
between writing and the absence of the father: "The *logos* is a son, then,
and he would be destroyed without the *presence*, without the present
assistance of his father. Of his father who responds. Who responds for
him and is responsible for him. Without his father, he is no longer any
more, precisely, than writing [*écriture*] [. . .] The specificity of writing
would, then, be directly related to the absence of the father."[7]

But, Derrida continues, the absence of the father can be desired as well as regretted: "This abjection is ambiguous: certainly it is the distress of the orphan who needs not only the assistance of a presence but also that assistance should be brought and he should be helped; but in pitying the orphan, we are also accusing him—and writing—of aiming to push the father away, to gain freedom from him with self-satisfaction and self-importance. From the standpoint of authority, the desire for writing is marked, designated, denounced as the desire to be an orphan and as parricidal subversion." Unlike Socrates, Plato writes; although writing is condemned in his texts, the very act of writing indicates a parricidal impulse toward his intellectual "father."[8] Writing, in this account, begins with—and evinces desire for—the death of the father.

There is a clear connection between the scheme described by Derrida and the discussion in the preceding section of this chapter. However, Derrida's account of writing derives from a reading of Greek texts and does not account for the very different attitude toward the written word that informs the Hebraic tradition to which Wiesel belongs. Derrida's reading of Plato depends on the primacy of father over son (speech over writing, Socrates over Plato), and the son's desire to overthrow that primacy. Derrida can deconstruct hierarchies only if they are—in the first instance—taken as established. This is a presumption that cannot be made if we turn from Greek to Hebrew, at least where the primacy of speech over the written word is concerned. The Torah, which in a restricted sense refers to the Pentateuch and in its extended sense to the whole of Jewish doctrine and law, is sometimes conceived as *preceding* creation, along with Israel, the Temple, and the name of the Messiah (see *CB*, 38); indeed, it is also taken as the *model* of creation.[9] In the beginning was the word, and the word was written. The written word, then, does not displace the father, since it was already in place before the father appeared. It is part of, not in opposition to, his authority. This is reflected in Wiesel's texts by the representation of the father as author or guardian of the Book: the community scribe in *La Ville de la chance*, the poet in *Le Testament d'un poète juif assassiné*, the author of letters in *Le Cinquième Fils*, and so on. The preeminence of the written text in Jewish thought brings with it a notion of truth unlike anything found in the Greek texts examined by Derrida. Rather than the object of unitary revelation, of reminiscence, or of abstract philosophical reasoning, truth is acquired through patient, attentive reading and interpretation of texts. In the final section of this chapter I discuss Wiesel's interest in the Jewish tradition of biblical exegesis and how it relates to his practice as storyteller and to the ambiguity of his literary writing.

In recent years the Hebrew Bible and rabbinical biblical exegesis have proved to be of great interest for the study of narrative art and modern literary hermeneutics. Robert Alter's *Art of Biblical Narrative* attests to the former, and Susan Handelman's *Slayers of Moses* to the latter. Such works emphasize the sophistication of both biblical narrative and Jewish exegesis. The latter is generated by what Robert Alter describes as the lacunary, indeterminate nature of the biblical texts: "Indeed, an essential aim of the innovative technique of fiction worked out by the ancient Hebrew writers was to produce a certain indeterminacy of meaning, especially in regard to motive, moral character, and psychology [. . .] Meaning, perhaps for the first time in narrative literature, was conceived as a *process*, requiring continual revision—both in the ordinary sense and in the etymological sense of seeing-again—continual suspension of judgment, weighing of multiple possibilities, brooding over gaps in the information provided." The indeterminacy of the text solicits interpretation; or, as David Banon puts it in his useful study of Jewish hermeneutics, "The enigmatic quality of the text is a demand for the production of meaning." The meaning of the text is not self-evident or fully revealed; it needs to be *produced* by the commentator. Hartman and Budick, borrowing a term from Derrida, describe interpretation (particularly midrashic interpretation) as the "originary supplement" of the Bible; it comes after the text, but is also required by the text, which in a sense would be incomplete without it. In the rabbinical tradition the revelation of God's truth does not take place independently from the interpretation of his word as written in the sacred texts.[10]

There can be no understanding without commentary. The very form of the Talmud gives evidence of the importance of commentary in the Jewish tradition; in the Talmud, the Mishnah, a codification of Jewish law established in the second century of the common era, is presented together with often contradictory debates and discussions on its interpretation. Moreover, the Talmud exists in two versions, the Jerusalem Talmud and the Babylonian Talmud, which contain the commentaries of different rabbinical academies. The Jewish tradition maintains both continuity and vitality through the proliferation of commentaries, and of commentaries upon commentaries. The Bible and the Mishnah are held to be texts that possess absolute authority, and it would be heresy to falsify their meaning; however, quite what that meaning is must be open to debate. Moreover, the revealed word of God is characterized by a plenitude that can only be diminished by translation into human words and actions. In consequence, contradictory interpretations of the divine word may, in different circumstances, be equally correct. Contradiction is not simply tolerated: differing views do not cancel one another out to reveal an absence of meaning, but are brought together in order to reveal the full and complex meaning of sacred texts (see *CT*, 15, 18). The philosopher Emmanuel Lévinas, who has devoted an important part of his work to commentaries on the Talmud, attributes an extraordinary authority to that text: everything has been thought, every situation and idea anticipated.[11] The Talmud is both authoritative and open, and the preservation of disagreements within it ensures the fullness of the word of God and the dynamism of commentary: "[The Talmud] keeps problems in the state of discussion. Theses are opposed to one another and yet remain, all of them, as it is said, 'words of the living God.' It gives credence to the idea of a unified spirit, despite the contradictions contained in inconclusive dialogues. An open dialectic."[12]

Wiesel, who studied with the same teacher as Lévinas, shares important aspects of Lévinas's conception of the Talmud.[13] He describes the Talmud as a great work, perhaps the greatest of all:

> The Talmud is a great masterpiece. Perhaps the greatest of all. No other civilization has produced such a marvel of literature and philosophy. Nothing can equal or even approach the biblical and talmudic texts. I love the ancient texts of Israel, especially for their concision. The Talmud is certainly the most concentrated of all texts. (*Qui êtes-vous?* 83)

For Wiesel as for Lévinas, all the important questions have already been posed:

> That is the very principle of the Talmud. All questions have a past that links us to our ancestors. (*Silences*, 21)

The authority that Wiesel seems prepared to invest in the Talmud does not exclude its openness to fresh interpretation; on the contrary, its authority seems bound together with its openness:

> It is wrong, and even dangerous, to see in Judaism a monolithic current. Jewish tradition is rather a symphony, a pluralist movement. In the Talmud I can find what I am looking for. By using quotations I can really demonstrate anything at all. (*Qui êtes-vous?* 44–45)

The Talmud justifies a plurality of interpretations; at the same time it constitutes a single, unified text, in which every part is in its place and necessary to the whole:

> At first sight the various treatises seem to contain disordered texts. By studying them more closely you can appreciate the organization and the system: no story is superfluous and all the examples are in the right place. (*Signes*, 214)

> All these stories, all these problems, all these conflicting ideas, all these quotations, these arguments and counter-arguments: how is it possible not to get lost in this confusion? It is possible. The confusion is only apparent. In truth, the Talmud is a perfectly structured edifice. Everything is in the right place. The connections, you will find them. The logic that maintains the whole is unshakable. (*CT*, 13; see also 348)

The Bible and the Talmud are, then, texts accorded absolute authority in the Jewish tradition. All truth is contained in them, but in the form of enigma; revelation comes about only through exegesis. Contradiction, rather than undermining the authority of the text, in fact attests to the unreproducible fullness of the word of God. The apparent disunity of the texts, which may be explained by the fact that their parts were composed by different hands at different times, is countered by the faith that both Bible and Talmud are in fact unified wholes. Lévinas describes the coherence of the Talmud as the hypothesis on which his commentary depends, and if he cannot find the coherence of the text he must attribute his failure to the shortcomings in his intellectual capacities rather than to the text itself.[14] And David Banon describes the unity of the Bible as the first and essential principle of biblical exegesis: "This process of investing and investigating meaning relies upon a certain number of guidelines. First of all, there is that of regarding the Bible as *one book* in which all the parts, far from opposing and contradicting one another, complete and mutually explain one another. This *global* vision of the biblical text governs analytical study. Moreover it allows a synthetic view of the whole development of history. In short, it is attentive to every detail, for *everything* in the text must have value and meaning."[15]

The form of exegesis known as Midrash is of particular importance to Wiesel. Writers on Midrash have shown an entirely comprehensible reluctance to define the term too narrowly. The following passage by James Kugel gives what will serve as a useful initial definition:

[The] Hebrew word *midrash* might be best translated as "research," a translation that incorporates the word's root meaning of "search out, inquire" and perhaps as well suggests that the results of that research are almost by definition recherché, that is, not obvious, out-of-the-way, sometimes farfetched. The word has been used to designate both the activity of interpretation and the fruits of that activity, and in Hebrew writings it was used extensively for the collective body of all such interpretations as well as in the name of certain collections of midrashic material (Midrash Rabbah, etc.). At bottom midrash is not a genre of interpretation but an interpretative stance, a way of reading the sacred text, and we shall use it in this broad sense.[16]

Midrash as interpretative stance involves a heightened attentiveness to the sacred texts, and especially to their "surface irregularities": it concentrates on problems such as unexplained motivations, apparent contradictions, unusual words, even unusual spellings of words.[17] Everything in the holy texts is motivated and needs to be explained. An important form of Midrash, known as aggadah, deals largely with the narrative parts of the Bible and often itself adopts a narrative form, as it amplifies and fills in the gaps in the original stories.[18] Wiesel himself gives a brief account of the meaning of aggadah in the glossary at the end of *Célébration hassidique*, where he describes it in the following terms: "Parables, commentaries, legends, adages, homilies, apologues, which, most frequently, springing from a biblical text or glossing its difficulties, constitute one of the aspects of the Talmud and the Midrash" (*CH*, 258; reprinted in *Mélancolie*, 219).

Wiesel's interest in the narrative aspects of Midrash is shown in particular in *Célébration biblique* and in the "Lecture midrashique de la Bible" in *Silences et mémoire d'hommes*. At the beginning of *Célébration biblique* he explains the sense in which he uses the term Midrash: "Midrash is here used in its broadest sense: interpretation, illustration, creative imagination" (*CB*, 10). This combination of interpretation and creation is essential to the midrashic stance; the tradition of reading is continued by a combination of fidelity to the source texts and the production of innovative readings of them. At the same time, the continuing relevance of the Torah to changing circumstances is assured.[19] Midrash operates in the gaps left by the biblical narrative; it offers verbose motivations for the actions described in the laconic, reticent manner of the Bible:

> The Midrash weaves its parables around the austere framework of biblical narrative, expands the portraits, strikes and provokes the mind and the heart [. . .] Sensitive to the tension that gives life to the biblical narrative, the Midrash, as usual, attempts to embroider it with details, with commentaries; the Midrash is to the Bible what imagination is to knowledge [. . .] It explores the heart and silence of its characters; it examines them from every angle; it hunts them down to the deepest parts of themselves; it thereby ends by imagining the unimaginable. (*CB*, 16, 50, 78)

Midrash, then, seeks problems within the Bible and attempts to resolve them. This can be illustrated by the chapter of *Célébration biblique* devoted to Cain and Abel. Using midrashic texts Wiesel asks a series of questions that are unanswered in the Bible: why does God accept the offering of Abel and not that of Cain? where are Adam and Eve while their children are quarrelling? what is the origin of the rivalry between the brothers? This last question gives rise to a series of partial solutions. First explanation: Cain and Abel are fighting over the inheritance that will be left by Adam and Eve. Second explanation: they are fighting over a woman. This hypothesis raises another question: if they are fighting over a woman, then who is the woman? Eve, suggests the Midrash; or, the twin sister of Abel, whom both brothers want to marry. A third explanation for the dispute is offered, according to which they are fighting over religious matters: in sharing out the universe Cain has chosen this world, Abel the world to come; now Cain wants a part in the world to come as well. Or, the brothers are fighting over the Temple of Jerusalem, since both of them insist that it should be on their territory (see *CB*, 50–53).

Midrash responds to the reticence of the biblical narrative and searches for the motivation behind the action. Although it is not entirely free from restraint, it does permit a large degree of boldness, even waywardness, with the biblical text.[20] In the supposition that the rivalry between Cain and Abel is due to a dispute over Abel's twin sister, for example, the midrashic author seems to have few qualms about inventing a child for Adam and Eve who is not mentioned in the Bible. Midrash embroiders, and may even dispute, what is said in the Bible: Wiesel refers to a midrashic text that, in explanation of a singular construction ("he returned") referring to Abraham's return from Moriah, supposes that the angel was too late in halting the sacrifice of Isaac, and that Abraham actually killed his son and returned alone (see *CB*, 86).

The explanations that Midrash provides are contradictory, seeming to cancel one another out. But Midrash does not aim to give *exclusive* truths, and the variety of interpretations offered attests to the *fullness* of the Bible, which produces innumerable readings and counterreadings. Indeed, the coexistence of opposed readings seems almost essential to the midrashic stance, as Wiesel implies at one point by his use of the word *forcément:* "Another source, inevitably [forcément], says the opposite" (*CB*, 34). The ambiguity of the Bible is not such that it requires the reader to choose definitively between competing readings; on the contrary, such a choice would diminish the word of God by reducing it to univocity. The Bible is ambiguous because all meanings are contained within it, and it is important to respect that ambiguity.[21] Wiesel insists that the midrashic stories should not be taken as offering final explanations for the events of the Bible; they reveal what the Bible *might* be about, and therefore in a sense what it *is* about, but never to the exclusion of other possibilities:

> Is it worth recalling once again that these accounts should not be taken literally? Cain and Abel are symbols, they serve as examples, illustrating the principal motives that, in human society, push individuals to hatred, bloodshed, war, and finally to self-destruction: sexual obsession, material power and religious fanaticism—or just plain fanaticism.
>
> But the event nevertheless remains unexplained; the file remains open. Logical or ingenious, none of the theses is presented as irrefutable. We are groping in the dark. We still don't know why Cain killed and why Abel let himself be killed. (*CB*, 52–53)

Although numerous explanations have been put forward, the event remains unexplained, "the file remains open," the text remains open to further investigation and exegesis; and this openness is in fact crucial to the survival of the Bible as a living text.

Wiesel's *Célébration biblique* aims to demonstrate this survival. It is not just a compilation of midrashic stories; in his discussion Wiesel continues the spirit of Midrash by his own creative rereadings of the Bible, and by drawing attention to the relevance of biblical figures to the modern world. Toward the end of the final essay of the book, entitled "Job ou le silence révolutionnaire," Wiesel protests against Job's ultimate submission to God. He prefers to think that the Book of Job should have ended differently: "Job died without repenting, without diminishing himself; he succumbed to his fate upright and undamaged" (*CB*, 196). Subsequently, however, Wiesel finds an ingenious way of reading his preferred ending into the text itself. Job, he suggests, gives way to God too quickly; he does not protest or argue, because he knows that he has no chance of winning, so he chooses instead revolt under the guise of submission:

> So, we can understand that, despite or because of appearances, Job continues to question heaven. If he repents of sins that he has not committed, if he accepts a suffering that he has not deserved, it is in order to signal to us that he does not believe his own confessions; they are only trickery. Personifying the unsatisfied quest for justice and truth, he has not given in. (*CB*, 198)

Wiesel's reading of the Book of Job exemplifies the tension that characterizes Midrash: the text is authoritative, but the ingenious midrashist seems capable of making it mean more or less what he wants. The stories of the Bible are explained by further stories; exegesis has become a pretext for more narrative.

Current interest in Midrash among those who are not primarily concerned with biblical exegesis can be explained partly at least by its relevance to some forms of modern fiction and criticism. Theorists of intertextuality could clearly learn a great deal from the interdependence of midrashic stories; and Midrash could also elucidate the fictional practice of a diverse range of writers and rewriters: Budick and Hartman's collection *Midrash and Literature* contains essays on Wallace Stevens, Milton, Defoe, Borges, Kafka, and Agnon. Moreover, the contorted ingenuity of some midrashic readings could throw light on much modern critical practice: Wiesel's demonstration that the end of the Book of Job means the exact opposite of what it seems to mean, for example, might remind us of the virtuoso performances of some recent critics. In the present context, I have dwelt so long on Midrash because it has a particular bearing on the notion of textual meaning and the practice of rewriting that informs Wiesel's thought and fiction. For Wiesel the question of Midrash is bound together with the question of fiction. He has characterized his fictional project in terms of Midrash:

> I think our generation needs a new language. So I am looking. I am looking for a new Midrash [*un midrash nouveau*] made of words that would not negate themselves. (*Qui êtes-vous?* 109)

Critics have not been slow to pick up on the midrashic aspect of Wiesel's work. Byron L. Sherwin has described Wiesel's writing as "a Midrash for our times"; like traditional Midrash it establishes a relationship "between an ancient text and a modern problem, between ancient events and contemporary experiences."[22] Michael Berenbaum and Emil Fackenheim have both taken Midrash as one of the central issues of Wiesel's writing; and it is worth comparing their differing accounts of the subject, since they serve to illustrate the difficulties of establishing the relationship between continuity and discontinuity in Wiesel's use of traditional forms.

In his book *Vision of the Void: Theological Reflections on the Works of Elie Wiesel* Michael Berenbaum argues that Wiesel's writing represents a crucial alteration in the practice of Midrash. Traditionally, Midrash and the Hassidic tales offer a way of exploring theological questions through storytelling; most importantly, they illustrate the fundamental Jewish belief in the continuing presence of God within history. For Wiesel, Berenbaum insists, "the most terrifying theological implication of the Holocaust is the collapse of the Midrashic framework." Berenbaum offers two explanations for this collapse: "First of all, the traditional images of God relating to the covenant of God's presence become so difficult and tortuous when applied to the reality of Auschwitz that we might prefer to abandon them entirely rather than retain them. Secondly, the covenant implies a posture of trust leading to an acceptance of historical reality as God ordained." To maintain the midrashic framework would require the intolerable belief that God himself was an actor in the Holocaust. So, although Berenbaum suggests that Wiesel's writing can be considered as "a Midrash on the Holocaust," such Midrash is severed from the belief system that spawned it, as it demonstrates "the incompatibility of previous midrashic traditions with the post-Holocaust world."[23]

Berenbaum contrasts Wiesel's stance with that of the Jewish theologian Emil Fackenheim, although he does not take account of the essay on Wiesel that appears in Fackenheim's *The Jewish Return into History*, published one year before Berenbaum's book (and acknowledged in his bibliography).[24] In his essay Fackenheim outlines a view of Midrash that he has developed in previous books. Midrash, he asserts, affirms the bond between God and the world, however fraught and paradoxical that bond might be. It accepts the tension, but refuses to choose, between belief in an omnipotent, omnibenevolent God and existence in a world that contains elements apparently in contradiction with such belief, namely evil and human freedom. Wiesel's work pushes this tension to its furthest conceivable point, as it maintains both a relentless self-exposure to the Holocaust and a Jewishness steeped in tradition. This combination produces what Fackenheim calls "the unprecedented phenomenon of mad Midrash."[25] Mad Midrash is ensconced within the antiworld engendered by Auschwitz. Instead of accepting the fraught bond between God and world, it protests against the antiworld and the anti-God who rules it. At the same time, mad Midrash keeps a link with the values that inform midrashic existence in as far as it turns into a determination to restore the world by overthrowing the antiworld that has replaced it. Mad Midrash desires and attempts to recover a world in which midrashic existence, an existence witnessing to the bond between God and the world, will again be possible. Inevitably, then, it cannot remain just a literary practice; it must point also to political praxis. Fackenheim sees a straight line of development from *La Nuit* to Wiesel's concern for human rights in *Les Juifs du silence* and the struggle for Israel recounted in *Le Mendiant de Jérusalem.*[26]

Berenbaum describes the collapse of the midrashic framework in Wiesel's writing; Fackenheim describes its survival, but in the transfigured form of mad Midrash. Despite the apparent contradiction of these views, the degree to which they correspond is striking. They agree on the importance of the Holocaust as a challenge to traditional Judaism; and while Berenbaum takes issue with Fackenheim, he associates the collapse of the midrashic framework, as Fackenheim associates mad Midrash, with Wiesel's defense of the Soviet Jews and his commitment to Israel.[27] The traditional function of Midrash to affirm the bond between God and the World has been disrupted; but Wiesel's post-Holocaust Midrash is accepted by both Berenbaum and Fackenheim as the production of tales with theological implications and moral consequences. The framework may have changed or even collapsed, but the focus of Midrash as theologico-ethical storytelling remains much the same. Fackenheim emphasizes that mad Midrash must not become purely aesthetic, that it must be transformed into praxis and the determination to remake the world. This is in fact equally the case for traditional Midrash. David Banon argues that the proliferation of meanings through Midrash is checked by an ethical injunction; its telos lies in its function as homily rather than the production of commentaries for their own sake. Exegesis finds its justification in ethics; or, as Banon suggests, "Midrash is an exeget(h)ical procedure [*une démarche exégét(h)ique*]."[28] In the unquestioned acceptance that Wiesel's writing has the moral urgency of traditional Midrash, both Berenbaum and Fackenheim keep Wiesel within the lineage that seemed challenged in its very existence by the Holocaust. Mad Midrash is still Midrash; the midrashic framework may have collapsed (I think this is less certain, or less definitive, than Berenbaum implies), but Midrash survives.

Midrash explores the fullness of the word of God. Stories and meanings proliferate, but they are arrested by the urgency of praxis. However, Fackenheim sees a danger in mad Midrash that is also present within its more traditional counterpart: "the Word is tempted to withdraw into inwardness, expand this inwardness into a self-contained quasi existence, and thus descend from literature into aestheticizing." Instead of being transformed into ethical praxis it runs the risk of being locked in the domain of aesthetics, forming a world of its own rather than engaging with the external world. For Fackenheim and Berenbaum, Wiesel avoids this danger; they take for granted— and I do not dispute—that Wiesel is a man of immense moral stature and commitment; where I disagree with them is over the question of continuity between his practice of storytelling and his work for human rights. Rather than one leading directly to the other (Fackenheim refers to "a clear road"),[29] the two seem in some respects at least to be in opposition. The polemical essays on human rights depend upon a sense of injustice; the characters in his fiction inhabit worlds in which justice is a redundant concept. Wiesel claims moral authority while his fiction enacts a disruption of authority; he demands truth and clarity while his fiction remains locked within ambiguity. Throughout this study I have resisted the reading of Wiesel's literary texts as examples of teaching through storytelling; instead, I have concentrated on the ways in which stories proliferate at the expense of meaning, disrupting and obscuring the "messages" that they have been taken to convey. This is precisely the "aestheticizing" that Fackenheim sees as the most dangerous temptation of mad Midrash.

In this context, what is radical about Wiesel's Midrash, in my view, is not that it is "mad" in Fackenheim's sense, nor that it abandons the "midrashic framework," in which God's presence in history is affirmed. Rather, Wiesel's use of midrashic and Hassidic stories entails a move away from the conception of meaning that underlies the theologico-ethical interpretation of Midrash. *Célébration biblique* comes close to privileging the creative richness of the midrashic stories over their explanatory power. Wiesel seems to prefer their imaginative verbosity to the laconic austerity of the Bible. The same can be seen in his use of

Hassidic tales. In the preface to *Célébration hassidique* he privileges the transmission of stories over all other considerations, ethical, pedagogic, or theological: the role of the storyteller is neither to teach nor to convince, neither to reveal nor to explain the past or the present (see *CH*, 13). The storyteller appeals to the imagination (see *CH*, 13), which may, Wiesel suggests, subordinate or deform knowledge rather than increase its purchase on the real (see *CH*, 21). The story is not a form of exegesis, as it is for the midrashist; on the contrary, when explanations cannot be found, *raconter* (to recount) replaces *expliquer* (to explain): "You can't explain Kotzk; with a bit of luck, you can only recount it [*On n'explique pas Kotzk; avec un peu de chance, on ne peut que le raconter*]" (*CH*, 254). There is no master text in which all truth is contained, there is only storytelling; the story does not explain, it offers a way of avoiding an issue that cannot be explained: "When a Jew, even if he is a Rabbi, cannot give an answer, he can at least recount a story" (*Mélancolie*, 9); "When a Jew cannot provide an answer, he at least has a story to recount" (*EDS*, 82). Storytelling appears here as a way of responding to unanswerable questions rather than as a form of didactic homily.

Wiesel describes how the Hassidic masters often distrusted the written word (see *CH*, 22, 74–75). Their distrust is reflected in his own texts. Moishe in *La Ville de la chance* declares that "What is written in books is false!" (*Ville*, 24); Moshe in *Le Serment de Kolvillàg* condemns the written word (see *Serment*, 172); and the narrator of *Le Cinquième Fils* refers to "novels where everything is false" (*Fils*, 197). Wiesel recalls his dislike for novels when he was a child: "I thought that novels were puerile: reading them was a waste of time" (*EDS*, 61), and he argues that "the truth will never be written" (*EDS*, 248). The written word, and in particular the language of fiction, is equated with falsehood. On the other hand, Wiesel's fiction constantly highlights the importance of the transmission of written texts: the theme emerges through the letter John Dawson writes to his son in *L'Aube*, and it dominates *Le Serment de Kolvillàg* and *Le Testament d'un poète juif assassiné*. The debate between Moshe and the father in *Le Serment de Kolvillàg* dramatizes the hesitation in Wiesel's texts between respect for the written word and rejection of it. The condemnation of writing is also a self-condemnation. Wiesel's essay "La Mémoire des livres" indicates his love for libraries and books; but it begins with an admission of anxiety over the unchecked proliferation of the written word:

But what about the books written by madmen, by skilful spinners of yarns, by writers thirsting for glory who have nothing to say—and who nevertheless speak.

It is with reference to them that King Solomon declared in *Ecclesiastes* that their works shall be the ultimate curse: "The profusion of books will have no end . . ." Curse? Solomon was a wise man, the most wise of all the kings. He knew. He knew that the time would come when more books will be published than it is possible to write. (*Signes*, 45–46)

It is significant here that Wiesel uses a book, the Bible, as authority for his condemnation of the proliferation of books. It is not certain, however, that even the Bible escapes Wiesel's anxiety about the falsehood that inhabits the word. It is included in Moshe's attack on writing in *Le Serment de Kolvillàg* (see *Serment*, 172); and, using a revealing metaphor, Wiesel indicates in *Le Chant des morts* that the Torah is like a child who has lost its father: "Today I believe that I have the proof that the Torah itself has been orphaned" (*Chant*, 40)

This reference to the Torah as orphaned brings us back to the question of paternity. Traditional Midrash relies upon a conception of the Bible as the paternal text par excellence, inexhaustible and authoritative, containing all meanings and guaranteeing the legitimacy of its commentators. Wiesel's Midrash, on the other hand, can no longer justify itself by the fullness of an original Word. The orphaning of the child brings with it the orphaning of the text. The death of the father, to which Wiesel's texts compulsively return, condemns writing to ambiguity. Moreover, Wiesel's later texts appear often as rewritings of his earlier works, as the same material is constantly reworked; he is becoming his own midrashist, retelling and reinterpreting stories from his own texts, stories that no longer originate in the plenitude of a divine word.[30] The ambiguity of Wiesel's fiction is the trace of an absence or loss of meaning rather than a hidden fullness awaiting realization through interpretation. If the Torah is orphaned, Wiesel's Midrash is doubly orphaned: the fatherless child of a fatherless child, deprived of explanatory power because no longer under the tutelage of the Original Text. What remains for Wiesel is a polarized attitude: as activist and essayist he often appears polemical and dogmatic, assured of his ground (even in his affirmations of doubt); as storyteller he undermines positions of interpretative or moral certainty. "Aestheticized" (in Fackenheim's sense: without finality in praxis), Wiesel's fiction is not the transcription of truth ("The truth will never be written");

neither teaching nor explaining, its telos is neither theological nor ethical; it perpetually commemorates (recalls, rewrites, and—through rewriting—obscures) its own inaugural moment, its severance from the paternal word. It discloses itself as false, but has no truth to offer in place of its conscious artificiality; indeed, Wiesel's civil rights work seems to depend on a tactical and wholly necessary *forgetting* of the pervasion of falsehood, of the sapping of moral knowledge, which his fiction insistently describes.

I end this chapter by offering my own speculative Midrash on a story recounted by Wiesel in his "Lecture midrashique de la Bible." The episode, taken from the Talmud, concerns events preceding the creation of man:

> During the afternoon of the sixth day, God informed the angels of his decision to create a man and to make him in his image. Some were happy, others opposed the decision. The Angel of Love imagined man as a vehicle of love and wanted to be near him, but the Angel of Truth foresaw the lies that man would spread and in consequence did not want him on earth. The same dispute took place between the Angel of Justice and the Angel of Peace. The first was convinced of the ability of man to practice justice, but the second was equally convinced of his inability to live in peace. God succeeded in pacifying the Angel of Peace, but had to expel the Angel of Truth: with him present, man had no chance of surviving.
>
> Other angels were opposed to man; God destroyed them with fire. Only their leaders—Michael and Gabriel—were saved. Moved by a feeling of understandable gratitude, they became the celestial protectors of Israel. (*Silences*, 181)

Like any Midrash, the story is subject to repetition and variation. In the version given in *Célébration biblique* all the angels who oppose the creation of man are burned (see *CB*, 19); in a version given earlier in *Silences et mémoire d'hommes* the dispute among the angels degenerates into a war, and all except Gabriel and Michael are destroyed in a fire that they lit themselves (see *Silences*, 167).

The story contains echoes of Wiesel's previous texts. The fire that consumes the angels recalls other fires, such as the one that destroys Kolvillàg:

> The cemetery was burning, the police station was burning, the cradles were burning, the libraries were burning. That night the work

of man was being submitted to the power and the judgment of fire. (*Serment*, 254)

And behind the flames of Kolvillàg is another fire, the one described in *La Nuit*, first seen in the train to Birkenau by the delirious Madame Schächter ("- A fire! I can see a fire! I can see a fire!" *N*, 34). This fire destroys the faith of Eliezer's childhood: "I will never forget those flames that consumed my Faith for ever" (*N*, 44). The fire in Wiesel's Midrash precedes, and makes possible, the creation of man; this parallels Eliezer's coming to manhood through the experience of the concentration camps, confirmed when he classes himself among the "free men" on the final page of the book (see *N*, 121). The fire that destroys the angels leaves two survivors, Michael and Gabriel, whose names recall those of two survivors from Wiesel's novels, Michael from *La Ville de la chance* and Gavriel from *Les Portes de la forêt*. In the version of the story given above, the destruction of the angels is attributed to God, not to the intensity of their own dispute. In this version the creation of man is preceded by a theological scandal, an act of violence for which God himself is responsible. God appears as powerful but brutal in his application of power; and once again we are reminded of *La Nuit*: "I had not denied His existence, but I doubted His absolute justice" (*N*, 54).

The story of the creation of man reflects and is elucidated by Wiesel's previous texts. It can also be read as an allegory of fiction, for what is at stake here is precisely *creation*. The work comes into being only when it has passed through an ordeal of fire; God the artist destroys his angels and thereby renounces his ethical supremacy so he can create a work that is "in his image." This theological scandal is accompanied by the expulsion of the angel of Truth, who foresees "the lies that man would spread." Once again, it is worth recalling the rabbi's words to the author: "you write lies" (*EDS*, 11). As an allegory of fiction, then, the story describes the origin of the work in violence and the expulsion of truth. It is striking also that Wiesel can be identified with each of the figures in the allegory, despite the conflict between them and the logical impossibility of such an identification. He is God the creator, whose fiction marks the absence of moral purity; he takes the side of truth and of love, of justice and of peace, although they seem incompatible; he can be identified with the angels who die in the flames, as part of him died in the Holocaust; and he is also, like Gabriel and Michael, the survivor who, by some incomprehensible dispensation, does not succumb to the common disaster.

The Angel of Truth is expelled, but the story does not specify where it is sent. In another version of the story, the angel is simply destroyed along with all the others, except Michael and Gabriel (see *Silences*, 167). Yet another version suggests that the angels were not destroyed: God created man while they were distracted in their discussion (see *CB*, 19). The stories contradict one another, leaving us unsure which to believe. Is truth expelled to some unknown location, is it destroyed or simply distracted? What is certain is that it is not to be found here, but elsewhere: not in the present but in the past or the future, not in the story but in the praxis, not in the praxis but in the story. As activist and author, Wiesel vacillates between the remnants of hope and the knowledge of despair; meanwhile he continues to write fiction that nostalgically recalls the lost unity of stories and anxiously anticipates the return of the Angel of Truth.

CONCLUSION: SECRECY

IRVING ABRAHAMSON has described Wiesel as an author who shares secrets with his readers; yet he also suggests that Wiesel is "simultaneously so self-revealing and so hidden" that he never discloses "the ultimate mysteries" of his world. He says that Wiesel "bears a message for all time," but quotes him as saying "I have no message—only tales." And Abrahamson argues later that the secret of Wiesel's text is never fully revealed "because it cannot be reduced to words."[1] The apparent contradiction is resolved by the implication that the secret of the text is beyond words, but nevertheless communicable through literature. Such a position can be neither proved nor disproved. Because the secret is not verbal it cannot by definition be brought to language, so there can be no way of verifying whether it is present in the text and received by a reader. Ultimately Abrahamson's argument (to which I refer here because it is typical of much that has been written about Wiesel) depends upon an act of faith. Throughout this book I have resisted such an act of faith: the secrets of the text are not messages beyond language, but lacunae or absences of sense that cannot be filled with any positive content.

Wiesel himself repeatedly refers to the secret of his texts as something that is retained rather than revealed:

> In [La Nuit] I tried to communicate a secret, a kind of an eclipse, and, in the Kafka tradition, even the eclipse is eclipsed. The secret itself is a secret. (quoted by Abrahamson, AS, 1:45)

> Let us tell tales: for children love to hear tales. But there is one tale that will never be told. And soon we will not even know its name—nor its secret. (AS, 2:93)

> So whether fiction or nonfiction, the core, the soul of the soul, the secret of the secret is in the tale [. . .] Again, a secret will be transmitted, but as a secret. You may try to enter it, but you will always remain on the outside. (AS, 2:112–13)

The interpreter remains on the outside; the secret is transmitted, but only as a secret, a vague contour rather than a revealed content. The final quotation above recalls Kermode's account of Kafka's "Vor dem Gesetz" parable, in which a man fails to gain entry to a court of law, and which Kermode takes as representing the situation of the interpreter who can never gain entry to the mysteries of the text. As Kermode puts it, using the same inside/outside dichotomy as Wiesel, "the outsider remains outside, dismayed and frustrated."[2]

L'Oublié refers repeatedly to secrets, and I now give a final consideration to the issue of secrecy by discussing how it is treated in that text. Tamar, Malkiel's partner for much of the novel, is particularly associated with secrets and their revelation: "Tamar senses that he has a secret. She loves secrets, Tamar" (*O*, 42). This chiasmus (Tamar-secret-secrets-Tamar) perhaps indicates that Tamar is in command of the secret; she contains and controls it. For her the secret is something to be revealed:

> That's her thing: she adores secrets. To penetrate them, to classify them, to digest them, to reveal them to the public, she loves all that as much as she loves to love. (*O*, 66)

Other characters do not share her view that secrets should be brought into the public domain: Malkiel is characterized by his ability to avoid direct questions (*O*, 22); Lidia, the interpreter and guide, insists on her right to have secrets ("I have the right to have secrets too, don't I?" *O*, 18); an SS officer orders "absolute secrecy [*le secret absolu*]" (*O*, 114); Elhanan wants his illness to remain secret (*O*, 150); and after the death of his lover Vitka he cries in secret (*O*, 170). As an adjective, the word *secret* appears in a variety of contexts in the novel. Talia, Elhanan's wife, lets her husband believe that she works for the "secret section" of a clandestine Jewish organization (*O*, 211); the father of Lidia's fiancé is a colonel in "the secret police" (*O*, 242); Malkiel is given instructions by a "secret voice" (*O*, 297). A striking number of references to secret passages also appear in the novel. On two occasions Elhanan enters the ghetto of Stanislav by a secret passage ("Itzik the Tall knows a secret passage linking the ghetto to the town" [*O*, 109]; "- I know a secret passage" [*O*, 174]); and the passage by which he enters the Jewish quarter of Jerusalem is mentioned several times:

> We need someone who knows the old city, the Jewish quarter. Someone who might perhaps remember a secret passage [. . .] I even remember a secret underground passage [. . .] Do you really know a secret passage? (*O*, 222, 225)

This passage was revealed to the boy Avshalom by his grandfather, described as "a great Kabbalist" (*O*, 222). The secret passage (and the word *passage* may also refer to a part of a text) makes it possible to penetrate to forbidden places; but, in keeping with Kabbalistic esotericism, it may be revealed only to the initiated. Knowledge of the secret must be restricted to an elite of insiders.[3]

There are, then, different sorts of secrets: those sought by Tamar, which should be made public, and the secret passages used by Elhanan, which must remain private. These different secrets can be related to the tension between revelation and concealment that is essential to Wiesel's writing and to his account of post-Holocaust aesthetics. They also recall Abrahamson's description of Wiesel as "simultaneously so self-revealing and so hidden" (quoted above). In the context of *L'Oublié* this is particularly interesting, as one of the major themes of the novel is Elhanan's attempt to reveal his past to his son. Elhanan's endeavor is anticipated at the end of a long series of interviews given by Wiesel; when the author was asked what he would like to pass on to his son, he replied, "Memory . . . All my memory [*La mémoire . . . Toute ma mémoire*]" (*Qui êtes-vous?* 127). The correction to "*All* my memory" is important; it suggests the desire for a complete transmission from which nothing is omitted. For Elhanan, this endeavor has a particular urgency because he has an illness that causes the loss of memory, and this is equated in the novel with a loss of identity ("I was going to forget what my existence was, who I am," *O*, 146). Elhanan wants to capture the past before it is too late, to organize experience and identity into a transmissible whole that will be preserved against oblivion; he is driven on by "an imperious need to say everything, to omit nothing" (*O*, 87).

The form of Wiesel's novel dooms this endeavor to failure; the use of extracts from journals, transcripts of tape recordings, a prayer, Talia's letter to Elhanan, and passages in italics draw attention to the fragmented nature of the text and resist the discursive unification that Elhanan requires. Different time scales intermingle, and first- and third-person narratives alternate, with the first-person being adopted by both Malkiel and Elhanan. The text never attains for anything more than short periods the assured, retrospective first-person narrative that would make it possible for the narrating subject to organize past experience into a coherent whole. On the most basic thematic level also, *L'Oublié* gives voice to contradictory points of view without offering reconciliation. As a student Malkiel has violent arguments with Leila, a future member of the PLO, about the rights of Palestinians (*O*, 141–43); Tamar and Malkiel have a bitter row about an article written by Tamar that criticizes Israel (*O*, 301–5); Elhanan and Itzik differ in their attitudes to the desire for vengeance (*O*, 191–92); Talia and Elhanan disagree about the value of terrorist action in the struggle for the foundation of Israel (*O*, 214–15). The novel frequently underlines the importance of memory, but both Inge (the German woman with whom Malkiel has an affair) and the woman whose rape Elhanan witnessed emphasize the value of forgetting the past (*O*, 89, 289–90). In each of these cases, one point of view may be given more weight than the other; but the presence of the alternative perspective in the text foregrounds the possibility of different, conflicting beliefs, and indicates that no single view is put forward with complete assurance.

L'Oublié never quite establishes a stable, consistent position that could assure its own unity and guarantee the success of Elhanan's attempt to preserve the past from oblivion. The uncertainty that pervades the novel can even be seen in some of its most intriguing sentences. Elhanan's wife Talia does not let her husband know that she belongs to a terrorist organization, and he expresses surprise at her ability to keep things hidden from him: "She hid [*cachait*] her game well, she who hid [*dissimulait*] nothing from me" (*O*, 211). It would be easy to neutralize the paradox of this sentence by supplying a contrast between Talia's normal behavior and her current practice: "She, who *normally* hid nothing from me, was *now* doing something different." But there is no such contrast in Elhanan's sentence, instead he flatly contradicts himself: "She hid nothing from me; she was deceiving me." The sentence suspends unambiguous affirmation; and the resulting hesitation parallels the tension within the text between the revelation and the preservation of secrets: whether Talia is on the side of revelation ("she who hid nothing from me") or preservation ("she hid her game well") is uncertain.

A similar uncertainty arises earlier in the text with respect to promises, a theme of great importance in the novel. Lidia, the interpreter, refuses to make a promise to Malkiel: "- When I was young I promised my mother never to make promises" (*O*, 23). The promise is made and broken; it is broken as it is made, and it is broken afresh by each subsequent promise. This recalls the impossible logic of the Cretan liar paradox: "All Cretans are liars," says the Cretan. Shortly afterward Lidia does however make a promise to Malkiel:

- No. It's a promise
And, after thinking for a moment:

- You see? I'm betraying my principles: I've just made a promise to you. (*O*, 25)

The following page returns once more to the theme; the only way not to break the promise is not to make it in the first place:

- Not tonight, Lidia. You mustn't hold it against me. Another time.
I promise you.
    After a hesitation, she cheered up:
    - I see that you didn't promise your mother to . . .
    - No, I didn't promise her anything. (*O*, 26)

These apparently frivolous exchanges are in fact of considerable importance to the development of *L'Oublié;* much of the novel revolves around the theme of promises, in particular Malkiel's promise to preserve his father's memory, and his inability to keep that promise:

    Yet, father, I had promised you to remember in your name and in your place; but I am not succeeding in doing it [. . .] I see and I hear everything you have done, everything you have seen, and yet, father, I know, yes, I know that it will be impossible for me to keep my promise. (*O*, 193–94)

Broken promises, untold secrets: these phrases could serve to summarize Wiesel's fiction as a whole. According to one of Wiesel's most radical comments on the Holocaust, God has broken his covenant with the Jewish people.[4] Wiesel's fiction bears traces of this broken covenant: the father breaks his promise to his son in *Les Portes de la forêt* as the son breaks his promise to his father in *L'Oublié;* and the promise of meaning in history or the text is also unfulfilled, leaving us with secrets rather than revelations. An important thematic illustration of this is given in *L'Oublié* by Malkiel's journey to the hometown of his father in Transylvania. The return to a transfigured home is an important theme in Wiesel's writing (see discussion in chapter 3 regarding *La Ville de la chance*). In *L'Oublié* Malkiel's evasiveness when asked why he has gone to Transylvania is explained by the fact that he himself does not know: "Why had Elhanan Rosenbaum insisted that son Malkiel go and visit his hometown? To bring back what secret?" (*O*, 94). Malkiel is offered two pseudosolutions. The blind mystic insists that the purpose of Malkiel's journey is to meet him:

> - Your father told you to come here and you do not know why. Me,
> I know. To see me. To receive my teaching. (*O*, 258)

Later Malkiel thinks he has discovered "the real motive of [his] stay" when he decides to look for the woman whose rape his father had witnessed (*O*, 285). After his encounter with the woman, however, he is still unsure whether he has fulfilled his mission:

> And now, father? How has my presence here been useful to you [. . .]
> By coming here, have I found answers to my questions? (*O*, 306, 308)

With its pseudosolutions and reiterated uncertainties, the text stutters toward a meaning that is never found. In this respect the final section of *L'Oublié*, entitled "Paroles d'adieu" (Words of farewell), can be taken as paradigmatic of Wiesel's fictional writing in general. It presents the parting words of the father before he falls into silence. The repeated use of ellipsis recalls the final speeches of Eliezer's father in *La Nuit:*

> - My son, water . . . I'm wasting away . . . My guts . . . (*N*, 118)

Corresponding to the heightened self-consciousness of Wiesel's later writing, the passage from *L'Oublié* makes the loss or breakdown of language an explicit theme:

> I raise my voice, at least I try . . . The words resist me . . . they don't
> come . . . (*O*, 314)

According to Malkiel, earlier in his life Elhanan "incarnated the power of the intelligence and the richness of the word" (*O*, 308); now, however, "he pronounces words that crumble away, dead words; the phrases that he utters are dead phrases" (*O*, 308). Fragments of memory and of sense emerge from the father's final speech; but he remains aware that something remains unsaid. Like Paltiel in *Le Testament d'un poète juif assassiné*, he will die without revealing to his son a crucial secret:

> But this is what I think I know: I have not told you the essential.
> Yes, Malkiel, I am still lucid enough to admit it: there is an important,
> vital thing that I wanted to tell you, a sort of testament, perhaps. Every
> time I said to myself: It can wait. I said to myself: This thing is so
> essential that I won't forget it, even if I forget everything else. Well,
> now I've forgotten that thing as well. (*O*, 316)

I don't even know why I sent you to that small distant town where, as a child and adolescent, I knew happiness, the evening of the Sabbath with your grandparents, and the anxiety which followed it, at midnight, when I heard the frozen laughter of the Tempter.

What message were you supposed to bring back?

What solution to what enigma? (*O*, 316)

The father does not deliver his final message; his text ends without punctuation ("And I who am speaking to you, I would no longer be able to speak, for," *O*, 318) and without revelation. Secrecy is no longer primarily located in the relationship between text and interpreter. It has become almost the sole subject of the text; and the fact that Elhanan cannot remember the secret he hoped to reveal represents a further stage in the eclipse of meaning in Wiesel's fiction. The withheld secret has now been lost forever; even its bearer no longer knows what it is. The messenger has forgotten his message.

This eclipse of meaning should deter us from looking for simple lessons in Wiesel's fiction. Throughout this book I have suggested that Wiesel's literary texts are not sense-bearing purveyors of clear messages; in them, on the contrary, meaning is precisely what is at issue; it is sought rather than transmitted. According to Kermode, irreducible secrecy has the consequence that texts are "perpetually to be interpreted" rather than definitively understood. However there is a danger of using Wiesel's texts too hastily to support a modern critical and theoretical affirmation of indeterminacy. Kermode, typically subtle in this respect, describes secrecy as "the source of the interpreter's pleasures, but also of his necessary disappointment."[5] In a context haunted by the specter of uninhibited hermeneutic freedom, it is possible that our pleasure in finding secrecy will outweigh our disappointment in being unable to elucidate secrets. But Wiesel's fiction describes the paralysis of the intellect rather than the joyous liberation of meaning. In discussion of Elhanan's "Paroles d'adieu" in *L'Oublié*, I drew attention to the withholding of secrets. This did not produce a proliferation of free interpretations; on the contrary, the disclosure that the text would not deliver its secrets in fact brought an end to interpretation. Once we have understood that the text will not tell us its "essential thing [*chose essentielle*]" (*O*, 318), we may be left speechless rather than empowered to speak.

Elhanan expresses a pious hope to his son and interpreter: "As I speak to you, I tell myself that, by your own means, you will discover after all what my lips have not been able or not known how to say" (*O*, 318). The choice presented by the text seems to be between believing that we can understand what has not been said, and accepting that we will never understand. Either way, there is little scope for free interpretation. Repeatedly and compulsively, Wiesel's fiction describes a loss of meaning that it simultaneously resists because such a loss cannot be envisaged as anything other than catastrophic. Interpretation may bring comfort (it protects us against epistemological terrors), but little else; and I am reminded of Wiesel's reference to storytelling: "That is no longer enough" (*CH*, 173). Hermeneutic freedom may be simply another name for our failure to understand, a refusal of enigmas too intolerable to leave unexplained.

So the speechlessness of the interpreter faced with secretive texts may turn out to be no less loquacious than those texts themselves; this book might be thought to be a case in point. In trying to analyze that which defeats understanding, we are in effect replicating the activity of the texts under study: Wiesel's fiction faces the challenge of speaking beyond the trial of speechlessness, of transmitting a message that it does not know how to formulate. Deeply conscious of themselves as fictional utterance, Wiesel's texts constantly remind us that their own verbal performance is endangered by a categorical self-rejection: "I said nothing" (*Ville*, 11); "I will not speak, said the old man" (*Serment*, 9); "the story that I have just recounted, it did not really happen!" (*Zalmen*, 174).

In a peculiarly acute and self-conscious form, Wiesel's fiction thus becomes the site where the imperative of testimony collides with the knowledge that experience is unrepresentable. In the remarkable book by Shoshana Felman and Dori Laub entitled *Testimony: Crises of Witnessing in Literature, Psychoanalysis, and History*, Wiesel is credited with isolating an essential aspect of modern literature: "If the Greeks invented tragedy, the Romans the epistle and the Renaissance the sonnet, our generation invented a new literature, that of testimony."[6] Following Wiesel, Felman and Laub accept that we are now living in the Age of Testimony; but the central paradox of the era is that testimony is precisely what cannot take place. The Holocaust is described as an event without a witness: potential outside witnesses did not wish to see or know; inside witnesses were brutally denied any possibility of "an unviolated, unencumbered, and thus sane, point of reference."[7] Survivors are attacked in their very ability to bear witness. Witnessing can thus no longer be taken as "the transparent mediation between seeing and telling, private experience and public testimony." The assault on the subject, the "assassination of experience" (in Lyotard's provocative term), the exposure of language as a cracked lens through which the subject views itself, all these ensure that the Age of Testimony is also the time of a crisis of witnessing.[8] Felman draws a bold comparison between this crisis and the forms of modern literature:

> I would suggest, now, that the cryptic forms of modern narrative and modern art always—whether consciously or not—partake of that historical impossibility of writing a historical narration of the Holocaust, by bearing testimony, through their very cryptic form, to the *radical historical crisis in witnessing* the Holocaust has opened up.
>
> This is why contemporary narrative—the narrative of that which, in the Holocaust, cannot be witnessed—has by necessity inaugurated a contemporary Age of Testimony, and why the *age of testimony* has also turned out to be, paradoxically enough, the somewhat unique *age of historical prooflessness:* the age of the professional denial, by "revisionist" historians, of the very *evidence* of the historical existence of the Holocaust.[9]

So-called revisionist historians have insisted that the Holocaust cannot be *proved*. The enormous number of Holocaust testimonies that have been published do not in themselves constitute proof; in the legal model, it can never be taken for granted that testimony is truthful, since its truth is precisely what the court is called upon to decide. The revisionists' insistence that the existence of the death camps has not been proved entails a prior choice about what they will accept as evidence. The testimony of survivors is not deemed acceptable; and if in the eyes of the revisionists testimony proves nothing, then Holocaust fiction is even further removed from the accredited disciplines of proof and demonstration. By drawing attention to its own fictionality it appears as less or other than true; and Wiesel's fiction in particular repeatedly foregrounds its proximity to the discourse of madness, which provides one more reason to dismiss its evidential value.

In Wiesel's fiction, the Age of Testimony is revealed most nakedly as the age of the crisis of testimony. In consequence, his texts are not commensurable with, and should not be judged according to, the revisionists' criteria for what constitutes evidence. Lyotard uses the word *tort* (wrong) to describe "a damage accompanied by the loss of the means required to prove the damage."[10] The Holocaust is one example of such a *tort*, when the ability of the survivors to bear witness is impaired by the very experiences they wish to transmit. Something that demands to be put into language has not yet found its proper idiom. According to Lyotard, it is the affair of philosophy, literature, and perhaps also of politics, to find the idiom in which the *tort* can be put into words.[11] This may involve new forms of narration or description, creating a regime of phrases that may not be reducible to the values of truth and reason. Wiesel, it should be remembered, is also looking for a new language, what he calls "a new Midrash" (*Qui êtes-vous?* 109): an idiom, perhaps, that, like the stories of the mad discussed in chapter 4, should not be understood in terms of empirical truth or falsehood. Perhaps it should not be understood at all in any sense that we can currently attribute to understanding. As Wiesel says in *Un Juif, aujourd'hui,* "the survivor expresses himself in a foreign tongue. The code that he uses, you will never break it" (*Un Juif,* 191).

This is where literature has a vital role to play. In Wiesel's fiction and, I am tempted to say, in Holocaust fiction and testimony in general, the idiom that accommodates both the need to testify and the crisis of testimony is precisely that of the secretive text. What is disclosed here is not the content of the secret, open to interpretation and verification, but the secret as such; or even, at the end of *L'Oublié,* the eclipse of the secret, its vanishing from the consciousness of its bearer. The subject or the text is not at liberty to disclose a secret that is not fully contained within any mind or any utterance. To understand Wiesel's secret would be to reduce it to familiar structures. His stammering, repetitive, contradictory, enigmatic, lacunary texts seek rather to preserve what Felman and Laub call "the shock of the unintelligible in the face of the attempt at its interpretation."[12] And this, they suggest (and I am persuaded), may be as close as we can get to reality itself.

NOTES

INTRODUCTION

1. Abrahamson, "Introductory Essay," 3; Berenbaum, "From Auschwitz to Oslo: The Journey of Elie Wiesel," 117. The word *Holocaust* has been criticized because of its sacred overtones, and Wiesel himself has tended to avoid it in recent years, preferring to use *Événement* (Event), *Shoah*, or *Hourban* (see *ME*, 112). Throughout this book I use the word *Holocaust* because it remains the most commonly used term.

2. Kermode, *The Genesis of Secrecy*, 32.

3. Kermode, *The Genesis of Secrecy*, 25, xi.

4. See for example Blanchot, *Après coup*, 96; Derrida, *Donner le temps: 1. La Fausse monnaie*, 193–94, 215.

5. Hirsch, *The Deconstruction of Literature*, 284.

6. Young, *Writing and Rewriting the Holocaust*, 3.

CHAPTER ONE

1. Estess, *Elie Wiesel*, 116; Brown, *Elie Wiesel*, 7. The theological aspect of Wiesel's writing has dominated most of what has been written on his work so far; see, for example, Brown's study *Elie Wiesel* and the following: Cargas (editor), *Responses to Elie Wiesel*; Berenbaum, *The Vision of the Void*; Walker, *Elie Wiesel*; Rittner (editor), *Elie Wiesel*.

2. On the importance of mystical silence in Wiesel's writing, see Cohen, *Elie Wiesel: Variations sur le silence*.

3. Camus, *La Chute*, 76–77.

4. See Ezrahi, *By Words Alone*, 3: "Even the most vivid presentation of concrete detail and specificity, the most palpable reconstruction of Holocaust reality, is blunted by the fact that there is no analogue in human experience."

5. See Katz, *Post-Holocaust Dialogues*, 144.

6. For discussion, see Berger, *Crisis and Covenant*, 22.

7. See "Jewish Values in the Post-Holocaust Future: A Symposium," 281. On Wiesel and covenantal Judaism, see Berger, *Crisis and Covenant*, 73.

8. For discussion, see Katz, *Post-Holocaust Dialogues*, and Cohn-Sherbok, "A Theology of Protest: Elie Wiesel."

9. Ezrahi, *By Words Alone*, 1; see Berger, *Crisis and Covenant*, 30–31.

10. Ezrahi, *By Words Alone*, 2, 6.

11. Langer, *The Holocaust and the Literary Imagination*, 1. The reference to Adorno is from Adorno, *Noten zur Literatur III*, 126.

12. Steiner, *Language and Silence*, 146; Michael Wyschogrod, quoted in Berger, *Crisis and Covenant*, 30; Cynthia Ozick, quoted in Berger, *Crisis and Covenant*, 194.

13. Derrida, *De l'esprit*, 87–88.

14. Derrida, *De l'esprit*, 87; Derrida does not explicitly make the connection with Nazism.

15. See Adorno, *Noten zur Literatur III*, 125–27.

16. Adorno, *Noten zur Literatur III*, 126 (my translation); Adorno, *Negative Dialectics*, 362, 367.

17. Friedlander, *Out of the Whirlwind*, 19. The note of hope here is echoed, for example, in Rosenfeld, *A Double Dying*, 15: "Its [Holocaust literature] birth must be seen as a miracle of some sort, not only an overcoming of mute despair but an assertion and affirmation of faith."

18. Ezrahi, *By Words Alone*, 217.

19. On Midrash, see chapter 6 of this book.

20. Berger, *Crisis and Covenant*, 67.

21. See Berger, *Crisis and Covenant*, 73, 79.

22. Fine, *Legacy of Night*, 80; Grossman, quoted in Walker, *Elie Wiesel*, 10.

23. Brown, *Elie Wiesel*, 99; Roth, in *Confronting the Holocaust*, edited by Rosenfeld and Greenberg, 66; Halperin, quoted in Brown, *Elie Wiesel*, 99.

24. Terence Des Pres, in Fine, *Legacy of Night*, xv.

25. Cargas, in *Responses to Elie Wiesel*, 291.

26. Walker, *Elie Wiesel*, v.

27. Roth, "Tears and Elie Wiesel," 48; quoted by Roth in "Elie Wiesel's Challenge to Christianity," in *Elie Wiesel*, edited by Rittner, 94.

28. Cohn-Sherbok, "A Theology of Protest: Elie Wiesel," 102, 103.

29. Fine, *Legacy of Night*, 3.

30. Freud, *The Interpretation of Dreams*, 120.

31. See Wardi, *Le Génocide dans la fiction romanesque*, 33: "Writers who conceive of the genocide as a mystery that must forever remain excluded from the human believe that it is not only unsayable but moreover unimaginable. They project their refusal to imagine on to what they preemptively qualify as unimaginable."

32. Brown, *Elie Wiesel*, 49.

33. On Wiesel's adoption of French, see *Qui êtes-vous?* 72–73; the connection between historical trauma and written style was suggested to me by Kristeva, "La Maladie de la douleur: Duras," in *Soleil noir*, 227–65.

34. See Engel, *Fou de Dieu ou Dieu des fous*, 71, 77; Brown, *Elie Wiesel*, 217–18.

35. See Brown, *Elie Wiesel*, 217–26.

36. For criticisms of Wiesel's staccato rhythms, see Ezrahi, *By Words Alone*, 119.

37. See Banon, *La Lecture infinie*, 204–16.

CHAPTER TWO

1. See Rousset, *L'Univers concentrationnaire*, 117, where Rousset describes how survivors are "separated from others by an experience that it is impossible to transmit"; see also Antelme, *L'Espèce humaine*, 9.

2. Fine, *Legacy of Night*, 29.

3. Fine, *Legacy of Night*, 30.

4. See Kermode, *The Genesis of Secrecy*, 23.

5. Kermode, *The Genesis of Secrecy*, 24, 27.

6. Kafka, *Der Prozeß*, 185 (my translation).

7. Wiesel himself compares Rabbi Nachman (or Nahman) and Kafka, and his comparison indicates his own affinity to his religious and literary forebears: "Their writing shares characteristics of both realist style and delirium. Their heroes live their lives by imagining them, their deaths by recounting them" (*CH*, 179); see also *Qui êtes-vous?* 97–98.

8. The passage is adapted from Nachman's story "The King and the Wise Man" in *Nahman of Bratslav: The Tales*, 117–19. Nachman's description ends differently from Wiesel's account of the laughing man; the man "performs all the jests and jokes of the country" (118), and jokes are associated in the story with lies and falsehood.

9. For an indication of the ambiguity of laughter in Wiesel's writing, see *Célébration hassidique*, 203 and *Qui êtes-vous?* 96–97. For a full discussion, see Friedemann, *Le Rire dans l'univers tragique d'Elie Wiesel*.

10. This is discussed further in chapter 6.

11. See also *Le Mendiant de Jérusalem*, 78–79: "Know that I have never set foot on the Holy Land. Know equally that I have never left it."

12. Scholem, *Major Trends in Jewish Mysticism*, 350, 349.

13. Buber, quoted in Scholem, *The Messianic Idea in Judaism*, 234.

14. See Fine, *Legacy of Night*, 2.

15. Lyotard, *Heidegger et "les juifs,"* 81.

16. Lyotard, *Heidegger et "les juifs,"* 82 and 128, referring to Heidegger's reading of Hölderlin.

17. See Lyotard, *Heidegger et "les juifs,"* 76, 130.

18. Lyotard, *Heidegger et "les juifs,"* 24.

19. See Lyotard, *Heidegger et "les juifs,"* 53.

20. Lyotard, *Heidegger et "les juifs,"* 51–52.

21. Lyotard, *Heidegger et "les juifs,"* 81.

CHAPTER THREE

1. Brown, *Elie Wiesel*, 51; Estess, *Elie Wiesel*, 17.

2. Boak, "Elie Wiesel's *La Nuit*, a Reconsideration," 86; Ozsvath and Satz, "The Audacity of Expressing the Inexpressible," 204.

3. See Lawrence S. Cunningham, "Elie Wiesel's Anti Exodus," in *Responses to Elie Wiesel*, edited by Cargas, 23–28; see Neher, "Le Silence et l'être: Elie Wiesel," 234; see Friedman, "Elie Wiesel: The Job of Auschwitz," in *The Hidden Human Image*, 106–34 and part 2 of *Abraham Joshua Heschel and Elie Wiesel: You Are My Witnesses*.

4. Neher, "Le Silence et l'être: Elie Wiesel," 234; Johnson, *A History of the Jews*, 2.

5. See also Wiesel's reluctance to describe his own survival as a miracle in Saint-Cheron, *Le Mal et l'exil*, 48: "No, I prefer to think that it's chance, and in effect it is chance. [. . .] It's simply by chance." See also Cargas, *Conversations with Elie Wiesel*, 147.

6. Berenbaum, *The Vision of the Void*, 172.

7. See Estess, *Elie Wiesel*, chapter 5, "Choosing Life."

8. Sartre, *La Nausée*, 63.

9. Beckett, *Molloy*, 239.

10. For an extensive discussion of this episode of the Talmud with particular reference to the role of Elisha and the question of interpretation, see Ouaknin, *Lire aux éclats*; see also Wiesel's *Célébration talmudique*, 179–94.

CHAPTER FOUR

1. For an indication of the importance of names in Wiesel's fiction, see the story recounted in both *Le Jour* (98) and *Le Crépuscule, au loin* (174). When Gavriel becomes Grégor he loses the constituent /el/ from his name: this is the Hebrew word for God, and it occurs twice in the name of Elie Wiesel. The name Grégor recalls that of Gregor Samsa, the protagonist of Kafka's story "Die Verwandlung" (The Metamorphosis); one reference to metamorphosis in *Les Portes de la forêt* highlights this derivation of the name: "Without realizing it, Grégor had been metamorphosed [*Grégor s'était métamorphosé*]" (*Portes*, 93). In effect, a man of God (Gavriel) is replaced by a character from Kafka (Grégor). On the significance of names in *Les Portes de la forêt*, see Sibelman, "The Dialogue of Peniel"; see also Wiesel's comments in Cargas, *Conversations with Elie Wiesel*, 52.

2. See Friedemann, *Le Rire dans l'univers tragique d'Elie Wiesel*, for example 145–46: "If there is a definition, it can only be multiple. How is it possible to reconcile, in effect, such different signifieds that arise in the work? . . . There remains a fundamental equivocation; and it is revealed at the level of writing as it is at the level of reading and interpretation."

3. See, for example, Kermode, *The Sense of an Ending*, 47.

4. See Scholem, *Major Trends in Jewish Mysticism,* 329–30, and *The Messianic Idea in Judaism,* 176–202. Scholem qualifies his view by saying that he is not referring to the later period of Hassidism beginning around 1800; see *The Messianic Idea in Judaism,* 179.

5. Felman, *La Folie et la chose littéraire,* 13; on madness in Wiesel's writing, see in particular Engel, *Fou de Dieu ou Dieu des fous.*

6. See also Cargas, *Conversations with Elie Wiesel,* 2–3, 128.

7. See R. D. Laing, *The Divided Self,* 33, 38: "It is just possible to have a thorough knowledge of what has been discovered about the hereditary or familial incidence of manic-depressive psychosis or schizophrenia, to have a facility in recognizing schizoid 'ego-distortion' and schizophrenic ego defects, plus the various 'disorders' of thought, memory, perceptions, etc., to know, in fact, just about everything that can be known about the psychopathology of schizophrenia or of schizophrenia as a disease without being able to understand one single schizophrenic. Such data are all ways of *not* understanding him. . . . The kernel of the schizophrenic's experience of himself must remain incomprehensible to us. As long as we are sane and he is insane, it will remain so."

8. Felman, *La Folie et la chose littéraire,* 12.

9. When asked by Cargas why he was not mad, Wiesel replied: "Maybe I am and I don't know it" (Cargas, *Conversations with Elie Wiesel,* 2); see also *Paroles d'étranger,* 7: "Why do I write? Perhaps in order not to go mad. Or, on the contrary, to touch the far end of madness."

CHAPTER FIVE

1. The evolution of the role of the *témoin* is discussed in Ellen Fine, *Legacy of Night,* where she argues that there is in Wiesel's writing "a general progression from witnessing to bearing witness" (3).

2. See Kant, *Critique of Practical Reason,* 17–19.

3. Quoted in de Lange, *Judaism,* 87.

4. de Lange, *Judaism,* 87.

5. Lévinas, *Éthique et infini,* 91.

6. See Friedman, *Abraham Joshua Heschel and Elie Wiesel,* 102.

7. Wiesel's texts refer almost compulsively to the moment of dawn. It is associated most importantly with the death of his father; see *La Nuit,* 118, and chapter 6 for discussion.

8. On 29 November 1947 the General Assembly of the United Nations voted to endorse a plan to establish independent Jewish and Arab states in Palestine; the implications and consequences of this decision are discussed in Johnson, *A History of the Jews,* 525.

9. The rape is in a sense repeated when the victim is obliged to describe and reexperience the crime; this is explained in Forrester, *The Seductions of Psychoanalysis,* 88–89: "In being asked to be a *witness* to this violation, she is being asked to *repeat* the experience of being deprived of this capacity [the capacity to

act as a subject]. In the nature of the legal functions of 'witness' and 'complain-ant,' she is being asked either to *repeat* the rape by alienating herself from the experience of being raped, or to *identify* with the position of the raped victim (herself). Either way, she is 'raped' again. No wonder that the victims, when acting as witnesses or as complainants, adopt evasive action."

10. Barthes, "Écrivains et écrivants," 151–52.

11. Barthes, "Écrivains et écrivants," 151–52.

12. Barthes, "Écrivains et écrivants," 153.

CHAPTER SIX

1. Fine quotes Lifton who relates survival guilt to "the process of identifica-tion—the survivor's tendency to incorporate within himself an image of the dead, and then to think, feel and act as he imagines they would" (*Legacy of Night,* 25; quoting Lifton, *Death in Life,* 496). Lifton also writes that "the survivor of sudden, overwhelming disaster, as in Hiroshima, experiences various kinds of *impaired mourning*—a general inability to accomplish the 'work of mourning'." (*Death in Life,* 484).

2. See Freud, "Mourning and Melancholia," 239–58.

3. Some of the parallels between the death of the father in *La Nuit* and the murder of John Dawson in *L'Aube* have been observed by Fine in *Legacy of Night,* 42–43, a text on which my discussion is partly based.

4. See Fine, *Legacy of Night,* 43, which refers to Lifton's *Death in Life.*

5. Paltiel's tears can be contrasted with his earlier inability to cry for the massacred Jews (see *Testament,* 234). This may be related to his refusal or inability to accept his father's death: "No, father. You did not die like that. You did not die" (*Testament,* 243). He finally cries not at the *birth* of his son, but at his circumcision, that is, the moment of his symbolic entry into the Jewish community.

6. Derrida, "La Pharmacie de Platon," 86.

7. Plato, *Phaedrus* 275d; Derrida, "La Pharmacie de Platon," 86.

8. Derrida, "La Pharmacie de Platon," 87, 170.

9. See Handelman, *The Slayers of Moses,* 37–38. In the absence of direct knowledge of the Hebrew Bible and of Jewish postbiblical texts, my own under-standing of the subject is entirely derived from the work of Handelman and others mentioned below.

10. Alter, *The Art of Biblical Narrative,* 12; Banon, *La Lecture infinie,* 90; Hartman and Budick, in *Midrash and Literature,* edited by Hartman and Budick, xiii.

11. See for example Lévinas, *Difficile liberté,* 101–2.

12. Lévinas, *L'Au-delà du verset,* 202.

13. The teacher was the enigmatic Rav Shushani, described by Wiesel in "Le Juif effant" (in *Le Chant des morts*) and "La Mort d'un juif errant" (in *Paroles*

d'étranger). Lévinas refers to his former teacher in *Quatre lectures talmudiques* (22): "But a prestigious master, M. Chouchani [*sic*], whose death in South America we have just heard of as the present collection is going to press, showed us the scope of the true method. For us, he made it impossible for ever to have a dogmatic access to the Talmud that was purely religious or even theological."

14. See Lévinas, *Du sacré au saint*, 167: "However my effort at commentary starts from the hypothesis that the Talmud is not a simple compilation. Moreover I am convinced of this, despite appearances to the contrary, and I always attribute my difficulties in finding the coherence and the profound logic of talmudic sayings to the poverty of my means."

15. Banon, *La Lecture infinie*, 89–90.

16. James Kugel, "Two Introductions to Midrash," in *Midrash and Literature*, edited by Hartman and Budick, 91.

17. Kugel, "Two Introductions to Midrash," 92.

18. On aggadah, and its relation to halakhah (prescriptive interpretation), see Banon, *La Lecture infinie*, 90–96; see also Joseph Heinemann, "The Nature of the Aggadah," in *Midrash and Literature*, edited by Hartman and Budick, 41–55.

19. See Heinemann, "The Nature of the Aggadah," 43: "The Jewish people sought, successfully, to continue living according to the dictates of the Torah. To achieve this, it was necessary that the Torah remain dynamic and open to varying interpretation in order to meet the challenges of drastically varying circumstances. By developing a method of 'creative exegesis' the aggadists were able to find in Scripture—which might otherwise have come to seem irrelevant to contemporary needs—the new answers and values that made it possible to grapple with the shifts and changes of reality." Wiesel echoes this view in his insistence on the continuing relevance of biblical stories: "It is by recounting them in the present, in the light of certain experiences of life and death, that one can understand them" (*CB*, 11).

20. See Judah Goldin, "The Freedom and Restraint of Haggadah," in *Midrash and Literature*, edited by Hartman and Budick, 57–76.

21. See Betty Roitman, "Sacred Language and Open Text," in *Midrash and Literature*, edited by Hartman and Budick, 174, quoting the introduction to a commentary on Leviticus: "Thus, whenever an expression can be read in [at least] two ways, our Sages have explicated both intentions of the text, for the Torah did not arbitrarily choose an ambiguous form [but rather chose one to indicate that both senses must be retained]."

22. Sherwin, "Wiesel's Midrash: The Writings of Elie Wiesel and their Relationship to Jewish Tradition," in *Confronting the Holocaust*, edited by Rosenfeld and Greenberg, 119, 117.

23. Berenbaum, *The Vision of the Void*, 129, 156.

24. See Berenbaum, *The Vision of the Void*, 154–60.

25. Fackenheim, "Midrashic Existence after the Holocaust," 266.

26. See Fackenheim, "Midrashic Existence after the Holocaust," 267, 268.

27. See Berenbaum, *The Vision of the Void*, 131–33.

28. Banon, *La Lecture infinie*, 251; on the ethical role of Midrash, see 219–55.

29. Fackenheim, "Midrashic Existence after the Holocaust," 268.

30. See Engel, *Fou de Dieu ou Dieu des fous*, 122, where he suggests that *Le Crépuscule, au loin* "is composed almost essentially of quotations and scenes taken from the preceding novels."

CONCLUSION

1. See Abrahamson, "Introductory Essay," in *Against Silence*, 9, where Wiesel is described as "The Secret Sharer"; Abrahamson, "Introductory Essay," 3, 11, 45.

2. Kermode, *The Genesis of Secrecy*, 27–28.

3. On the esotericism of Kabbalism, see Scholem, *Major Trends in Jewish Mysticism*, 21: Jewish mysticism "is a secret doctrine because it treats of the most deeply hidden and fundamental matters of human life; but it is secret also because it is confined to a small élite of the chosen who impart the knowledge to their disciples."

4. See Wiesel's contribution to "Jewish Values in the Post-Holocaust Future: A Symposium," 281.

5. Kermode, *The Genesis of Secrecy*, 143, xi.

6. Wiesel, "The Holocaust as Literary Inspiration," 9; quoted by Felman, in Felman and Laub, *Testimony*, 5–6. (With the exception of the foreword, each of the chapters of this book is authored by either Felman or Laub individually.)

7. See Laub, "An Event Without a Witness: Truth, Testimony and Survival," in *Testimony*, 75–92; Laub, *Testimony*, 81.

8. Felman, "The Betrayal of the Witness: Camus' *The Fall*," in *Testimony*, 193; the phrase "assassination of experience" is used in the title of Lyotard's *L'Assassinat de l'expérience par la peinture, Monory*; on the problems of talking about "experience" in relation to Auschwitz, see Lyotard, *Le Différend*, 133–35.

9. Felman, "The Betrayal of the Witness: Camus' *The Fall*," in *Testimony*, 201.

10. Lyotard, *Le Différend*, 18.

11. See Lyotard, *Le Différend*, 29–30.

12. Felman and Laub, *Testimony*, xx.

BIBLIOGRAPHY

The Bibliography is divided into three principal sections: Works by Wiesel, Criticism on Wiesel's Writing, and General Works.

WORKS BY WIESEL

In this study I have used works published originally in French, with the exception of *Against Silence* (see below), which contains many articles and essays available only in English. All references are to the original editions unless otherwise indicated.

Autobiography

La Nuit. Paris: Minuit, 1958; references are to the 10/18 edition.

Fiction

L'Aube. Paris: Seuil, 1960; references are to the Points roman edition.
Le Jour. Paris: Seuil, 1961.
La Ville de la chance. Paris: Seuil, 1962.
Les Portes de la forêt. Paris: Seuil, 1964; references are to the Points roman edition.
Le Mendiant de Jérusalem. Paris: Seuil, 1968.
Le Serment de Kolvillàg. Paris: Seuil, 1973.
Le Testament d'un poète juif assassiné. Paris: Seuil, 1980; references are to the Points roman edition.
Le Cinquième Fils. Paris: Grasset, 1983.
Le Crépuscule, au loin. Paris: Grasset, 1987.
L'Oublié. Paris: Seuil, 1989.

Theater

Zalmen ou la folie de Dieu. Paris: Seuil, 1968.
Le Procès de Shamgorod tel qu'il se déroula le 25 février 1649. Paris: Seuil, 1979.

Essays and other texts

Le Chant des morts. Paris: Seuil, 1966.
Les Juifs du silence. Paris: Seuil, 1966.
"Jewish Values in the Post-Holocaust Future: A Symposium." With Emil Fackenheim, George Steiner, Richard Popkin. *Judaism* 16 (1967): 266–99.

Entre deux soleils. Paris: Seuil, 1970.

Célébration hassidique. Paris: Seuil, 1972; references are to the Points sagesses edition.

Célébration biblique. Paris: Seuil, 1975.

"The Holocaust as Literary Inspiration." In *Dimensions of the Holocaust: Lectures at Northwestern University.* Evanston: Northwestern University Press, 1977.

Un Juif, aujourd'hui. Paris: Seuil, 1977.

Contre la mélancolie: Célébration hassidique II. Paris: Seuil, 1982.

Paroles d'étranger. Paris: Seuil, 1982; references are to the Points sagesses edition.

Against Silence: The Voice and Vision of Elie Wiesel. 3 vols. Selected and edited by Irving Abrahamson. New York: Holocaust Library, 1985.

Signes d'exode. Paris: Grasset, 1985.

Job ou Dieu dans la tempête. With Josy Eisenberg. Paris: Fayard-Verdier, 1986.

Discours d'Oslo. Paris: Grasset, 1987.

Silences et mémoire d'hommes. Paris: Seuil, 1989.

Célébration talmudique: Portraits et légendes. Paris: Seuil, 1991.

Interviews

Cargas, Henry James. *Conversations with Elie Wiesel.* South Bend, Ind.: Justice Books, 1992; expanded edition of text originally published by Paulist Press, 1976.

Cohen, Brigitte-Fanny. *Elie Wiesel: Qui êtes-vous?* Lyon: La Manufacture, 1987.

Saint-Cheron, Philippe-Michaël de. *Le Mal et l'exil: Rencontre avec Elie Wiesel.* Paris: Nouvelle Cité, 1988.

CRITICISM ON WIESEL'S WRITING

Abrahamson, Irving. "Introductory Essay." In *Against Silence: The Voice and Vision of Elie Wiesel.* 3 vols. Selected and edited by Irving Abrahamson. 1: 7–83. New York: Holocaust Library, 1985.

Abramowitz, Molly. *Elie Wiesel: A Bibliography.* Metuchen, N.J.: Scarecrow Press, 1974.

Alter, Robert. "Elie Wiesel: Between Hangman and Victim." In *After the Tradition: Essays on Modern Jewish Writing,* 151–60. New York: E. P. Dutton, 1969).

Alvarez, A. "The Literature of the Holocaust." In *Beyond All This Fiddle: Essays 1955–1967,* 22–33. London: Allen Lane, Penguin Press, 1968.

Banon, David, et al. *Présence d'Elie Wiesel.* Geneva: Labor et Fides, 1990.

Berenbaum, Michael. *The Vision of the Void: Theological Reflections on the Works of Elie Wiesel.* Middletown, Conn.: Wesleyan University Press, 1979.

————. "From Auschwitz to Oslo: The Journey of Elie Wiesel." In *After Tragedy and Triumph: Essays in Modern Jewish Thought and the American Experience*, 117–25. Cambridge: Cambridge University Press, 1990.

Berger, Alan. *Crisis and Covenant: The Holocaust in American Jewish Fiction*. Albany: State University of New York Press, 1985.

Boak, Denis. "Elie Wiesel's *La Nuit*, a Reconsideration." *Essays in French Literature* 24 (November 1987): 86–93.

Brown, Robert McAfee. *Elie Wiesel: Messenger to All Humanity*. Notre Dame: University of Notre Dame Press, 1983.

Cargas, Henry James, ed. *Responses to Elie Wiesel: Critical Essays by Major Jewish and Christian Scholars*. New York: Persea Books, 1978.

Cohen, Myriam B. *Elie Wiesel: Variations sur le silence*. La Rochelle: Rumeur des Ages, 1988.

Cohn-Sherbok, Dan. "A Theology of Protest: Elie Wiesel." In *Holocaust Theology*, 92–103. London: Lamp Press, 1989.

Davis, Colin. "Understanding the Concentration Camps: Elie Wiesel's *La Nuit* and Jorge Semprun's *Quel Beau Dimanche!*" *Australian Journal of French Studies* 28 (1991): 291–303.

Engel, Vincent. *Fou de Dieu ou Dieu des fous: L'Oeuvre tragique d'Elie Wiesel*. Brussels: De Boeck-Wesmael, 1989.

Estess, Ted L. *Elie Wiesel*. New York: Ungar, 1980.

Ezrahi, Sidra Dekoven. *By Words Alone: The Holocaust in Literature*. Chicago: University of Chicago Press, 1980.

Fackenheim, Emil. "Midrashic Existence after the Holocaust: Reflections Occasioned by the Work of Elie Wiesel." In *The Jewish Return into History: Reflections in the Age of Auschwitz and a New Jerusalem*, 252–72. New York: Schocken Books, 1978.

Fine, Ellen S. *Legacy of Night: The Literary Universe of Elie Wiesel*. Albany: State University of New York Press, 1982.

Friedemann, Joë. *Le Rire dans l'univers tragique d'Elie Wiesel*. Paris: Nizet, 1981.

Friedman, Maurice. "Elie Wiesel: The Job of Auschwitz." In *The Hidden Human Image*, 106–34. New York: Dell, 1974.

————. "Elie Wiesel's Messianism of the Unredeemed." *Judaism* 38 (1989): 310–19.

————. *Abraham Joshua Heschel and Elie Wiesel: You Are My Witnesses*. New York: Farrar-Straus-Giroux, 1987.

Garber, Frederick. "The Art of Elie Wiesel." *Judaism* 22 (1973): 301–8.

Langer, Lawrence. *The Holocaust and the Literary Imagination*. New Haven: Yale University Press, 1975.

Neher, André. "Le Silence et l'être: Elie Wiesel." In *L'Exil de la parole: Du silence biblique au silence d'Auschwitz*, 228–45. Paris: Seuil, 1970.

Ozsvath, Zsuzsanna, and Martha Satz. "The Audacity of Expressing the Inexpressible: The Relation between Moral and Aesthetic Considerations in Holocaust Literature." *Judaism* 34 (1985): 197–210.

Rittner, Carol, ed. *Elie Wiesel: Between Memory and Hope*. New York: New York University Press, 1990.

Rosenfeld, Alvin H. *A Double Dying: Reflections on Holocaust Literature*. Bloomington: Indiana University Press, 1980.

Rosenfeld, Alvin H., and Irving Greenberg, eds. *Confronting the Holocaust: The Impact of Elie Wiesel*. Bloomington: Indiana University Press, 1978.

Roth, John K. "Tears and Elie Wiesel." *Princeton Seminary Bulletin* 65 (December 1972): 42–48.

Sibelman, Simon P. "The Dialogue of Peniel: Elie Wiesel's *Les Portes de la forêt* and Genesis 32: 23–33." *The French Review* 61 (1988): 747–57.

Walker, Graham B., Jr. *Elie Wiesel: A Challenge to Theology*. London: McFarland, 1988.

GENERAL WORKS

Adorno, Theodor. *Noten zur Literatur III*. Frankfurt am Main: Suhrkamp, 1965.

———. *Negative Dialectics*. Translated by E. B. Ashton. London: Routledge and Kegan Paul, 1973; first published in German in 1966.

Alter, Robert. *The Art of Biblical Narrative*. New York: Basic Books, 1981.

Antelme, Robert. *L'Espèce humaine*. Paris: Gallimard, 1957.

Banon, David. *La Lecture infinie: Les Voies de l'interprétation midrachique*. Paris: Seuil, 1987.

Barthes, Roland. "Écrivains et écrivants." In *Essais critiques*, 147–54. Paris: Seuil, 1964.

Beckett, Samuel. *Molloy*. Paris: Minuit, 1951; Collection double.

Blanchot, Maurice. *Après coup*. Paris: Minuit, 1983.

Camus, Albert. *La Chute*. Edited by B. G. Garnham. London: Methuen, 1971; first edition 1956.

de Lange, Nicholas. *Judaism*. New York: Oxford University Press, 1986.

Derrida, Jacques. "La Pharmacie de Platon." In *La Dissémination*, 69–198. Paris: Seuil, 1972.

———. *De l'esprit: Heidegger et la question*. Paris: Galilée, 1987.

———. *Donner le temps: 1. La Fausse monnaie*. Paris: Galilée, 1991.

Felman, Shoshana. *La Folie et la chose littéraire*. Paris: Seuil, 1978.

Felman, Shoshana, and Dori Laub. *Testimony: Crises of Witnessing in Literature, Psychoanalysis, and History*. New York: Routledge, 1992.

Forrester, John. *The Seductions of Psychoanalysis: Freud, Lacan, and Derrida*. Cambridge: Cambridge University Press, 1990.

Freud, Sigmund. *The Interpretation of Dreams. The Standard Edition of the Complete Psychological Works of Sigmund Freud.* Edited by James Strachey. Vol. 4. London: Hogarth Press and the Institute of Psycho-Analysis, 1953–74.

———. "Mourning and Melancholia." In *The Standard Edition of the Complete Psychological Works of Sigmund Freud.* 14: 239–58.

Friedlander, Albert. *Out of the Whirlwind: A Reader of Holocaust Literature.* New York: Schocken Books, 1976.

Handelman, Susan A. *The Slayers of Moses: The Emergence of Rabbinic Interpretation in Modern Literary Theory.* Albany: State University of New York Press, 1982.

Hartman, Geoffrey, and Sanford Budick, eds. *Midrash and Literature.* New Haven: Yale University Press, 1986.

Hirsch, David. *The Deconstruction of Literature: Criticism after Auschwitz.* Providence: Brown University Press, 1991.

Johnson, Paul. *A History of the Jews.* London: Weidenfeld and Nicolson, 1987.

Kafka, Franz. *Der Prozeß.* Frankfurt am Main: Fischer, 1982.

Kant, Immanuel. *Critique of Practical Reason.* Translated by Lewis White Beck. New York: Macmillan, 1956; originally published in 1788.

Katz, Steven T. *Post-Holocaust Dialogues: Critical Studies in Modern Jewish Thought.* New York: New York University Press, 1983.

Kermode, Frank. *The Sense of an Ending.* London: Oxford University Press, 1966.

———. *The Genesis of Secrecy: On the Interpretation of Narrative.* Cambridge: Harvard University Press, 1979.

Kristeva, Julia. *Soleil noir: Dépression et mélancolie.* Paris: Gallimard, 1987.

Laing, R. D. *The Divided Self: An Existential Study in Sanity and Madness.* Harmondsworth: Penguin, 1969.

Lévinas, Emmanuel. *Difficile liberté.* Paris: Albin Michel, 1963 and 1976; Biblio essais edition.

———. *Quatre lectures talmudiques.* Paris: Minuit, 1968.

———. *Du sacré au saint: Cinq nouvelles lectures talmudiques.* Paris: Minuit, 1977.

———. *L'Au-delà du verset.* Paris: Minuit, 1982.

———. *Éthique et infini.* Paris: Fayard and Radio-France, 1982; Livre de Poche edition.

Lifton, Robert J. *Death in Life: The Survivors of Hiroshima.* London: Weidenfeld and Nicolson, 1967.

Lyotard, Jean-François. *Le Différend.* Paris: Minuit, 1983.

———. *L'Assassinat de l'expérience par la peinture, Monory.* Paris: Flammarion, 1984.

———. *Heidegger et "les juifs."* Paris: Galilée, 1988.

[Nahman]. *Nahman of Bratslav: The Tales.* Translation, introduction, and commentaries by Arnold J. Band. New York: Paulist Press, 1978.

Ouaknin, Marc-Alain. *Lire aux éclats: Eloge de la caresse.* Paris: Lieu Commun, 1989.

Rousset, David. *L'Univers concentrationnaire.* Paris: Minuit, 1965; first published 1946.

Sartre, Jean-Paul. *La Nausée.* Paris: Gallimard, 1938; Folio edition.

Scholem, Gershom. *Major Trends in Jewish Mysticism.* 3d ed. New York: Schocken Books, 1946.

———. *The Messianic Idea in Judaism and Other Essays on Jewish Spirituality.* New York: Schocken Books, 1971.

Steiner, George. *Language and Silence: Essays 1958–1966.* London: Faber and Faber, 1967.

Wardi, Charlotte. *Le Génocide dans la fiction romanesque: Histoire et représentation.* Paris: Presses Universitaires de France, 1986.

Young, James E. *Writing and Rewriting the Holocaust: Narrative and the Consequences of Interpretation.* Bloomington: Indiana University Press, 1988.

INDEX

Abel, 164, 165
Abraham, 27, 53, 152, 164
Abrahamson, Irving, 2, 175, 177, 185
Adam, 152, 164
Adorno, Theodor, 17, 18, 24, 186
aggadah, 163, 191
Agnon, Shmuel Yosef, 166
Akiba, Rabbi, 41
Alter, Robert, 160, 190
Antelme, Robert, 31, 187
Auschwitz, 1, 17, 18, 20, 21, 24, 25, 28, 29, 30, 48–49, 50, 53, 56, 59, 62, 104, 118, 167, 168, 185, 188, 192

Baal Shem Tov, Israel (the Besht), 27, 44–45, 46
Banon, David, 160, 162, 168, 187, 190, 191
Barthes, Roland, 138–39, 190
Beckett, Samuel, 75, 188
Berenbaum, Michael, 2, 64, 167, 168–69, 185, 188, 191, 192
Berger, Alan, 2, 16, 17, 20, 185, 186
Besht, the. See Baal Shem Tov
Birkenau, 32, 55, 173
Blanchot, Maurice, 4, 17, 185
Boak, Denis, 53, 188
Borges, Jorge Luis, 166
Brown, Robert McAfee, 2, 7, 20, 26, 28, 52, 185, 186, 187, 188
Buber, Martin, 39, 45, 53, 187
Buchenwald, 1, 20, 55, 56, 143, 146
Budick, Sanford, 160, 166, 190, 191

Cain, 152, 164, 165
Camus, Albert, 10, 14, 79, 128, 185, 192
Cargas, Henry James, 185, 186, 188, 189
Carter, Jimmy, 2
Cohen, Arthur, 16
Cohen, Miriam, 185
Cohn-Sherbok, Dan, 22, 185, 186
Cunningham, Lawrence, 188

Defoe, Daniel, 166
de Lange, Nicholas, 121, 189
Derrida, Jacques, 4, 18, 158–59, 160, 185, 186, 190
Des Pres, Terence, 186
Duras, Marguerite, 17, 186

Eichmann, Adolf, 8, 12
Eisenberg, Josy, 33
Elijah, 63, 91, 126
Engel, Vincent, 3, 28, 186, 189, 192
Estess, Ted, 7, 20, 52, 185, 188
Eve, 164
Ezrahi, Sidra Dekoven, 2, 16, 17, 19, 185, 186, 187

Fackenheim, Emil, 167–68, 169, 171, 191, 192
Felman, Shoshana, 103, 108, 182, 183, 184, 189, 192
Fine, Ellen, 2, 20, 23, 34–35, 48, 146, 186, 187, 189, 190
Forrester, John, 189–90
Foucault, Michel, 103
Freud, Sigmund, 24, 143, 186, 190
Friedemann, Joë, 3, 89–90, 187, 188
Friedlander, Albert, 19, 186
Friedman, Maurice, 2, 125, 188, 189

Gide, André, 10
Goldin, Judah, 191
Greenberg, Irving, 186, 191
Grossman, Edward, 20, 186

halakhah, 191
Halperin, Irving, 20, 186
Handelman, Susan, 160, 190
Hartman, Geoffrey, 160, 166, 190, 191
Hassidism, Hassidic stories, 1, 5, 27, 35, 42, 44–51, 80, 90, 114, 167, 170, 189
Heidegger, Martin, 18, 49, 187
Heinemann, Joseph, 191
Heschel, Abraham Joshua, 2, 188, 189
Hillel, Rabbi, 121
Hiroshima, 29, 30, 118, 146, 190
Hirsch, David, 5, 185
Hölderlin, Friedrich, 187

Isaac, 27, 53, 164
Israel, 1, 8, 66, 104, 107, 119, 123, 124, 125, 129, 133, 137, 159, 161, 168, 172, 178

Jabès, Edmond, 17
Job, 32–33, 53, 165–66, 188
Johnson, Paul, 53, 188, 189

Kabbalism, 32, 54, 59, 69, 82–83, 91, 177, 192
Kafka, Franz, 26, 37, 39, 166, 175, 176, 187, 188
Kant, Immanuel, 189
Katz, Steven, 15, 185
Kermode, Frank, 3–4, 12, 37, 90, 175, 181, 185, 187, 188, 192
Khmer Rouge, 125
Kristeva, Julia, 186
Kugel, James, 162–63, 191

Laing, R.D, 106, 189
Langer, Lawrence, 17, 186
Langfus, Anna, 27
Laub, Dori, 182, 184, 192
laughter, 3, 39–40, 69, 87, 89–90, 94, 103, 181, 187, 188
Lévinas, Emmanuel, 122, 161, 162, 189, 190, 191
Lifton, Robert Jay, 146, 190
Lyotard, Jean-François, 49–51, 182, 183–84, 187, 192

madness, 3, 23, 33, 48, 57, 68, 80–85, 90, 103–12, 113, 183, 189
Maimonides (Moses ben Maimon), 61, 91
Malraux, André, 79
Mauriac, François, 1
Messiah, 90–92, 93, 103, 123, 152, 159
Midrash, 19, 35, 46, 142, 158–74, 184, 186, 191
Milton, John, 166
Mishnah, 160
Mitterand, François, 2
Monowitz-Buna, 8, 55, 56, 57
Moses, 41, 124, 152, 160, 190

Nachman (Nahman), Rabbi, 39–40, 42, 43, 187
Neher, André, 188

Orwell, George, 29
Ouaknin, Marc-Alain, 188
Ozick, Cynthia, 186
Ozswath, Zuzsanna, 53, 188

Perec, Georges, 17
Plato, 158, 159, 190
Proust, Marcel, 63

Rawicz, Piotr, 27
revisionist historians, 183
Rigaut, Jacques, 139
Rittner, Carol, 185, 186
Roitman, Betty, 191
Rosenfeld, Alvin, 186, 191

Roth, John, 20, 186
Rousset, David, 31, 187
Rubenstein, Richard, 16, 20

Saint-Cheron, Philippe-Michaël de, 123, 188
Sartre, Jean-Paul, 10, 74, 79, 188
Satz, Martha, 53, 188
Scholem, Gershom ,45, 46, 90, 187, 189, 192
Semprun, Jorge, 27
Sherwin, Byron, 167, 191
Shushani, Rav, 190–91
Sibelman, Simon, 188
Sighet, 1, 32, 33, 34, 39, 42, 54, 55, 56, 60, 61, 72, 73, 101
Six-Day War, 104, 107, 109
Socrates, 158, 159
Solomon, 171
Steiner, George, 186
Stevens, Wallace, 166

Talmud, talmudic stories, 27, 54, 81, 91, 121, 131–32, 160, 161–62, 163, 188, 191
témoignage, témoin, 31–35, 48–49, 78–80, 85, 95, 98–99, 100–101, 103, 115–16, 138, 182–84, 189
testimony. *See témoignage*
Torah, 40–41, 121, 159, 163, 171, 191
Treblinka, 28, 50

Walker, Graham, 2, 185, 186
Wardi, Charlotte, 186
Wiesel, Elie, writings of
—*Against Silence*, 175, 192
—*L'Aube*, 1, 5, 10, 49, 52, 62–67, 73, 82, 85, 86, 113, 124, 125–29, 132, 138, 140, 144–46, 149, 150, 151, 156, 170, 190
—*Célébration biblique*, 33, 35, 40–41, 53, 163–64, 165–66, 169, 172, 174, 191
—*Célébration hassidique*, 35, 39, 44–45, 47, 49, 50, 51, 163, 170, 182, 187
—*Célébration talmudique*, 41, 161, 162, 188
—*Le Chant des morts*, 1, 4, 7–15, 16, 21, 23, 30, 72, 103, 111, 144, 155, 156–57, 171, 190
—*Le Cinquième Fils*, 2, 10, 48, 49, 114, 123–24, 125, 141, 144, 145, 147, 148–49, 150, 151, 156, 157–58, 159, 170
—*Contre la mélancolie*, 35, 163, 170
—*Le Crépuscule, au loin*, 5, 49, 86, 103–12, 141, 152–53, 157, 188, 192
—*Discours d'Oslo*, 123
—*Elie Wiesel: Qui êtes-vous?*, 25, 26, 72, 104, 118, 161, 166, 177, 184, 186, 187
—*Entre deux soleils*, 23, 25, 27, 65, 78, 97, 114, 170, 173

—"The Holocaust as Literary Inspiration,"
192
—"Jewish Values in the Post-Holocaust Future: A Symposium," 185, 192
—*Job ou Dieu dans la tempête,* 33
—*Le Jour,* 5, 20, 22, 52, 62–67, 73, 77, 85, 86, 188
—*Les Juifs du silence,* 2, 113, 115–22, 168
—*Le Mal et l'exil,* 123, 186, 188
—*Le Mendiant de Jérusalem,* 2, 5, 35–44, 52, 86, 104–11, 125, 168, 187
—*La Nuit,* 1, 5, 6, 19, 20, 21, 31–35, 37, 50, 52–62, 63, 64, 85, 86, 95, 110, 115, 141, 142–44, 145, 146, 147, 149, 150, 151, 152, 153, 156, 168, 173, 175, 180, 190
—*L'Oublié,* 5, 10, 113, 119, 124, 125, 129–38, 141, 150, 157, 176–82, 184
—*Paroles d'étranger,* 27, 28, 30, 86, 113, 118, 119, 120, 121, 123, 133, 189, 190–91
—*Les Portes de la forêt,* 20, 44–45, 46–47, 49, 64, 86–97, 113, 141, 173, 179, 188
—*Le Serment de Kolvillàg,* 5, 29, 47, 48, 78, 86, 97–103, 125, 147, 170, 171, 172–73, 182

—*Signes d'exode,* 29–30, 59, 113, 117–18, 120, 162, 170–71
—*Silences et mémoire d'hommes,* 25, 26, 113, 117, 125, 127, 144, 161, 163, 172, 174
—*Le Testament d'un poète juif assassiné,* 2, 62, 125, 141, 144, 145, 147–48, 149, 150–1, 153–6, 157, 159, 170, 180, 190
—*Un Juif, aujourd'hui,* 1, 23, 24, 29, 49–50, 57, 113, 117, 118, 123, 125, 127, 184
—*La Ville de la chance,* 2, 5, 20, 52, 67–85, 86, 115, 125, 143–44, 146–47, 149, 157, 159, 170, 173, 179, 182
—*Zalmen ou la folie de Dieu,* 48, 115, 125, 182
Wyschogrod, Michael, 186

Yom Kippur War, 123
Young, James, 6, 185

Zionism, 126, 128
Zohar, 46